INDIA AND WEST ASIA

IIC's Asia Project : Other Publications

1. Religion, Politics and Society in South and South-east Asia (Konark, 1998)
2. Culture, Society and Politics in Central Asia and India (Shipra, 1999)
3. Culture, Democracy and Development in South Asia (Shipra, 2001)
4. India and East Asia Culture and Society (Shipra, 2002)

History, Culture and Society in India and West Asia

Introduction by
Dr. Karan Singh

Edited by
N.N. Vohra

SHIPRA

India International Centre

ISBN 81-7541-123-6

First Published in India in 2003

History, Culture and Society in
India and West Asia

Published by :
SHIPRA PUBLICATIONS
115-A, Vikas Marg, Shakarpur,
Delhi-110092 (India)
Ph. : 2458662, 2200954 Fax : 2458662
Email : siprapub@satyam.net.in
Website : www.shiprapublications.com

Laser Typesetting by :
R.S. Prints,
New Delhi

Printed at :
Choudhary Offset
Delhi-110006

Contents

Preface
N.N. Vohra vii

A Message
Prince El Hassan bin Talal ix

Introduction
Karan Singh 1

Conceptualising India-West Asia Relations
The Macro-Historical Perspective
A.K. Ramakrishnan 9

Kuwait and India: Historical, Cultural and Social Bonds
Rasha Al-Sabah 17

Afro-Asian Relations: The Sudanese Perspective
Jaffar Mirghani Ahmed 21

Contemporary Indo-Sudanese Relations
Hassan Mekki 24

Indo-Arab Relationship: The Syrian Perspective
Waiel S. H. Awwad 28

Yemen and India: Development of
Historical Relationships
Saleh Ali Basurrah 32

Egypt: A Link between India and the Mediterranean
Mostafa El-Abbadi 37

India and West Asia: Sharing History and
Future Challenges
Abdulaziz Othman Altwaijri 46

India and the Arab World: Retrospect and Prospects
Faisal Odeh Al-Rfou'h 54

Personal Reflections on Indo-Arab Relations
Rafiq Zakaria 60

Enduring Relationships: Maritime Contacts
in the Western Indian Ocean
Himanshu Prabha Ray 77

Cultural Implications of Trades between South Asia, the Gulf and Mesopotamia in the Bronze Age
Shereen Ratnagar 102

Arabian Gulf During the British Era: The Impact of India
Abdulla Elmadani 109

India and West Asia Relations: The Changing Economic Matrix
Girijesh Pant 125

Population Dynamics in West Asia and North Africa
Prakash C. Jain 141

Minorities in the Middle East: An Inquiry
P.R. Kumaraswamy 163

Globalisation and Literature
Sadik J. Al-Azm 179

Exploring Composite Culture in India
Neera Chandhoke 197

Sanskrit's Legacy to the Arab Intellectual Heritage
Abdul Ali 220

Indo-Arab Cultural Relations: Glimpses of Medieval Arabic Texts
Abdul Bari 232

South India and the Gulf: Trade and Diplomacy During the Late Eighteenth Century
A.K. Pasha 237

Medieval West Asian Critical Appreciation of India
M.A. Saleem Khan 250

India-West Asia Interaction
Akhtarul Wasey 269

Unitary Histories, Epistemological Divides: A Summing Up
Gulshan Dietl 282

Contributors 293

Preface

For the past four decades and more the India International Centre has been organising a continuing series of discussions, presentations and expositions to promote awareness and deeper appreciation of past and present cultures. These activities have been undertaken with the essential objective of promoting understanding between different world communities.

With the onset of globalisation there has been growing concern about the emerging economic scenario and the consequential disturbing of the traditional equities and societal harmonies. The continuing debates on the need to alter the existing policy approaches to secure sustainable development have led to a renewed interest in the preservation of the cultural roots of societies which are imbedded deep in ancient history.

Asia is the cradle of the world's oldest civilisations and home to the world's dominant religions. For thousands of years, Asian countries enjoyed extremely creative inter-linkages which saw the efflorescence of the arts, architecture, science, engineering, medicine, philosophy and religion. Internal disunities, invasions and wars and various disruptive factors generated decline and paved the way for the prolonged period of colonial domination.

The deprivations resulting from the subjugation and exploitation by the colonial masters led to the shattering of socio-cultural traditions and value systems which had provided the bedrock for civilisational advancement.

To recall, and hopefully revive, the centuries-old cultural roots and intellectual linkages the Centre established an Asia Project to commence a structured dialogue between scholars, researchers and eminent persons from Asian countries. Since 1997, under the aegis of the Asia Project, we have organised five seminars which have focused on the societal, religious and spiritual, cultural, political, democratic and developmental aspects of the historical inter-relations among the countries in Asia. To obtain a meaningful outcome, each of these seminars was so organised as to secure participation from the distinct geo-political regions of Asia: South Asia, Southeast Asia, Central Asia, East Asia and West Asia. A dialogue with countries in Australasia, the last in the ongoing series, is planned to be held later this year.

This volume relates to the most recent seminar organised under the aegis of the Asia Project, 'India and West Asia: History, Culture and Society'. Thirty participants from Bahrain, Egypt, Jordan, Kuwait, Saudi Arabia, Sudan, Syria, Yemen and India held intensive discussions at this two-day seminar (1-2 March 2002).

This volume contains twenty-three papers presented at the seminar and a summing-up chapter by Professor Gulshan Dietl which provides a broad over-view of the discussions held.

The concept paper for the seminar was drawn up by Prof. Dietl, who was also the Convenor of the Steering Committee which comprised Sh. J. N. Dixit and Sh. I. P. Khosla, both distinguished former Ambassadors, and Sh. M. H. Ansari, Vice-Chancellor of Aligarh Muslim University. We received valuable support from Sh. R. N. Abhyankar, Secretary, Ministry of External Affairs. I am indebted to all of them for their kind help. Our thanks are also due to Sh. Hifzul Rehman and Dr. Irshad Ahmad, officers in the Ministry of External Affairs, for their assistance in Arabic-to-English interpretation.

The IIC-Asia Project has continued to function fruitfully under the mature direction of Dr. Karan Singh, a Life Trustee of the Centre and an eminent scholar, thinker, author, diplomat and parliamentarian. We are grateful for his sustained support.

For the timely publication of this volume, I thank Ms. Bela Butalia, Deputy Editor in the Centre's Publication Division, and Shipra Publications.

N.N. Vohra
Director
India International Centre
New Delhi

August, 2002

A Message

This important and timely international seminar bears strongly upon the issues of regional cooperation and the dialogue between cultures which I have worked to promote over the past thirty years and more. It is, therefore, all the more a matter of regret for me that I cannot be with you in person, in this beautiful and varied country; but I look forward very much to reading your contributions in the near future.

On this theme, it was only a fortnight ago that I had the pleasure and honour of announcing the institution in Istanbul of a 'Parliament of Cultures' as a forum for international dialogue at a cultural level. Dialogue between cultures is particularly appropriate to this meeting, as western Asia and the Indian subcontinent have always grappled with numerous cultural identities—and become great civilisations as a result of the noble effort to respect differences, cherish commonalities, and fight against the stirring up of hatred.

At a time when international anxieties threaten increasing estrangement—not only between Muslims and others but between the different Muslim communities themselves—it is necessary to remind ourselves of the deep-rooted ties, the scholastic and cultural exchanges, and the shared values of the Indian subcontinent and the West Asian heritage.

Many scholars attending this seminar will surely dwell upon the long history of exchange between the West Asian and Indian subcontinental civilisations: the great scholars of high Islamic culture who were born in India or travelled there, such as Ibn Batuta and Al-Biruni; and the mathematicians, philosophers, physicians, poets, scholars and financiers from Sindh who made outstanding contributions to the society of the Arabs, and who translated numerous texts from Sanskrit on mathematics, astronomy, medicine, literature and ethics to the benefit of the world. On the topic of cultural exchange, I might mention the use of ceramic tiles in construction in India, inspired by Iraqi, Iranian and Central Asian architectural traditions; or the famous exports from Sindhi towns of manufacture: brassware from Moradabad, carpets from Mirzapur, printing from Farrukhabad, fine leather and shoes from Mansur, not to mention a wide variety of agricultural produce and cash crops from the whole subcontinent.

Muslim rulers of Sindh brought with them new legal and administrative systems, and some imported cultural practices from Turkey, Central Asia, Persia or Iraq; but others preferred to study Sanskrit, encourage indigenous arts and employ Hindus in their administration. Some came to understand Indian geographic and climatic conditions and invested in vital water-works such as canals, dams, artificial lakes, step-wells and underground water transportation.

These contacts and exchanges deserve further study and—perhaps more importantly—further imitation today. An alternative to a traditional 'Orientalist' view is provided by the Japanese scholar Professor Yuzo Itagaki, who considers western Asia to have made extensive civilisational contributions to the rest of the world, but also to have faced incessant invasions, interferences and penetrations from outside. The very geographic centrality and accessibility that had helped enrich the civilisations of West Asia and the Indian subcontinent were also their bane as they repeatedly attracted ambitious conquerors and marauders.

The history and geography of western Asia and the Indian subcontinent has thus been characterised by a continuous flow—of people, ideas, goods, services and cultures travelling back and forth in a two-way process. Yet western Asia and the Indian subcontinent were also engaged in other processes of contact and exchange with other cultural and geographic entities, from Morocco to Mongolia; and, no less importantly, smaller western Asian and Indian regions were engaged in *intracultural* dialogue and exchange within the larger regions.

Today, India has the second-largest Muslim population of the world, after Indonesia. In a flourishing democratic system, Muslim men and women have reached high positions in society as entrepreneurs, experts, and figures of authority in the political, legal and military systems of the country. Just as many Hindus and Muslims have succeeded not only in coexisting but in working positively together, different but equal, so we must continue to make efforts to complement each other, as parts of one human universe. Acceptance of 'the other' has to begin with recognition of differences whilst enhancing similarities. I am proud to count myself a pluralist, and I regard with admiration India's pluralist society which can respect many cultures within a framework of universal values.

Yet the wider world today, our international and global existence, stands in urgent need of change if we are to begin to achieve the universal ideals of human dignity, justice, respect for life and solidarity to which all cultures have always subscribed. Unintended consequences of international actions, and the tensions inherent in the 'arc of crisis', pose challenges to the welfare and future of all.

When I speak of the 'arc of crisis' I refer to a region extending from the Horn of Africa through the Congo and western Asia to Central Asia and the Indian subcontinent. This extensive region, rich in oil and natural gas, is plagued by a variety of conflicts and potential conflicts; but it has no crisis-avoidance centre of its own. As President and Patron on the Arab Thought Forum, as Moderator of the World Conference on Religion and Peace, as President of the Club of Rome, and as a member of the International Crisis Group, I call for the establishment of such a crisis-avoidance centre. It is time to move from a culture of mere survival into a culture of non-violence, of participation and thence to a culture of peace. Peace and democracy are interlinked. The effort towards peacefulness by every individual contributes to the national democracy.

As Sher Ali Palaudi wrote, political rivalries leave deep rifts of misunderstanding. All religions teach *insaniyat* (humanity) as a fundamental principle. To achieve this is possible and, therefore, a *modus vivendi* among religions is possible. The legitimacy of an ideology should be demonstrated by its capacity to improve well-being for all—it cannot be demonstrated by recourse to the jungle law of 'might equals right'.

Our codes of humanitarian behaviour are at present all based upon the circumstances and risks of war. Peace has to be worked for continuously in its own right. West Asia and the Indian subcontinent now face a variety of similar challenges to which we could and should seek common solutions. We presently struggle alike with issues of distributive justice, gender and human rights, civil society, environment and education. We are equally anxious concerning the increasing availability of medium-range missiles and weapons of mass destruction, and the sale of arms to the region. The politicisation and securitisation of religion and culture bring parallel threats to us all, which increase with the prevalence of arms at both an individual and at a national level. Extremism in all religions, policies and creeds must be curtailed in the interests of an overarching ethic of human solidarity which embraces each and every individual in the broader western Asian and Indian subcontinental region—and, indeed, the world.

I believe that a stepping away from parochial outlooks can only be achieved by enhancing what is universal and respecting what is different. The right to life and human dignity is universal and yearned after by us all; yet, we still have to find ways of dealing with cultural differences and disagreeing in a civilised manner. We can have dialogues without idealogues; we can have conversation without conversion. We *can* agree without compromising faith or culture.

Events during the past five months have brought further challenges not only to Muslim thought and communities but to all international relations. If we accept a global civilisation and that our one world faces interconnected, global threats and shares similar (human) interests, then we will rationally appreciate that international values and standards *must* be unanimously and strictly respected if we are to survive. History shows that there is always progress if risks are recognised early enough. The rich and participatory culture within Indian society is a leading example. The international relationships put to the test by recent events must surely emerge stronger and more beneficial to all if the basic standards of human behaviour are not only observed but actively and broadly promoted through individual example, education, media and policies.

The shared history and many similarities between the Indian subcontinent and western Asia give us links to understand one another readily and draw upon common heritage in our conversations. To set aside immediate political gain in order to work for longer-term peace and stability is a difficult act. For different countries and peoples to come together as a region by reconciling local differences and visualising a future of two-way traffic in ideas, commerce, technology and people is a high goal. To realise a universalisation of human values all around the globe means rejecting one single cultural approach and stressing instead that all cultures embrace certain civilisational values—not just *civitas*, but *humanitas*—which will serve as the basis for a global code of conduct. We need Parliaments of Culture; centres for crisis avoidance; improved communication and education; and sustained, high-level policy promoting variety and tolerance amongst all peoples.

A single world with a single agenda formulated according to the value system of one culture—to the exclusion of others—will be a world in which injustice and marginalisation will inevitably lead to conflict and further to war. However, 'one world of ten thousand cultures'—a world in which commonalities are the foundation and particularities are the cornerstones—will be characterised by cooperation.

H.R.H. Prince El Hassan bin Talal

1 March 2002 (The Hashemite Kingdom of Jordan)

Introduction

Karan Singh

Living as we do in a democratic society, it is of tremendous importance that there should be areas which are totally free from any kind of governmental control. Governments keep changing in a democracy, whereas the freedom of expression and creativity cannot in any way be linked to the fortunes of any particular government. The India International Centre (IIC) is a unique institution; it is entirely self-supporting; does not get any grant from the government, and thus enjoys complete freedom.

We have been particularly interested in Asia, because we felt that while there were many lectures here by the people from the West, not enough interest was being taken in our relations with Asia and between Asian countries inter-se. Asia has been the cradle of many of the world's oldest civilisations, be it on the banks of the Nile, the Euphrates, the Indus or the Ganges. All the world's great religions, without exception, were born in Asia, whether the four Indic religions—Hinduism, Jainism, Buddhism and Sikhism—or the religions that have come to us from West Asia, the religion of Zarathustra, Prophet of Iran, Judaism, Christianity and Islam, and now the Baha'i faith. India has in fact been a meeting place of all the great religions of the world.

Asia was in the forefront not only of philosophy and religion, but of science, mathematics, astronomy, medicine and engineering. I do not think one could build the pyramids today even with all the computers in the world, or the Taj Mahal or the magnificent Ellora Temples of Aurangabad or the great Shiva temple in Thanjavur. These are great engineering feats, which bespeak a very high level of scientific development. There had been in history a creative interaction between many Asian countries, but unfortunately due to our own weaknesses and lack of unity, Asia came under a long spell of colonial domination, either directly under colonial rule or indirectly under the control of one or other of the colonial powers. That subjugation, coupled with exploitation in many ways, impoverished the Asian experience. As a result, all the great efflorescence that had taken place over thousands of years, in India, in Egypt, in Iran and in Arab countries, gradually began to be thrown into the background and Western concepts, Western civilisations, became predominant.

When the freedom movements began there was again a great efflorescence. Mahatma Gandhi and Jawaharlal Nehru spearheaded the Indian freedom movement. I remember meeting President Nasser on several occasions at Jawaharlal Nehru's house. Many of the Arab leaders looked to him and to India for inspiration. There was a lot of interchange and exchange of ideas and concepts. I also remember when Jawaharlal Nehru, President Nasser and President Tito of Yugoslavia, all three of whom I knew personally, founded what later became known as the Non-Aligned Movement. That movement also helped to re-establish links between the Asian countries.

Now, after the end of the Cold War, we face a whole series of new challenges and fresh opportunities. It is in order to focus on the deeper civilisational roots and relationships that we have structured these seminars. These are not involved in security matters or immediate problems. They are trying to look into the deeper linkages between the Asian countries. The four seminars which have already been held were on: (i) Religion, Politics and Society in South and Southeast Asia; (ii) Culture, Society and Politics in Central Asia; (iii) Culture, Democracy and Development in South Asia; and (iv) India and East Asia: Culture and Society. This fifth one is 'India and West Asia: History, Culture and Society'. Each one of these is a significant contribution towards the re-establishment of intellectual linkages between these countries.

Our seminars have some special features. The first is that the participants are drawn only from Asian countries. We took a policy decision that howsoever distinguished Western experts may be-and there are very fine experts on Asian languages and cultures in the West—we would not invite anybody from outside Asia. We took the decision not because we are being in any way parochial—after all, we are global citizens and the whole world now is a unity—but because we do feel that our seminars are for Asians and therefore must be attended only by Asians.

Second, the participants are invited in their personal capacity, and not as representatives of their countries. I would like to stress this. This is not a United Nations seminar where you have your country in mind and have therefore to say what your Foreign Ministry wants you to say. I think this is an important point, and is in fact one of the reasons why we do not generally invite diplomatic representatives, except to the social functions, because we feel that these seminars are intellectual seminars and there should be no kind of inhibition.

Third, as I said, we deal not so much with contemporary issues, problems of strategies or economic growth, as with deeper civilisational, historical, archaeological, philosophical and religious linkages. And each seminar ends with a publication so that we do have a permanent record of what has been done during these meetings. Apart from the papers which are presented, some friends like to make verbal contributions, and there is a recording system, so that later on we can use that material also.

Looking through some of the papers, I found Professor Abdul Ali's paper on 'Sanskrit's Legacy to the Arab Intellectual Heritage' particularly interesting. Although we already know about mathematics, engineering and astronomy, I did not realise that many of the basic Sanskrit texts had been translated into Arabic, be it the scientific texts, or the Charaka or Sushruta texts on medicine and, of course, the *Hisab-ul-Hind* on the decimal system. When my American friends talk about intellectual property rights, I always say, fine, if you give us one cent for every time you use the 'zero', we are prepared to give you all the intellectual property rights that you need!

It is most interesting how philosophy went to the Arab world and I am sure there were inflows from the Arab world also into India, particularly on the coastal areas where there were settlements. India has not always been a poor country. In fact, India was one of the richest countries in the world, and it was the riches of India that attracted the unwelcome attention of invaders, not its poverty. We became poor because we were exploited and invaded; it is not the other way around.

Everybody now-a-days assumes that the developing countries were always poor. I do not think Egypt would have been poor when the pyramids were made there. India was certainly not poor. India's wealth was known throughout the world. So this whole mindset that we were always poor countries has to change. It is true that we are depressed now, but that does not mean that we were always poor, nor that we will always be poor. If we can only get our own act together in Asia, if we could sort out our own problems, the day is not far when Asia could once again rise in the world and play its due role in the rapidly developing global society.

I am particularly interested in the relationship between Islam and Hinduism. My friend and colleague, Dr Rafiq Zakaria, had written some extraordinary books about the impact of Islam. He has written a book titled *Discovery of God*. I myself happen to come from a Muslim-majority state in India, where the Sufis played a major role. For example, Shah Hamadan came with 700 followers to Kashmir and there was this confluence between Hinduism and Islam. I often give the example of Humayun's Tomb and the *dargah* of Hazrat Nizamuddin, both of which are only one kilometre from where we are meeting. Now, Humayun was one of the great Moghul Emperors, but if you go to Humayun's Tomb you will find that not a soul is there. On the other hand if you go to the *dargah* of Hazrat Nizamuddin, a great Sufi saint, you will find tens of thousands of people flocking there every year, regardless of whether they are Hindus or Muslims or from any other religion. In this country we have always preserved our greatest reverence not for great kings and emperors, but for the saints, the Sufis, the *rishis*.

As another example, take the city of Aurangabad, which has the tomb of Aurangzeb, the last Moghul Emperor. Hardly anybody goes there. But at the *dargah sharif* of Hazrat Moinuddin Chishti at Ajmer hundreds of thousands of people flock every year. So it is not only a question of being Muslim, it is a question of what sort of Islam interacted and at what point in time with Hinduism, and how the creative interaction was established.

This is in fact a fascinating area. Some of the papers in the present volume have touched upon this. The interactions have been unpleasant, but have also been creative in the field of architecture, in the field of cuisine, in the field of dress, in the field of dance, in the field of music, in the field of language, in so many different fields. The Hindu-Muslim interaction has resulted in immense creativity. On the other hand, where there were invasions and where there was fanaticism and intolerance, that has created scars. What I am saying is that this is the Indian experience. I am sure all of you in your own countries will have similar experiences in different ways. I think what we now have to do is to try and see where our roots lie, where the creativity lies and whether we cannot once again tap the sources of the harmony and compassion, love and creativity that lie hidden beneath all the encrustation of the last thousand years.

You may have noticed that we have totally banned the use of the word 'Middle East'. It irritates me intensely. Whenever anybody in America asks me what is happening in the Middle East, I say, 'Oh, Bangkok is fine'. They say we are talking about the Middle East. I say, 'Well, Bangkok for us is the Middle East'. For heaven's sake why should we define ourselves in Western terms? For the West it is Middle East, Far East and Near East and therefore we also fall into that trap. It is a mindset we have got to get out of. For us it is West Asia, it is South Asia, it is Southeast Asia, and it is Central Asia.

During the discussions several important points were raised. One is this whole question of minorities. In India, for example, the question of minorities is built into our Constitution. It is an awkward problem for the majority everywhere. Even in America, which is very unicultural, they are beginning to realise it. In Florida, in California and in Texas, the Spanish-speaking people are growing to become a majority and therefore, for the first time, they have moved into bi-lingualism. Earlier they were totally against bi-lingualism, but they are also being forced by demography to move into a bi-lingual situation.

This question of minorities is something which has to be tackled by all countries. Prof Kumaraswamy has pointed out something which is not generally known, that Islam is also not a monolith. There are several versions of Islam. There are Shias and Sunnis and other offshoots, the Wahhabis, the Sufis, the Barelvis, the Nakshbands, and so on. So maybe in the years to come the countries of West Asia and North Africa will also have to creatively address the problem of minorities, as we have tried to do in India, not with entire success, by giving certain special minority rights in the Constitution.

We are now witnessing a process of globalisation, which in some ways is an irreversible process. But in the midst of that globalisation, the old identities are beginning to be threatened and there is a re-assertion of ethnic, linguistic and national identities. So on the one hand you have the process of regionalisation and globalisation; on the other you have the reassertion of ethnic and linguistic minorities. This is one of the major problems confronting political scientists and thinkers in the twenty-first century.

The other concept that needs to be articulated is this concept of multiple identities. My own view is that the old concept of a single identity is now obsolete. If you look upon identities as concentric circles around a self—I am coming here to the field of spirituality—then it does not matter how many concentric circles you have. We have to get out of the outmoded concept that one's identity is only either as a Muslim or only as a Malayali, or an Indian. We are moving into a new kind of civilisation. The world that we have known, the world that we belong to, the world in which we have studied has disappeared. We are now moving into a new kind of civilisation, whether you like it or not, whether it succeeds or not. And in that civilisation the key is going to be the concept of multiple identities, and the challenge is going to be whether we can have a harmonious development of these identities or whether there would be perpetual conflict which might destroy the world. That is the challenge for humanity in the twenty-first century.

It seems to me that at the core of all these questions lies the concept of human dignity. If every human being is given the dignity and the respect which he or she deserves as a human being, then that is the basis upon which all the other identities must revolve. You cannot deprive a human being of the dignity and respect that they deserve because they happen to fall or not fall into one or the other identity. My concentric circles of multiple identities revolve around a core of spiritual identity, which is inherent in every human being. I do not want to go into the theology of Hinduism, although this is something in which I am deeply interested. I am also involved in the Interfaith movement which seeks to bring together people of different religions, but all religions ultimately believe that there is within each human being something which is very special, whether you call it a divinity, or divine reflection or whatever. And therefore the dignity of an individual is to be respected, then the identities have to be respected.

I found particularly interesting this definition of areas. It seems that West Asia is certainly not sufficient, but we do not want to revert to using the term Middle East. Maybe we should work out some new nomenclature. This is a creative experiment; WANA, which means West Asia and North Africa, is how the Indian Ministry of External Affairs calls this area. It just shows that the whole region we are dealing with is much more complex than might appear at first sight.

I am often asked about the follow up to these seminars. This is a question I have been unable to answer from the very first seminar to this one. There is nothing that we as the India International Centre can do by way of follow up. We try to act as a catalytic agent. Many of our participants meet each other here for the first time. I remember when we had the Central Asian seminar, the participants from countries like Kazakhistan, Kirghistan, Turkmenistan, Tajikistan, Uzbekistan and others met for the first time in this very room. Similarly, it is quite possible, that some people even among the Arabs may not have met those from other Arab countries, and surely the Indians may not have met the Arabs. The follow up can be at two levels. One is the individual level. Individual scholars who have been here can keep in touch with their colleagues or individual scholars from the Arab world can keep writing to us. The second follow up can be at the institutional level. We have four major Indian universities involved here—the Delhi University, the Jawaharlal Nehru University, the Aligarh Muslim University and scholars from Jamia Millia Islamia of Delhi. Perhaps our seminar can be of help in some way to encourage further contacts between the scholars who are here from the other countries.

It is in the clash of ideas that the truth emerges. A seminar that is too bland does not fulfill its purpose. All of us are in the academic and intellectual fields, and as one goes around the world attending seminars they are always interesting provided there is a basic commitment to certain fundamental theses. As far as this seminar is concerned, there are three major assumptions: (a) that India and the Arab world have in the past had very close and creative relationships; (b) that the relationships today are not satisfactory in terms of intellectual exchange or anything else; and (c) that we should try and work in the future towards strengthening these relationships in the context of the emerging global society. It is my sincere hope that this publication will be a modest but significant step towards achieving this goal.

Conceptualising India-West Asia Relations
The Macro Historical Perspective

A.K. Ramakrishan

The history of India-West Asia relation is so multi-faceted and long ranging in both scope and time that a piecemeal approach becomes extremely restrictive in grasping its scale and significance. Historians have traditionally been concentrating on trade relations, cultural contacts, political and foreign policy aspects, etc., of the India-West Asia relationship, especially in a bilateral framework. While such studies are very important in understanding different shades of the history of that relationship, a macro-historical approach is essential to comprehend the threads of substantial linkages between the entities. A macro-historical approach is well served by analysing the systemic character of such linkages rather than by looking into each and every particularity of the long-standing relationship. What is attempted in this paper is not a study of the history of relationships proper, but a broad approach to comprehend the relative positions, associations and linkages between India and West Asia within different and changing world systems. The basic thrust of this paper is to provide a brief assessment of the significance of macro-historical world system perspectives by critically evaluating the contributions of a variety of scholars such as Janet Abu Lughod, Immanual Wallerstein, Andre Gunder Frank, Barry Buzan and Richard Little.

The inextricable linkage between historical writing and the idea of the modern 'nation' brought forth history as national history. Those regions, peoples and entities outside the modern nation and the international system based on nation-states were viewed as having no history of their own. Anti-orientalist and reverse orientalist positions and critiques of modern historiography advanced by Said, the Subaltern Studies group, and others have their own limitations in overcoming the colonial discourse that dichotomizes modern Europe and the contemporary but pre-modern non-West. The world historical *long duree* notions are extremely significant in breaking the shackles of both unitary national/societal histories and the West/non-West colonial epistemological divide. It becomes imperative to talk about systemic aspects of history so that linkages rather than perceived hierarchies of temporal and spatial dimensions could be studied.

Foucault proposed that there are no grand or meta-histories, but only history in 'patches' or only genealogies of the particular. Foucault's rejection of universalism especially of the modern kind, as inherently hegemonic made it more or less impossible to look at human civilisations in their world historical linkage. Why should one after all pose the universal against the particular? Ideas of historical international systems, where civilisational cores and other units interact and give shape to a wider pattern of networks in definite order, are useful in circumventing the dichotomous notions described above.

Andre Gunder Frank argued for a 'globological' perspective on world history.[1] This may seem to be an alternative to the particularisms of conventional treatment of India-West Asia relations. But there are a variety of conceptual and methodological problems that one has to confront in adopting a global perspective. One important problem is that the global denotes an unmediated entity, unmediated by state, civilisation, society, economic process, or any agency of peoples and societies. One way out obviously is to resort to a systemic analysis of a historical nature so that questions of agency/structure are not addressed in a simple dichotomous way, but in the dynamics of an agency-induced historical perspective.

Any systemic theory should have to delineate the nature of the system (whole) with regard to its units (parts). The world system approach that Wallerstein popularised in academic circles conceives economic entity as the unit of analysis rather than state, society or individual.[2] Frank would agree with this proposition, though of late, he has become more long-stretching and ephemeral about the unit of analysis. World economy is Wallerstein's and Frank's take on the unit. Barry Buzan and Richard Little in their recent book, *International Systems in World History*: *Remaking the Study of International Relations,* try to identify various units for different international systems at different points of time: city-states, empires, nation-states, non-state entities, etc.,[3] and thereby move away from the Wallersteinian analysis. What seems to be feasible for our purpose is to identify both the economic structure and the socio-political entities at different historical junctures as strategic units of analysis, keeping in mind both the convergence and divergence that we seek to obtain with the analysis of the above writers.

The long fixation with the *modern* world system arguments of Immanuel Wallerstein has in a way undermined the possibility of studying the world system in a much longer time scale as well as in a much broader civilisational anchorage. Understanding long-term India-West Asia relations demands an approach that is beyond Wallerstein. One could hold on to his world economy argument, but yet not be satisfied with the five hundred year modern world system as *the* world system. The world economy itself can be understood from a longer historical terrain that the five hundred years that Wallerstein holds dear.

One has to acknowledge now the existence of world systems before the European-dominated one that started from the 'long sixteenth century' (as Fernand Braudel calls it). Janet Abu-Lughod stresses on the dynamic nature of world systems. She has suggested that the thirteenth century is a plausible beginning of a world system that was in no way 'inferior' to the sixteenth century one.[4] Frank and Barry Gills extend the scope of the world system further by tracing its origins as far back as five thousand years.[5] They argue, 'the same features that characterize Wallerstein's "modern" five-hundred-year-old world system can also be found in the same system going back at least five thousand years.'[6] Frank has been very skeptical of the qualitative difference between the capitalist modern world system and the previous ones by asserting the continuity of the world system from five thousand years to date. This seems to be too generalized an approach. What I call 'historical world systems' in their similarities and differences could be approached from their multiplicity rather than a unitary notion of a world system. Interestingly enough, certain conceptual notions of world systems defined by

Wallerstein fit more or less with previous world systems, whose qualitative difference from the modern one he wants to portray. According to him, world systems 'are defined by the fact that their self-containment as an economic-material entity is based on extensive division of labour and that they contain within them a multiplicity of cultures'.[7]

One of the main arguments of Janet Abu-Lughod is that, 'the century between A.D. 1250 and 1350 constituted a fulcrum or critical "turning point" in world history, and in terms of space, the Middle East heartland region, linking the eastern Mediterranean region with the Indian Ocean, constituted a geographic fulcrum on which West and East were then roughly balanced.'[8]

This points to the need to look at the period's India-West Asia linkages within the contours of the world system rather than simply as a bilateral process. And we have to extend the argument to include such relations in the previous world systems as well.

Buzan and Little point out that the ancient and classical world 'fits into the picture of overall human progress'[9] as if one needs to say this in black and white. They argue that the ancient and classical era witnessed 'several distinct full international systems operating at the same time, and over the course of the era all of these systems tended to expand, sometimes merging with others in the process'. They say that they were not 'global' international systems.[10]

Whether one agrees with the particularities of the arguments put forward by Abu-Lughod, Frank and Gills or Buzan and Little, arguments that extend the temporal scale of the world system, they are significant in understanding Indo-West Asian relations not as appendages of the European world system, but as integral and most often as core realms of historical world systems.

Reservations on this kind of 'taking the world system back' may arise out of the notion that the gap between the centres and peripheries of classical and ancient systems are so big that a systemic perspective really might not yield any tangible results. But one is struck by the discrepancy and unevenness of even the modern capitalist world system that one can view the cleavages of different world systems as a matter of degrees.

The thirteenth century world system was 'extremely *uneven*, integrating into the network only an archipelago of "world cities" elevated above a sea of relatively isolated rural areas and open stretches'. But, as Abu-Lughod points out, 'such spottiness was not unique to the thirteenth century'.[11] It is well evident in the present-day world system in numerous ways and levels. Blaut describes the mode of production in those cities as 'incipient capitalism', and he insists that it was definitely not feudalism. It was a sort of 'protocapitalism... with wageworkers being, apparently the largest working-class sector, merchants, merchant-landlords, or merchant-manufacturers the ruling class, and economic activity a mixture of trade (movement of commodities, banking, and so on), manufacture (both large-scale and small-scale), and commercial agriculture'.[12] While agreeing with Blaut on several counts, Frank questions the use of the term proto-capitalism and other similar usages: 'The incessant discussions about non-, pre-, proto-, blooming-, full blown-, declining-, post-, or any other "stage" and quantity or quality of capitalism or the lack thereof have led us down the garden path and diverted us from analyzing the real world.'[13]

The debates on the Asiatic mode of production have also shown the same weariness of describing non-Western societies in terms of underdevelopment, etc. While for Frank, such a stage-wise representation would undermine his notion of a continuous world system for five thousand years, Blaut's proposition is significant in showing the capitalist-seeming tendencies within earlier world systems. Frank, Blaut and Abu-Lughod point towards the possibility of turning the wheel of world system analysis back in order that for us the grasping of India-West Asia relations from a broader canvas is possible.

While writing the history of the theoretical traditions of International Relations, Torbjorn Knutsen attempted at distinguishing between a 'historical tradition' and an 'analytical tradition' and argued that even though historical traditions of International Relations scholarship were available in a number of instances in both the West and the East, an analytical tradition was the contribution of Europe in the so-called Dark Ages. But, while noting the contributions of medieval civilisations, he noted, 'it is quite conceivable that the Arabs sustained an analytic tradition of International Relations.'[14] It is imperative that both in the historical practice of International Relations and in the intellectual tradition of International Relations, one has to look beyond medieval modern Europe, not only to the medieval Arab world, but also elsewhere in a larger historical scale.

This India-West Asia axis in world history is a significant pointer in understanding the whole dynamics of historical world systems. There was no single hegemonic power in the thirteenth century world system. Nor was this system hierarchical in character.[15] There were multiple centres of trade and civilisation such as China, India, various centres in West and Central Asia, and Europe (which was the least developed of the rest, 'an upstart peripheral' in Abu-Lughod's words). Arab-Persian imperial centres, the Mongol empire, the Delhi Sultanate, trading centres of coastal India, etc., along with the towns of western Europe formed nodal points of such a system. If we go further back, West Asian, Indian and Chinese cities and empires and their mutual trading and civilisational links formed a major core activity in earlier world systems.

Buzan and Little suggest that in the existence of international systems the following are significant criteria; interaction and its pattern and scale. Whether India-West Asia relations historically formed the core of a world system or not, it is crucial to think about the extent and type of interaction and the two entities' capacity and potential for multiple ways of mutual intercourse. India and various centres in West Asia were proved to be showing significant capacity and scale of interaction in the world systems that existed at various temporal junctures.

If in the ancient and classical world systems India-West Aisa Relations acted as nodes or even as fulcra of the systems, both the entities lost out to the European-dominated capitalist world system of the modern era. As Abu-Lughod suggested, 'there was no *inherent historical necessity* that shifted the system to favour the West rather than the East, nor was there any inherent historical necessity that would have prevented cultures' of the East from initiating growth of the contemporary world system.'[16] Buzan and Little suggest the following regarding the transformation from the pre-modern to the modern world system:

> The ancient and the classical world provided the foundation on which the European development was built. If the rise of Europe had not intervened, it is easy to imagine that the process of slow expansion from several cores of civilization might have continued. Trade and contact might have increased as the different zones of civilization overlapped more with each other, eventually resulting in a global system. This system would have been quite different from that which the Europeans eventually created.[17]

Once the capitalist world system under European hegemony expanded to South and West Asia and subdued the regions to machinations of accumulation and control, the resistance to imperialism became the shared and combined legacy of both India and West Asia, as their response to the hegemonic modern world system. The anti-imperialist struggle was obviously the assertion of the weak against the dominant in the world system. It was a way of empowerment and of seeking legitimate national and regional space within the global order. The Non-Aligned Movement and politics of solidarity during the immediate post-colonial context were further attempts at this retrieval of power and freedom.

If nation-state politics (imagining and constructing a free nation-state) was integral to the India-West Asia relationship during imperialist rule, the contemporary neoliberal politico-economic climate does not allow for nation-centric linkages anymore. There is need to address how neoliberal globalisation of the contemporary capitalist world order are shaping and reshaping the subservient status of both India and West Asia in the world system.

What is extremely significant is the necessity to evolve economic and trade linkages that compel the capitalist world system not only to shift geographically, but also to promote alternate centres of production and trade. China, a power that no historical world system could do away with, will be a player to be reckoned with in evolving regional and trans-regional politico-economic arrangements. The events of September 11 and the projection of an unscientific and unrealistic 'clash of civilization' logic which never applied to India-West Asian relationship in the past historical world systems, should make us more receptive to ideas of evolving greater cooperative interaction. Regional economic and trade regimes and joint intellectual endeavours have to be evolved on a wider scale. If there has to be a shift in the core of the world system, centres of production, technology and trade have to shift. Given the potential of the natural resources, markets, strategic commodities, and the technological potential, etc., of India, China and the West Asian region, a shift cannot altogether be dismissed.

Notes

1. Andre Gunder Frank, *ReOrient: Global Economy in the Asian Age,* New Delhi: Vistaar Publications, 1998, p.xv.
2. Immanuel Wallerstein, *The Modern World System,* New York: Academic Press, 1976, p.xi.
3. Barry Buzan and Richard Little, *International Systems in World History: Remaking the Study of International Relations,* Oxford: Oxford University Press, 2000.
4. Janet L. Abu-Lughod, *Before European Hegemony: The World System A.D. 1250-1350,* Oxford : Oxford University Press, 1989.
5. Andre Gunder Frank and Barry K. Gills, *The World System: Five Hundred Years of Five Thousand?* London: Routledge, 1993.
6. Andre Gunder Frank, p.xxi; emphasis in the original.
7. I. Wallerstein, p. 230.
8. J.L. Abu-Lughod, p. 12.
9. B. Buzan and R. Little, p. 240.
10. Ibid., p.239.
11. J.L. Abu-Lughod, p. 353.
12. J.M. Blaut, *The Colonizer's Model of the World,* New York: The Guilford Press, 1993, p. 167.
13. A.G. Frank, p. 331.
14. Torbjorn Knutsen, *A History of International Relations,* Manchester: Manchester University Press, 1997, p. 20.
15. J.L. Abu-Lughod, pp. 364-65.
16. Ibid., p. 12; emphasis in the original.
17. B. Buzan and R. Little, p. 240.

Kuwait and India
Historical, Cultural and Social Bonds

RASHA AL-SABAH

'Arabia and India have been friends since the beginning of history. A sea is named after Arabia and an ocean after India. Between us we account for some of the most ancient and glorious of human civilizations.'

Indira Gandhi, 11 May 1981[1]

The people of Kuwait, a small state wedged at the north western corner of the Arabian peninsula between Saudi Arabia to the south and west, Iraq to the north, and the Arabian Gulf to the east, proudly profess a certain knowledge about India and the Indian people. This sense of intimacy, acquired during the course of active commercial, cultural and political interaction between Kuwait and India, particularly in the pre-oil period, cannot understandably be returned by India, a huge country with a far vaster population, separated by geographical distance and lack of knowledge regarding the customs, habits, history and lifestyle of the people of Kuwait.

For this purpose, it is worthwhile to present a brief introduction describing Kuwait and its people from the time of Kuwait's foundation as an entity in the Arabian peninsula until its emergence as a full-fledged nation-state over forty years ago.

In the mid-eighteenth century, around the year 1752, several nomadic tribes emigrated from the heart of the Arabian peninsula and settled in Kuwait, an Arabic term denoting 'small fort'. In the year 1756, the elders of these tribes alongside the tiny indigenous population collectively voted Sabah the First as the ruler of their community. This process of the election of a leader by means of tribal consensus is the earliest historical record showing Kuwaitis practicing democratic principles in their most primitive form, a tradition that has continued to this day.

The conditions of a barren desert and a mercilessly hot environment for most of the year dictated the exploitation of the sea outlet as the most viable means of subsistence for Kuwaitis. This they used with amazing skill and fortitude and gained universal renown as first-class ship makers, pearl divers and sea merchants, braving the seas to reach the shores of East Africa and the Indian subcontinent. With the discovery and exportation of the first shipment of oil towards the middle of the twentieth century came the gradual decline of Kuwait's seafaring activities, as the merchant and the fast emerging middle classes leaned towards more home-based economies. Moreover, the vast revenues accruing from the sale of oil allowed the state to provide essential health and education services free of charge to its citizens and residents, and encouraged it to become the largest and most favoured employer for the vast majority of its citizens, providing jobs with attractive salaries and generous fringe benefits.

However, despite the gradual and eventual cessation in Kuwait's seafaring activities in the wake of its emergence as a welfare state, the bonds created between Kuwaitis and their former trading partners overseas have never been interrupted. On the contrary, influences deriving from Kuwait's interaction with these distant lands and peoples are heavily impressed and remain acutely visible in the customs, habits and lifestyles of modern Kuwaitis. No truer can this be than witnessed in the relations between Kuwait and India. Aspects of Indian culture and heritage, borne by intense trading and cultural interaction, have been cordially and effectively subsumed in our national culture and social norms. These all-pervasive influences have affected our language and terminology, our literature, our music and arts, our cuisine, not only on the national level, but indeed on our entire civilisational heritage as citizens of a nation-state belonging to the larger Arab and Muslim world.

On a more particular level, there is no doubt that the former subjection of both Kuwait and India to the spherical jurisdiction of the same political and military foreign power (Great Britain) is a common denominator shedding further insights into the bilateral ties linking both nations. The fact that Kuwait used the Indian rupee as the principal source of monetary exchange until its independence, indicates that Kuwait's economy was inextricably tied to the economy of India. Furthermore, prior to the independence of both nations, Kuwaitis expressed great sympathy with and supported the movement for liberation and independence from the colonising power here in India, professing their great admiration and acclamation of the leadership of Mahatma Gandhi. From the Indian perspective, the emergence of Kuwait as a sovereign nation was a welcome issue. On 30 June 1961, soon after Kuwait gained its full independence, Prime Minister Jawaharlal Nehru stated that 'he was glad that Kuwait had become independent' and added: 'India had treated Kuwait as a separate entity for a considerable time past and we propose to continue to treat it as an independent identity.'[2] Not only did India support Kuwait's entry into the United Nations later in the same year, but it was the first non-Arab country in Asia and Africa to recognise Kuwait as a sovereign independent state.

Despite the common denominators and similarities between Kuwait and India, there remain, however, certain points of divergence and disparity. The most obvious, from the point of view of this speaker, is the status of women in both nations. Whereas India, as the largest democracy in the world, has long resolved the issue of women's participation in political life, boasting a woman prime minister, the struggle to attain women's political rights in Kuwait remains a path fraught with enormous obstacles. Since independence and the promulgation of the Constitution in 1962, the question of the right of Kuwaiti women to enter the political arena and to exercise their constitutionally ordained civil rights as full-fledged Kuwaiti citizens, to elect their candidates and stand for parliamentary seats, has not been settled.

All efforts to reclaim this right, stipulated in Article 29 of the Constitution, by amending the Kuwaiti election law, have so far failed. Even the historical initiative made by His Highness the Amir of Kuwait on 16 May 1999, when he issued an Amiri decree granting full political rights to Kuwaiti women who constitute over half the population of Kuwait, was rejected by a two-vote margin when put to the vote by Parliament in October of the same year.

Since its era of independence, India decided that it cannot

truly boast a full-fledged democracy with the isolation of half of its populace. Kuwait has still to follow suit, not only for the sake of legitimising its status as a true democratic nation but also in order to continue building a modern state by expanding the base of political participation for all its citizens.

During the pre-oil period, when many male members of the Kuwaiti community spent several months of the year away from home, travelling on their merchant ships to the shores of distant lands, including India, it was the women of Kuwait who held the fort. In their own way and during the long periods of absence of their husbands, fathers and brothers, the women of Kuwait played the multiple roles of ministers of the interior, the economy, and social affairs, in their respective homes. This resilience and fortitude during times of hardship and adversity demonstrated by Kuwaiti women in the course of history, came to their advantage during the bleakest hour of Kuwait's history, that is, during the seven-month invasion and occupation of Kuwait by the Iraqi regime, which began on 2 August 1990. It was the women of Kuwait who staged the first demonstration against the aggressor army on 5 August 1990, and it was they who laid their lives for the sake of freedom and the sovereignty of their nation. Many of these women are still kept, alongside their male compatriots, in unknown places of detention in Iraq. The Iraqi regime remains obstinate in its refusal to provide any information regarding their whereabouts to their families and loved ones in Kuwait, despite their capture and abduction by the Iraqi forces over a decade ago.

I have mentioned these facts about the heroism and sacrifices of Kuwaiti women in order to stress that they have long reached the age of political maturity, a condition that merits placing them on a similar status of parity with their Indian counterparts.

Notes

1. A.K. Pasha, *India, Kuwait: Strategic, Economic and Political Developments*, Gyan Sagar Publications, New Delhi, 1999, p. 258.
2. Ibid., p. 298.

Afro-Asian Relations
The Sudanese Perspective

Jaffar Mirghani Ahmed

A truth of human social history, mostly ignored, is that seas and even oceans are the oldest and best means of strong contact. Wherever there is a sea, wide or narrow, you are sure to find that the people occupying both coasts have age old intercourse and even ethnical ties. Thus, as an example, the Mediterranean African coasts were from early times in contact with the Mediterranean's European coasts. Phoenician (Cana'anites) vessels had traversed it from times immemorial. History tells us that it is they who built ancient cities all around its coasts, such as Tyr, Beirut, Cartage, Cordoba, Madrid and Venice. It is they, in the times of the Pharaohs, who sailed all around the coasts of Africa, starting from the Delta coast and ending in the Suez Canal.

The widest water basin of the whole world is the Pacific Ocean. Yet it did not severe human societies from contacts and ties going back to prehistoric times. Anthropology tells us that the so-called Red Indians and the aborigines of Australia have racial relations with the peoples of East and Southeast Asia.

The Indian Ocean is not an exception. Witnessing the fact that the oldest habitats of the human race are to be found scattered over lands surrounding its coasts and those of seas and gulfs linked to it, we may conclude that these are the waters in which humanity in its earliest infancy first learned sailing and sea faring.

Our notion of a modern world torn between two poles of East and West have much blurred our memory of history. The natural division of a cold North and a warm South—hence variety in products—founded the basis of mercantilism upon which the economy and traditional and commercial transactions used to rest. Sea liners of the Indian Ocean and the water courses open to it (the Red Sea and the Gulf) were linked by caravan routes to those of the Mediterranean.

Commodities from different parts of the Indian ocean traversed the routes of West Asia and North East Africa to Europe where they were greatly needed and highly valued. Caught in active currents of far distant trade and worldwide transactions, lands of warm climates extending from the western and eastern coast of Africa to West, South and Southeast Asia became so intermingled to such familiarity of contact, as depicted in the famous book of travels of Ibn Batuta. Journeying all those quarters of warm climates and even some of the near reaches of cold ones from Morocco to China, Ibn Batuta (as Gibb rightly pointed out), wherever he travelled or landed, was sure to find brothers and friends ready for him.

Prehistoric contacts and the ever growing commercial conduct evolved into common trends of culture and a holistic outlook, which viewed these vast lands of warm climates as an integrated and somehow unified world. Subsequently, and naturally enough, a generic name was coined. In ancient Greek and classical literature this whole world of warm climates around and in-between the tropics was named Ethiopia. To this Homer pointed in his famous *Iliad*:

The Ethiopians utmost of mankind
These Eastward situate, those to the West

In Arabic literary works and traditions the idea of a whole Afro-Asian warm world is to be found. In the oldest extant history book named *Sira* (Biography of The Prophet) it is mentioned that King Saif of Yemen, speaking in front of the Emperor of Persia, said: 'We have been conquered by the Sudan.' To that the Persian Emperor answered, 'Whom do you mean by the Sudan? The Indians or the Abyssinians.'

Gahiz, a renowned ancient Arab writer, entertained the same idea and elaborated on it in his book entitled *The Glory of the Sudan*. Under the generic name of Sudan he counts the Chinese, Indian, Abyssinians, Nubians, Copts, Berbers and all peoples living in-between. To Gahiz it is not a matter or colour or race. He points out that Indians are more fair in colour than the Arabs yet they are to be counted among the people of Sudan.

The Bible classifies Cana'anites as Kushites (Hamites), whom other histories classify as Semites. The Berbers of North

Africa and the Nubians of North Sudan are related in some works of history to the Homerites of ancient Yemen. For the Greeks, Arabia starts from the Eastern banks of the Nile, while Yemen, Abyssinia and East Africa come under the name of India in some of their works. It is of interest to mention here that the word 'Sudan' in Arabic bears the same meaning as Ethiopians in Greek. In Tubdawi (a language of the Sudanese Red Sea coast) the word Hindi means green or dark-colored. An old patriotic Sudanese song has a verse saying:

That I love most
From Berno (Nigeria) to India
My Sudan

All the above notions and terms, agreed upon or disputed, spring from a kind of profound bond felt between those lands and peoples of warm climates in different phases of history, no matter how inadequately it was interpreted. One may conveniently interpret it, in accordance with the modern phrase, into 'Pan'-'Sudan', 'Pan' 'Ethiopian', 'Pan'-'Indian', or even better, 'Pan'-'tropical'.

The cultural and economical aspect of our world has much differed since the European advent of discovery and colonisation. Rivalry in the cold North over the riches of the warm South caused in less than a quarter of a century two sad World Wars and a dual polarization which left little choice to the glorious Pan-Sudan world of the past except to try to accommodate itself in a movement with a newly coined name derived from a passive notion of non-alliance. A term which blocked our thoughts to the extent that when the Cold War came to an end we made little use of the rich legacy of our past, a legacy which if properly made use of in a revived strategy of action, could not only have provided the movement with a positive name, but also established ideals and recognised trends so that what was once 'Pan-Sudan' or Pan-Indian' could be spelled as 'Pan-Sudanism', 'Pan-Indianism', 'Pan-tropicalism' or, any such appropriate name with the suffix 'ism'.

Contemporary Indo-Sudanese Relations

HASSAN MEKKI

The main focus of my contribution is on Sudanese-Indo relations from three major perspectives, namely, political, economic and socio-cultural, and intellectual.

To begin with I am very pleased to underscore that in Sudanese memory there is full awareness of the political developments of the contemporary history of India, starting from the time of Mahatma Gandhi, passing through that of Jawaharlal Nehru up to the present Indian leaders who, with their wise leadership and farsightedness, have put India at the rightful place that it now occupies at both the regional and international levels.

The Sudanese also still remember the historic visits paid in the past by some of those great leaders to the Sudan, among which were those paid by Nehru, one of the founding fathers of the Non-Aligned Movement (NAM), and the late former Indian President Fakhruddin Ali Ahmed.

It is with our strong belief in the principles of NAM that the conscience of the Sudanese political elite stands for the unity of the Third World countries as a pre-requisite to the formation of a common ground among them that could assist in achieving true political independence, economic development and social prosperity for all.

Coming to the cultural aspect, history indicates that the cultural ties between the Sudan and India date back to the time when the ancient civilisations and kingdoms in both countries interacted. Many aspects of culture and tradition in the two countries had a common origin.

In the Sudan the Indian community is known to have been the only foreign community that has undergone complete social integration. Though small in number, it has undertaken various organised activities which are reflected in the Sudanese media.

Both the Sudan and India share a common cultural heritage traditions and civilisation ever since they were striving to liberate their people from the yoke of colonialism.

In the economic field, light and heavy Indian industries as well as advanced Indian technology have entered the Sudanese market decades ago. Many Indian modes of transport have dominated the highways, streets and by-lanes of most of the Sudanese cities and towns.

I am very pleased to note that the economic cooperation between Sudan and India is developing faster and faster with genuine and remarkable efforts being exerted by both the countries to further strengthen this cooperation.

Indian Universities have contributed immensely in educating many Sudanese elite in the past and they continue to impart scientific and social science education to thousands of Sudanese students currently pursuing their education in various Indian higher institutions of learning.

In the intellectual field, the Indian Islamic mode of thinking such as that of Dahlawi, Maududi and others, have remarkably affected Islamic intellectual activity in the Sudan. This influence has actually been based on an early historic literary influence dating back to the age of translation, where many Indian works like *Sindbad*, *Taj Mahal*, and others have influenced the conscience of many Sudanese poets and novelists.

A most far-reaching influence of Hindustan was the intellectual influence on West Asia and the Arab world. This is well embodied in the scholarly impact of the Indian Islamic movement and in shaping the mentality and activities of Muslim and Arab thinkers. The Tablihgi Jama'at is well known since decades to Egyptian Sudanese and indeed to many Muslim Asian elites. Over 150 Muslim countries are influenced by the Jamaat Tablighi. In Sudan the Jama'at Tablighi is one of the most active movements whose spiritual and moral guidance is generated from Jama'at headquarters in Nizamuddin in New Delhi.

On the other hand Maulana Muhammed Elyas and his son Muhammed Yousuf of Kandhli established a Tablighi Jama'at Centre, where Arabic language was spoken and the practice of the Prophet and his companions was strictly adhered to. Through their purely religious activities the Tablighi Jama'at was able to work uninterruptedly for years. Many Indian Muslim writers attracted the attention of many renowned Muslim scholars in West Asia. Shah Walyullah was the first Muslim writer to introduce the concept of review in the theory of ijtihad in Shari's in the eighteenth century.

Moreover, Sir Sayid Ahmed Khan was known to be the first to advocate modern trends in Islamic thought. Books authored by Maulana Asad of Jama'at ul Ulema on Al Fatiha were widely read by Arab and Muslim readers. Similarly, other writers' works, like Zakir Hassain, the former President of India who vigorously advocated Hindu-Muslim peaceful life, were also widely read by Muslim and Arab scholars.

In his own address to the conference, my colleague Jafar Mirghani, tried to avoid using the term 'India and West Asia' since many Arab participants were sceptical about the term West Asia because it is meant to split the Arab world into two, while many Indians were sceptical about the term Middle East as it is a Western concept that reflects the European or Western view that divides the East into Near, Middle and Far. Indeed, it might be far to the Europeans but as far as we are concerned we are all Easterners and the Middle East to us might mean Bangkok. What is important here is that Jafar Mirghani used new terms, i.e. 'The Tropical League', the 'Sudanese League' or even the 'Indian League', properly relying upon the classification of Al-Jaghiiz, an early Muslim of scholar who classified the globe into hot and cool. Jafar's suggestion, though appearing peculiar to some, was actually given much preference by many, since we all live in a hot zone and to the whites we are all coloured nations anyway.

With all this in mind, I earlier touched on the impact of India on Sudanese life, starting with the role of the political elites in Sudan who were very vocal in appreciating the contribution made by the great leaders of India.

The Sudanese political elites, who were at a loss in the early thirties of the previous century, had either to choose the Mahdiya military struggle to liberate their country or the peaceful political struggle, of which Gandhi was the pioneer. The latter was their choice when the Graduate Conference emerged.

The spiritual influence and Tag Din Al Buhari cannot be forgotten. He visited Sudan in the fifteenth century as a guest of the family of Al Hindi (the Indian), a renowned religious family in Sudan. Thereafter he established the Tabligh Society that plays a great role in Sudan today (Kadri Sufi Group).

In conclusion, I would like to reiterate the importance of such academic interaction between our two countries. I hope to see my colleagues in India in the Sudan for a similar interaction in order to further strengthen the cultural cooperation between the Sudan and India, particularly in the academic field.

Indo-Arab Relationship
The Syrian Perspective

WAIEL S.H. AWWAD

The world will remember the twenty-first century as the century of humanity and equality among humans. If we are able to rise above selfishness and egoism then we can acquire the greater consciousness that we are all part of the Divine Being, one father.

The impact of colonial thinking was visible from day one, especially among historians, some of whom politicized history to suit themselves. The famous French researcher Pierre Russi had said, It is not enough we talk, but we should talk what is correct and useful.'

Indo-Arab relations have their roots dug deep in history, since human discovery in the Arab world and in the subcontinent had proved beyond doubt the continuity of humans' and their achievements in one place over eons. This phenomenon is supported by archaeological discovery and linguistically it has been asserted that there is a deep link between Mesopotamia and the Indus Valley Civilisation.

Wall Diwarnt says that more than six thousand years have passed since the beginning of written history and during half of that era the Far East was the centre of human affairs; this includes all the Southwest Asian countries which extend from the South of Russia and the Black Sea to India and Afghanistan.

The presence of two similar civilisations in the two different places and times leads us to the belief of either the transfer of this phenomenon, or the independent indigenous birth of each of these two similar civilisations. But the presence of one language in two different places and times cannot but imply the movement of people who speak the same language and impose it on others to prove their superiority.

We strongly believe in the unity of human history on earth and this will highlight all the oppressive methods and selfishness in writing history. This will unite humanity and brighten the track of civilisation and highlight noble and humane values.

There is a belief in the Arab world that India or Hind derives its name from the mountain Nid, the centre of which we believe was our father Adam, the first man who was sent from heaven to earth. Scientists have confirmed the phenomenon of Ice Melting from Europe at the beginning of the contemporary warm era which started 14,000 years ago, which led to the creation of seas and oceans over 10,000 years. The Arabian sea came into existence and advanced into a region called the Arabian Gulf which pushed the Arab Syria into two directions, one to the South Arab and the other to western Indian shores. This is the contention of environment experts like Jack Labem and the American archaeologist Goris Zairians and the German research unit (Meteor) which has been working in the Gulf areas for a long time. Therefore, we can safely conclude that the Dravida language and the Sanskrit language in India are the twin sisters of the old Arabic language.

Kandortof said that linguists will find a lot of similarity between the Dravida language and Assyrian language (slaves' language). These slaves came from Mesopotamia and kept talking about their submerged ancestor's land and about the kingdom which was swallowed by the sea waters. The Indus Valley Civilisation is a mixture of Sumerian and Dravidian and hence the interchange between the civilisations has never been based on political enmity but on fraternity and friendship.

I may be allowed to say that the old religion of Syria has a lot in common with the basic tenets of the Indian religion and archaeological findings prove a striking similarity between the two civilisations.

Contemporary Relations

Recent developments in the world scenario have introduced a new element in the relations between nations. While the relations between the Arab countries and India remained steady, in the normalising of relations between India and Israel India's perception was that this will give New Delhi a leading role in the Middle East peace process. But recent developments in Tel Aviv, the halt in the peace process due to the refusal to implement the UN Security Council Resolutions 242, 338 and the Madrid peace conference reference, i.e. 'Land For Peace' and the uprising in the occupied territories against the Israeli occupation brought the right wing Likud party to the helm of power in the Jewish state.

The atrocities against the Palestinian people went parallel with strengthened ties between New Delhi and Tel Aviv, especially in the security and military fields and in the suspected relations in the nuclear field. All this raised the concern in the Arab World that India was drifting from the old traditional relations with the Arab world and that the warm relations with Israel were at the cost of the Arabs. Despite New Delhi's efforts to calm the Arab concern, this did not help much in practical terms for many reasons including the secrecy of the relations with Tel Aviv. The repeated visits by high level delegations and experts from both sides, and New Delhi not keeping its Arab allies aware of the extent of such relationships made many Arab countries believe that Israel had succeeded in shifting the balance to its side and India would be used as the bridge for Tel Aviv to spread its hegemony on the Arab world, especially the Gulf states.

The enemy of strong ties harps on the Arab stand in OIC and other forums by distorting facts and rumoring that Pakistan is being appeased by the Islamic countries, in general, and the Arab world in particular, whenever the question of Kashmir is raised, so that short-term political gains can be achieved, and the long-term goals for the peace and tranquillity of the whole region get ignored.

Therefore to implement the legacy of the past in shaping the future relationship certain measures need to be taken and irritant factors eliminated.

India and the Arab world should play an active role in shaping the international relationship in the current world scenario. They are the natural candidates for it as they have a rich contribution to make to humanity.

Certain steps should be taken such as:

1. Enhancing interaction and greater cooperation in all fields.
2. Formation of joint consulting groups to deal with current issues and holding of periodic meetings to

defuse crises and exchange views on issues of mutual interest.

3. Formation of a Parliamentarian's forum to stress on the values of democracy, freedom of expression and human rights.
4. Enhancing of cultural ties by exchanging delegations in various fields like education, communications, literature and languages. It is of vital importance to learn each other's language so that greater understanding and people-to-people contacts can be established.
5. Increasing people-to-people contacts and greater interaction between the non-governmental organisations to consolidate the old ties.

One might argue that most of these measures already exist. But in order to realise their importance and priority such steps should be stressed upon by the political establishments in India and in the Arab countries.

I will leave it to the decision makers on both sides to do a retrospective analysis, and introspect on the importance of this relationship, and block any attempt by parties to create tensions and divisions between us under any pretext. After all, we do not sell weapons. We gift friendship, fraternity and brotherhood.

Yemen and India
Developent of Historical Relationships

Saleh Ali Basurrah

The geographical proximity across the Indian Ocean has provided the Indian subcontinent and the Arabian Peninsula, especially Yemen, with favourable circumstances/conditions conducive for civilisational contact and commercial exchange. In addition to this, another factor, with a geographical and navigational/maritime component, made the relationship between India and Yemen from ancient times and until the present, more important and beneficial. This was that Yemen is a country overlooking the Arabian Sea and the Indian Ocean, and hence controls the southern gate of the Red Sea (Babel-Mandab and Perim Island). This is a strait of utmost importance for mercantile traffic between India and the countries overlooking the Red Sea, and also between India and the countries of North Africa and Europe, especially after the opening of the Suez Canal in 1869.

In addition, the sailing ships were owned by some Yemenis and some Omanis, and their skills in navigation and good knowledge of the monsoons in the Arabian Sea and the Indian Ocean were unequalled. These ships used to cross the Indian Ocean carrying products and commodities to India and sailing back to Yemen or Oman with Indian goods.

These factors were very fruitful in establishing cultural and economic relationships between India and Yemen during the period of the ancient Indian civilisation and the ancient Yemeni kingdoms (Hadramount Qataban, Ousan and Sheba, until the unification of these kingdoms under the Hemiarite Kingdom). Indians and Yemenis exchanged the Yemeni myrrh and incense and Indian silk, textiles and spices.

With the emergence of Islam and its spread, and the establishment of the Islamic State in the Arabian Peninsula and beyond it, the commercial and cultural relationships continued between India and the Caliph state. Yemeni ports (like Shihr, Aden, Mokha) were the point of connection. Some of the results of these relationships were: (a) the conversion of some of the population in the Indian subcontinent to Islam, (b) mutual cultural influences and c) two-way migrations between the two nations. Some Yemenis migrated to India, especially Hyderabad, from Hadramout, and some Indians migrated to Yemen, especially to the port towns of Shihr, Mokalla, Aden, Mokha, Hodeida, and even Socotra. This resulted in the appearance and establishment of Yemeni communities in India and Indian communities in Yemen. Many Indian Muslims coming to Mecca as pilgrims, or on their way back, settled in Yemen.

With the beginning of the era of geographical explorations, accompanied by the Western colonial activities in the Asian and African countries, the European colonial powers made plans to dominate the mercantile route between India and Yemen. Their aims were: (i) to dominate over navigation in the Red sea, the Arabian Sea and the Indian Ocean; (ii) to monopolize the spice trade; (iii) to spread Christianity; (iv) and to reach India as a gate to eastern Asia.

The Portuguese Empire was the first to move in this direction, and their attacks on ports overlooking this maritime route and on Indian ports are well-known. These were not merely attacks, but attempts to colonize these ports.

The end of the sixteenth and the beginning of the seventeenth century witnessed the decline of the Portuguese and the rise of the British Empire. The British established what became known as the East India Company in 1600 to fulfill the task of dominating India and the maritime routes leading to it. It could be said that a turning point in the relationships between India and the Yemen coast occurred from the very day that this company came into existence, and continued until 1937.

During the period 1600-1839 Great Britain was trying to find and establish commercial agencies and military posts along the Yemeni coast, when Napoleon Bonaparte threatened, from Egypt, the British existence in India and in the coasts of the Red Sea and the Arabian Sea. Britain occupied Perim Island in 1799 to block the infiltration of French influence. Later, it signed commercial and military treaties with the rulers of Lahj and Aden in 1802 for the same reasons. When naval transport started to use coal, Britain decided to occupy Aden to make it an important coal depot for its ships and as a base which could be used to face the threats against its interests.

Aden was eventually occupied in 1839 by a combined British and Indian force. The British Governor of Bombay wrote in a letter to the Council of Directors of the East India Company on 27 February on the importance of Aden to British interest:

> Aden is of great value to us. It is very suitable as a coal depot throughout the year. It could be a meeting place for all ships using the Red Sea route, and as a military base from which we can protect our activities. Aden is like Gibraltar, once in our hands will be difficult to take neither from land nor from sea. There are two great nations conspiring against us and seek to eliminate our influence in the East The first is Russia which tries to advance through Iran, and the other is France which is coming via Egypt. To confront these threats Britain must have defense post outside its borders.

After the occupation of Aden, the British expanded their influence along the coasts of the Arabian Sea—Aden to Hadramout and Mahara, and on the coasts of the Gulf of Oman and the Arabian Gulf—through what came to be known as the Protection and Consultation Treaties.

The British existence in Aden and its eastern and western Protectorates in the Yemen hinterland was tied closely to the British Administration in Bombay, and to the Viceroy in India until 1937.

During the period—about 100 years—when Aden was politically and administratively under the authority of Bombay, there was a rapid growth of Indian commercial, cultural and demographic influence in Aden. New buildings and houses were built according to the Indian style. The British officer, Harold Jacob, in his book. *The Kings of Arabia* says, describing the Indian influence on life in Aden: 'Aden is painted Indian, the post office have their notices and instructions written both in Arabic and Hindi and Gujarati. Many of the school teachers are Indians. The resonance of Bombay hypnotizes Aden.'

The intensification of the liberation movement in India compelled Great Britain to take measures to ensure the continuation of its presence in the Arabian coasts, and that was when Aden and the Protectorates were put under the direct administration of the colonial ministry in London, severing its ties with Bombay. But that did not last long, for only after three decades were the people of southern Yemen able to drive the British out. During British rule in Aden and the Protectorates there was an increase of Yemeni presence in India.

While those Yemenis interested in commerce or religious guidance migrated to countries like the Malayan and the Indonesian archipelagos, those interested in military service migrated to India. They were recruited in the armies of Indian rulers, both Hindu and Muslim—especially on the western Indian coasts of Kutch, Junagarh (e.g. the Bafaqih family), Kathiawar, Gujarat, Baroda (the Jamadar Al-Fadhli family), Khandesh, Indore and Puna, and lastly in Hyderabad Deccan, to which some Yemenis shifted from the western provinces. Some Yemenis reached high military ranks, and some were able to make large fortunes which they used to consolidate their influence in their original country and even established states like the Kathiris, the Quwaitis, the Aulakis and the Harhara.

The Alawi families, e.g., the Aidroos, the Mihdhars and the Shihabs, and individuals belonging to these families were high-ranking army officers, or conducted religious guidance on Sufi lines, or were counsellors/ministers to the kings of Hyderabad.

The above account shows that Yemeni-Indian relationships have a wide historical and geographical background. This provides a good prospect for the growth and expansion of these relations. They could support the formation of an economic group for the countries overlooking the Indian Ocean. While India is the biggest among these countries— the large population and area, the degree of industrial, agricultural and technological development—Yemen is also of importance, situated as it is on the gate linking these countries with those overlooking the Red Sea and the Mediterranean.

The crucial factor is that this economic group must not weaken any other group in Asia or the Arabian Peninsula. On the contrary, such a group could be an important factor in strengthening and consolidating the already existing regional groups in Asia and the Arabian Peninsula.

Today's world is one of alliances and groupings, a world of mutual interests and mutual benefits. India, through such a group, could be influential in boosting the scientific, educational and technological development of the other members of the group, including agriculture, scientific research and information technology.

Egypt: A Link between India and the Mediterranean

MOSTAFA EL-ABBADI

The establishing of a direct connection in antiquity between Egypt and India was a difficult and protracted process. I shall try to present a brief analysis of Egypt's historical experience. The earliest traceable relations between India and East Asia were first evident in the Gulf area and in Mesopotamia. Indian objects and Indian influences infiltrated from Mesopotamia by land through the hands of several intermediaries to other West-Asian countries including Egypt.[1]

On the other hand, we have ancient records of a long chain of sea voyages and expeditions that set out from the Egyptian coast on the Red Sea for the Indian Ocean, yet the range and ultimate destination of those voyages have repeatedly been disputed. For example, the German geographer, Heinrich Quiring, once argued in 1952 that there existed in the past a persistent legend of a Gold Island in the East Indies and that expeditions were being sent out until early in the sixteenth century to find the magical golden island. He then suggests that in order to identify the Golden Island, we must shift our viewpoint back to ancient Egypt. After surveying Egyptian records of the journey to Punt, he suddenly attributes to Herodotus the fact that those voyages set out from the Red Sea in long ships for the Indies. Quiring next asserts: 'In the whole circumference of the Indian Ocean, Sumatra is the only island for which gold mining is demonstrable.' He finally concludes that the Ramessides of the twelfth century B.C. in search for gold were chiefly responsible for those expeditions; he also adds that after the death of Ramses III (c. 1166 B.C.) the Egyptian decline began to set in; soon after, this relationship was broken, probably 1090 B.C.[2]

More recently in 1975, another geographer, George Carter, noted in a supporting paper, 'Quiring shifts from Punt-in-Africa to Punt-in-the East-Indies. If Punt referred to the distant gold yielding land, it could have been both, or perhaps first one and then the other. The subject has long been debated.'[3] We shall have occasion to consider the location of Punt later on.

The above hypothesis appears to be rather speculative and cannot be fully substantiated on available historical evidence as the direct sea voyage between Egypt and India during the third and second millennia B.C. was fraught with many uncertainties and unknown dangers, e.g: a) unexplored sea routes, b) total ignorance of the prevailing wind-system over the Indian Ocean, not to speak of the Pacific, where the Monsoon winds can become too violent for sailing ships, and c) the hazards of piracy which constituted a serious menace to navigation. The overcoming of these obstacles was gradual, one step after another. We can trace the following three major stages in the development of Egyptian activities and trade in the Indian Ocean.

In the first place, during the third and second millennia B.C., Pharaonic Egypt seems to have directed its commercial marine activities towards the western side of the Indian Ocean, namely, East Africa; this activity appears to have started at the time of the Old Kingdom around the middle of the third millennium B.C. and was maintained throughout ancient history. The climax of Egyptian activities in this direction was undoubtedly the great naval expedition of Queen Hatshepsut to Punt and several other East African locations (c.1500 B.C.). The description as illustrated by the text and scenes of the Deir-el-Bahari Temple in Luxor, impresses upon us the magnitude of the expedition and its wide-ranging field of operation.[4] An indication of the magnitude of such expeditions can be found in the great Harris Papyrus,[5] composed later on by Ramses IV, on his accession to the throne (1166 B.C.) in memory of his father Ramses III and his achievements. Among the great deeds of Ramses III is recorded a naval expedition to Punt composed of 10,000 men. In a sense, it was a military force capable of confronting any opposition, a formation such as Hatshepsut may have used for her expedition. Another point worth mentioning is the duration of the voyage. On two earlier occasions in the sixth dynasty and again in the twelfth dynasty, we are told that the round journey to Punt required three years.[6] This lengthy journey implies either a long sojourn at the destination or several stops on the way, a customary practice among merchants in antiquity and the Middle Ages.

In view of the long-standing controversy around the location of Punt between Africa and Asia, I would like to consider a text that I believe should settle the question once and for all. It is a partly damaged inscription addressed to King Psamtik of the seventh century B.C. that records a startling climatic observation on conditions in the land of Punt that, to my mind, has not been sufficiently taken note of. It reads as follows:

> ...a great marvel took place in thy reign, such as has not been seen or heard of; the heavens rained upon the mount of Punt, rain being scanty in the fields of the south... in this month the rainfall took place at a time when rain was out of season even in the north land, thy mother Neith of the temple of Sais came to thee to conduct to thee the Nile, giving life to your men.[7]

This is so far, the earliest known observation recording the Monsoon rain upon the mountains of Punt. The fact that this text explicitly states that the flooding of the Nile in summer was caused by rain on Punt proves beyond any doubt that Punt could only be in East Africa; it could not be anywhere else in Asia, neither east nor west. In view of this evidence, I find it unacceptable to shift earlier Egyptian expeditions from East Africa to the Indies in the Pacific without conclusive evidence.[8] Yet it is conceivable that smaller naval units could have sailed east from the strait of Bab-el-Mandeb, hugging the coast as far as India. Unfortunately we have no clear indication that it was a regular practice until the end of the second millennium B.C.

Second, around the year one thousand B.C. major changes took place in both the Eastern Mediterranean and the Indian Ocean. The Eastern Mediterranean suffered a commotion of several migrating peoples both by land and sea. In consequence, several older kingdoms fell and new ones emerged. Egypt had its share of suffering due to a succession of neighbouring foreign dominations. In the western Indian Ocean, South Arabia, Yemen of today, emerged rather suddenly as a leading trading centre. This development was the direct result of the discovery of the peculiar faculties of the camel who could subsist without food and drink for up to four days. Consequently, South Arabians were able to establish their caravan trade across the Arabian Peninsula and thereby become chief participants in the valuable North-South trade between the Mediterranean and the Indian Ocean. Enhanced further by their unique geographical location in command of the strait of Bab-el-Mandeb, they were able to impose their own terms on the other principal participants in that trade: India, Egypt and East Africa. Thus no ship, Indian or Egyptian, was allowed to sail north or south beyond the strait of Bab-el-Mandeb without the approval of the Arab authorities. As an alternative, the various parties were required to bring their respective wares and products to the Arabian ports and markets where they could conduct their exchange and business, to the profit of Arabia Felix (Eudaemon Arabia) as it came to be known. This arrangement, however, allowed—perhaps for the first time—closer encounters and direct dealings between Indian and Egyptian merchants and sailors.

This situation continued for several centuries and each party maintained its role without any known violation until the fourth century B.C., when the global campaign of Alexander the Great brought about drastic changes. For the first time, India became directly and better known to the Mediterranean people. As a result of the geographical explorations initiated by Alexander and maintained by his immediate successors, India in particular attracted the attention of Hellenistic scholars, most eminent among them being Eratosthenes and his colleagues of the Alexandria school. With the combined better knowledge of the land of India and better realisation of its fabulous commercial possibilities, Alexandrian sailors and merchants in Egypt tried to continuously increase their profit from the exchange trade with India in order to satisfy the ever-increasing demand in the Mediterranean market. Thus in the then prevailing conditions in the Indian Ocean, Alexandrian merchants controlled the sea-borne trade up and down the Red Sea while Nabataeans and South Arabians controlled the over-land caravan trade across the Arabian desert whereas Indian and Arabian merchants strictly kept to themselves complete control of traffic in the Indian Ocean.

This delicate balance was maintained and jealously guarded till the middle of the second century B.C. by the South Arabians who profited and prospered by being the main entrepôt centre for the North-South trade.

This commercial set up is very clearly reflected in two pertinent statements, the one by Diodorus Sicilus (mid-third century B.C.) when he speaks of 'The prosperous islands near Eudaemon Arabia which were visited by sailors from every port and especially from Potana, the city which Alexander founded on the river Indus.'[9] The other statement is of a later date (around A.D. 40) in the so-called *Periplus of the Erythraean Sea* by an unknown author. It reads as follows: 'The port of Eudaemon Arabia (Aden) was once before a full fledged city, when vessels from India did not go to Egypt, and those of Egypt did not dare sail to places further on, but came only this far.'[10] Any attempts by Alexandrian ships to sail beyond the port of Eudaemon Arabia were strongly discouraged; if they did sail, it was by laboriously hugging the coast, and in the words of the *Periplus,* 'sailing round the bays'.[11]

This situation however was upset by a drastic change in the balance of power in the Mediterranean basin. The prominent position of South Arabia in the Indian Ocean was more than counterbalanced by the unforeseen rise of Rome as a dominant power in the Mediterranean after her victory over Carthage in 202 B.C.[12] It was then that Rome adopted a policy of expansion and supremacy in the Eastern Mediterranean, while the island of Rhodes had been enjoying a central role in trade and navigation, and had maintained close friendly relations with all trading centres in the region. Rome, however, looked with disfavour upon the prosperity of independent Rhodes. Not wishing to resort to the use of force against that powerful distant island, Rome launched what can be called a policy of economic blockade, by inducing or coercing other countries to transfer their route and agencies from Rhodes to the nearby poor island of Delos. Under growing Roman pressure, Alexandrian merchants gradually moved their warehouses and agencies in accordance with the wish of Rome. There is ample evidence from the second century B.C. testifying to the close trade connections between Alexandria and Delos.

Significant in this respect is a dedicatory inscription set up in Delos by 'The chiefs of the union of Alexandrian merchants'.[13]

In the direction of the Red Sea and the Indian Ocean, there was another development. With the growing awareness in Rome of the possibilities of the North-South trade in incense, spices, aromatics, precious stones, gold, ivory, ebony, medical herbs and later on silk, Roman businessmen thought of investing more in this line of trade through Alexandria. Consequently, more Roman capital was pumped into the Alexandrian market. Accumulating evidence substantiates this point.

A papyrus of the mid-second century B.C. reveals the formation in Alexandria of a multinational company for the import of aromata from 'the incense-bearing land' (Punt). The papyrus is a maritime loan contract in which the various parties (I creditor, I banker, 5 debtors and 5 guarantors) belong to at least 7 diferent civic affiliations: Rome, Carthage, Messalia, Elea, Thesalonica and Macedonia. It is significant that the Roman, named Gnaeus, was the banker through whose bank the transaction was made.[14]

Other inscriptions from Delos of the second half of the second century B.C. indicate that Romans and Italians were already firmly established in Alexandria in no small numbers. In one example, a dedication was made by 'Italians at Alexandria' (*Alexandreae Italicei*).[15] In another, we find Roman ship-owners and merchants dedicating to Apollo and expressing their gratitude to King Ptolemy VIII and to a certain Lochos who was a high ranking official at the royal court in Alexandria on the occasion of the King's recovery of his throne in Alexandria'.[16] The occasion referred to in the dedication was when the King was expelled from Alexandria during a civil war (132-127 B.C) and was reinstated through the intervention of the Roman senate.

The presence of this class of Romans and Italians was not confined to Alexandria since we meet them traversing the whole of Egypt up to the island of Philae, near Aswan. A small group of Latin inscriptions attest to this fact; they are written by four Roman citizens, three of them wrote down the date of their visit according to the Roman calendar (26 August 116 B.C.).[17] The date 126 B.C. of these Latin inscriptions is of special interest because it coincides with an event of global significance, namely, the discovery of the Monsoon winds in the Indian Ocean by Alexandrian navigators. The story of the discovery was first recorded by Poseidonius (c.130-51 B.C.) and was later on recorded by Strabo (36 B.C.-22 A.D.).[18] We are told that a shipwrecked Indian sailor was found half dead by Egyptian coast guards of the Red Sea and brought to King Ptolemy VIII. To gain favour, the Indian sailor promised to guide any of the King's navigators on a direct sea voyage to India. The King immediately assigned an adventurous seaman in his service, Eudoxus of Cyzicus with the mission. Poseidonius mentions two direct journeys to India undertaken by Eudoxus, the first in 118 B.C. guided by the Indian sailor; it proved a success and Eudoxus brought back a cargo of aromatics and precious stones. The second, under the sole guidance of Eudoxus, occurred in 116 B.C. when the King had just died and his wife Queen Cleopatra III was still reigning.

Although Strabo disbelieved the entire story of Eudoxus, modern scholarship has accepted the historicity of the facts of Eudoxus' two voyages.[19] They fit in with the international situation at the time. The enormous increase in the demand for Oriental and Southern goods in the Mediterranean market whetted the appetite of Alexandrian merchants to increase their share in the North-South trade. They also realised that their only chance lay in bypassing the Arabian ports and in sailing off directly across the ocean to the rich Indian market. Such an undertaking could not be attained without the substantial and powerful support of the Romans who were more than ready for the opportunity. It was not surprising therefore that Ptolemy VIII and his wife, both friends of Rome, demonstrated personal zeal and involvement in the project. The expertise of an Indian pilot with a thorough knowledge of the secret of the Monsoon winds would therefore be very much in demand.

The discovery of the Monsoon winds and their use for navigation by Alexandrian sailors had a very marked effect on the Egyptian scene. Not long after Eudoxus a new important office was created, for the first time in the Egyptian administration, of 'Commander of the Red and Indian Seas', probably under Ptolemy XII in the first half of the first century B.C. The creation of such an office implies that the utilization of the Monsoon led to a marked increase in the regular commercial transactions with India. The new office was needed to ensure the safety of navigation for those engaged in that trade. Also, the fact that Rome decided in 56 B.C. to send a permanent Roman force to Alexandria to ensure the safety of King Ptolemy XII against any uprising by the population, confirms the magnitude of Roman capital invested in that trade.

The importance that Rome attached to that line of trade is confirmed still further, even after Augustus conquered and made Egypt a Roman province in 30 B.C. Soon after, in 26 B.C. Augustus commissioned his prefect in Egypt, Aelius Gallus, to invade South Arabia by land. This land onslaught brought about considerable damage to the Sabaeans as far south as the city of Ma'reb, but did not completely cripple the commercial activity of the Arabian ports on the ocean.[20] Not satisfied with this result, Augustus later on in one A.D., launched another devastating naval attack,[21] that resulted, in the words of the *Periplus* 'in sacking the port of Eudaemon Arabia (Aden)' which declined into a mere village after having been a full-fledged city (*polis*).[22]

Now that the port or Eudaemon Arabia was out of action, Alexandrian navigators of the Roman period enjoyed unrivalled dominance in the Red Sea and the Indian seas, a fact that rendered Egypt the main link between India and the Mediterranean.

Notes

1. Shereen Ratnagar, *Understanding Harappa Civilisation in the Greater Indus Valley*, New Delhi: Tulika, 2001, pp. 43-54; C.J. Gadd, *The Cities of Babylonia*, Cambridge Ancient History, 1(2), 3rd ed. Cambridge, 1971, pp. 132-3; V. Gordon Childe, 'Notes on Some East lranian Pottery', in *Egypt and the East*, 1-2 (March-June 1933) pp. 15-25.
2. H. Quiring, *Die Goldinsel des Isidor von Sevilla*, 'Aegypter der 20 Dynastie als Entdecker und Kulturbringer in Ostasien', Petermanns Geographische Mitteilungen 96 Jahrgang,2, Quartalsheft (1952) pp. 93-5.
3. G.F. Carter, 'Egyptian Gold Seekers and Explorations in the Pacific', The Epigraphic Society. Occasional Publications, Vol. 2, no. 27 (February 1975) 1-10.

4. J.S. Breasted, *Ancient Records of Egypt*, Vol 2, Chicago, 1905, p.187 ff.
5. Ibid., Vol 4, 15-412.
6. Cf. G.F. Carter, loc.cit. p.2.
7. W.M. Flinders Petrie and F.L.I Griffith. *Tanis*, part 2, 'Nebesheh and Defeenh', London, 1888, pp.107-8.
8. As argued by Quiring and Carter, nn. 2&3 above.
9. Diodorus 3. 47. 9.
10. *The Periplus*, 26, lines 26-32. ed. L.Casson, Princeton 1989.
11. *Periplus*, 57; also see editor's introduction and comm. pp.71-2.
12. For points discussed in this section in greater detail, see my paper 'Geographical Explorations', Saryu Doshi, ed. *Marg* Bombay, 1993, pp. 22-37.
13. F. Durrbach, *Choix d' Inscriptions de Delos*, Paris, 1922, 108 (127-116 B.C.).
14. *Sammelbuch Griechischer Unkunden aus Aegypten*, ed. F. Preisigke, Berlin, 1913-22, 7169.
15. Durrbach, op.cit. 107.
16. Ibid. 105-106 (127 B.C.).
17. A.Rocat, *Nuove epigrafi grechi e Latine da file, Homage Vermaseren III*, 988-996, esp. 994 ff. nos. 5-6; also published in *Anneé Epigraphique* (1977) 838-9; and *Supplementum Graecum*, 28, no. 1485. Also see Diod. 1. 83,8-9.
18. Strabo 2.3.4-5.
19. J. Thiel, *Eudoxus of Cyzicus*, Groningen, 1966, passum; W. Otto and H. Bengton, *Zur Geschichte des Niederganges des Ptolemaerreiches*, München, 1938, pp. 1-22.
20. *Strabo*, 16.4.23-24.
21. Pliny, *Natural History*, 4.32.160 & 12.30.55.
22. *Periplus*, 26 & Commentaries, p. 160.

India and West Asia
Sharing History and Future Challenges

ABDULAZIZ OTHMAN ALTWAIJRI

I start with an analysis of the very wording, especially the duality of the title of the seminar India and West Asia. It is already stated elsewhere that West Asia refers to what is otherwise known as the Middle East, but no need was felt to make explicit what 'India' refers to.

From this and from my standpoint as an Arab Muslim, and in order to better grasp the cultural and social linkages between the two areas, I think that both terms need to be clarified.

Even if 'West Asia' was used by many eminent politicians, outstanding scholars and famous thinkers, the term 'Middle East' remains the most popular, without gainsaying whether it is the most appropriate term to cover the concerned area. This area actually includes countries from Africa, from Southwest Asia and also Southeast Europe. On this basis, which term can be considered the most accurate? Is it a geographical reference that limits the area, or a locational term that does not specify the 'Middle' of what, and the 'East' from where?

Shall the word 'Asia' when applied to the region, exclude other countries which have always been considered a part of the 'Middle East' while they do not belong to the continent of 'Asia', like Egypt, for instance. What are, in short, the geo-strategical consequences of the new delimitation of the area that West Asia implies?

On the other hand, in the Middle Eastern countries, especially in Arab Muslim countries, what is known today as 'India' was never covered in history by one term: 'Sind' and 'Hind' are in fact the two terms which have always been used to this part of the world. 'Far East' or 'Indian subcontinent' were also used for this region.

We consider these preliminary remarks important since they will help us in identifying to a certain extent the historical and geographical delimitations of the two areas.

The scope of the analysis of this paper, and I believe the seminar's perspectives, are actually built on these considerations.

However, I will concentrate in this paper on the Arab world, instead of the whole region of 'West Asia'.

Historical Contacts

It is not an easy task to trace the history, or rather the story, of the first contacts and early links between the Arab world and India. The memories of the pre-islamic era, to begin with, are still alive in the cultural and social heritage of the Arabs, and took different forms.

We are all aware of the place that the swords occupy in the life and consciousness of the Arabs. 'Indian' swords were actually considered among the best. Diamonds, gold and pearls, cotton cloth were also prestigious commodities for which India was famous in the Arab peninsula. It is not also a meaningless detail that families gave to their daughters the names of 'Hind', to recall the magic of beauty, the mysteries of the spirit that 'India' ignited in the collective imagination of the Arabs.

These linkages actually developed through trade activities that the Arab navigators transmitted from one generation to another. But when Islam came, these links radically changed and a new form of relationship came to be established between these two regions. Both regions got connected, if not united, by one faith and came in a way to belong to what is known as the Muslim Ummah.

This holy link will mark the beginning of very rich and deeply instructive civilisational exchanges, where cultural and scientific disciplines will flourish, and political and social systems will emerge, creating a new entity that knew no boundaries and still ignores any frontiers.

As early as the first century of the Islamic era, precisely in A.D. 711, Islam penetrated in this part of the world, under the rule of the Umeyyads, and in the person of Mohamed Ibn Al-Qacim. Islam was attracted to parts of this regions for many reasons and it spread relatively quickly, despite the barriers of language, the remoteness from the central Authority and the diversity and strength of the local religions and faiths.

Broadly speaking, it was the egalitarian principles of Islam in opposition to the local caste system which can be considered as the main key to the success of Islam in India. Its lofty spiritual aspirations and the quest for self-knowledge and transcendent tendencies also facilitated its dissemination in Indian society, since these aspects were already present in Hindu precepts and other local faith teachings.

This first stage of Islam's penetration in India took about two and a half centuries before the establishment of the first dynasty (the Ghuznids: 977-1186), and a series of other dynastic rules started in India, enrooting the religion in the region and consolidating the relationships with other parts of the Islamic world. The Sultanate of Delhi (1206-1555), the Sultanate of Bengal (1336-1576), the Sultanate of Kashmir (1346-1589), the Sultanate of Gujarat (1391-1586) and the Sultanate of the Mughals (1526-1858) were outstanding instances of the presence of Islam in India and also a wonderful opportunity for cultural exchange and civilisational inter-penetration.

During this period, we can give some examples which show the nature and extent of the close and deep relationships between the two regions:

- Historians report that the Sadatis Dynasty (1414-1451) was given this name since they were the descendants of the Prophet Mohammed (PBUH). We all know the social and spiritual place that the family of Mohammed (PBUH), otherwise called the Ashrafs, occupies in the hearts of the Muslims. That a branch of his family ruled a part of India should certainly be understood as a 'symbol' of the fluidity of power that Islam established in the region.
- The king Ultumich (Ultutmish) was recognised by Al-Muntassir, the Abbassid Caliph (1226-1242), and he manufactured the local currency coins with the Caliph's name, which was kept until the end of the Abbassid's Caliphate in A.D. 1258.
- The Ghurids' dynasty had very close relationships with

the Egyptian Mamluk rulers, and a prestigious historical monument still bears the name 'Ghuria' in Cairo.

- It is also historically attested that the official inscriptions of the Delhi Sultanate were in Arabic. Other Muslim nation' languages were also prominent at that time, namely, Persian and Turkish, whose mergence with Hindi gave what is known today as Urdu.

On the cultural level, it is worth noting that the presence of India in the Islamic heritage is consistent and substantial. Researchers insist on the fact that the famous Muslim scholar Al-Biruni was one of the first scientists who defended the theory that India had been a sea in the geological period, and was certainly the only Muslim geographer who embraced this point of view.[1] Other forms of interest of Muslim scholars in India could be felt through the biographies that the Muslim historians wrote on the most eminent Indian Muslim figures.

Ibn Hajar, Shawkani and Sakhawi, in their biographic compilations, inform us of the life and scientific works of at least 2,000 outstanding Indian Muslim scholars.

Al-Hassani, the famous Indian historian, in his book, *Biographies of the Muslim Scholars in India*, mentions about four thousand names, in all different branches of Islamic studies and Arab culture.[2]

The cultural contacts between the scholars in both regions, in the absence of means of communication and information, came through the annual pilgrimage gathering, where the Muslims not only sought to perform the acts of Hajj, but also tried to meet other scholars, to learn from them, to submit to them their views and standpoints on controversial issues and to check with them the foundations of any Fatwa they had ever to deliver or to enforce.

With the interaction between Islamic and local Indian cultures, new styles of architecture appeared, specially in the mosques, mausolea, tombs and palaces; new forms of music also emerged combining the spirituality of local music to the glamour of the Arab melodies, and many scientific disciplines flourished and developed under the impetus of this interaction.

In this context, besides these aspects of 'formal' culture, we believe it is also important to give examples of the presence of India in the 'popular' Arab Islamic cultural heritage.

The adventures of Ibn Battuta in India, in the thirteenth century, certainly constitute what feeds the most the popular Arab memory about India. He described the Sultans' way of life, costumes, and horses, and gave very insightful details on the women's social and political position in their society and reported extensively on the traditions of the various regions he went through. The fact that a young traveller, who came from the remote Tangiers was nominated as Qadi (Judge) in Delhi, spelled at that time 'Dehli', is still perceived in the Arab world both as a symbol of openness and also unity of the Muslim Ummah.

Ibn Battuta's description of the wives burning themselves after the death of their husbands remains one of the most striking portrayal of examples of loyalty and sacrifice.

The book, *Kalila wa Dimna*, which speaks with implicit symbolism on Animals, was translated from Hindi to Arabic by Ibn Al Muquaffa, and the famous *Arabian Nights* (One Thousand and One Nights) not only contained references to the kings, princes and traditions of India, but was also claimed by some to be of Indian origin.

Yaqut Al Hamawi, in his Atlas wrote that 'Sind' and 'Hind' are true twin brothers and were grandsons of Adam, and that is why they are always mentioned together.

'Qadi Abul-Qassim Al-Andalusi, in his book *Tabaqat Al Uman*, which enumerates the history of science in different nations, put the Indian nation at the top of the nations devoted to science and learning. He also reported a very significant distribution of attributes to some nations, including the Indian one. He says that there are five kings: (a) The King of China, and he is the 'King of his people' since the Chinese are very disciplined and loyal to their kings; (b) The King of Turkey, and he is the 'King of lions' since the Turkish are well-known for their courage; (c) The King of Persia, and he is the 'King of kings' for his prestige; (d) The King of Rome, and he is the 'King of men' since the Romans are keen on their appearance and looks; (e) And last but not least, the King of India who is the 'King of wisdom' because India is the cradle of science, wisdom and learning.

New Common Challenges

We saw that the first stage of relationship between the two regions was one which preceded Islam and it was very limited. With Islam the second stage of the common links started which was very strong, rich and constructive. We can say that the third stage of common relations started when both areas were colonized about the same time and by the same colonizers. Both the regions were in fact 'united' in the eyes of the colonizers, since they all constituted *their* territories, and certainly shared the same mechanisms of exploitation and submission. Then, the whole process of decolonization and nation-building after independence, the modern challenges of poverty, illiteracy, social welfare, constituted a common ground for more relationships between the two regions. Needless to insist here on the role India played, hand-in-hand with some of the Arab leaders, to found the Non-Aligned Movement, and also on its position regarding Palestine.

More recently, globalisation has become another common challenge that these two regions have to synchronize their efforts to face. Both regions actually possess valuable cultural reserves which constitute the richest contributions to the universal heritage. Dialogue among civilizations and peaceful coexistence among people are also modern challenges to both regions. In fact, despite the geographical distances and cultural differences, both regions were and will stay connected, not only because they historically built strong foundations in their relationships, but also because their future is inter-dependent, and concrete actions should be taken in this regard.

It is not enough to state the common history of the two regions and to insist on the fact that they share a common future; we need to go beyond this and establish practical and institutional initiatives that will consolidate the relations and guarantee their promotion:

1. In my view, and in my standpoint as head of an intergovernmental specialized organisation, the first recommendation we should make is that India should strengthen its ties with the Member States of the Organization of the Islamic Conference (OIC), which is the global frame that unites not only the Muslim

countries but also other countries which comprise Muslim communities.

2. The role India plays together with the Organization and the interaction with other Member States will benefit the Organization and also the sub-region.
3. Consolidate the partnership between specialized institutions, Universities and Research Centres in both regions as the key to mutal understanding and the basis of the sound exchanges between cultures and civilisations.
4. Promote translation and research activities on the common history of the two regions and also on the future horizons of cooperation in order to develop inter-cultural exchanges.
5. Hold more conferences, symposia and seminars on subjects related to the development of linkages and interaction of the two regions, to substantially contribute to strengthening and implanting of cooperation, solidarity and understanding within the region.

The Islamic Educational, Scientific and Cultural Organization (ISESCO) will be more than honoured to help and assist in the achievement of these lofty goals and noble objectives.

Notes

1. See *Encyclopedia of Islam*, article on 'Hind'
2. الإعلام بمن في تاريخ الهند من الأعلام. عبد الحي الحسني، دار ابن حزم، 1999
   (Al Hassani, *Biographies of the Muslim Scholars in India*, 1999)

Select Reading

R.C. Majumdar, H-C Ray Chaudhuri and K. Datta, *An Advanced History of India*' London, 1960.

Clifford Edward Bosworth, *Islamic Dynasties,* London, 1967.

Stanely Lane Pool, *The Mohammedan Dynasties*, London, 1893.

Ebouard Von Zambaur, *Manuel pour 1'histoire de I'Islam*, Hanovre, 1927.

C.H. Philips, ed, *Handbook of Oriental History*, London, 1951.

Arabic Sources:

نب يحلا دبع ،" مالعألا نم دنهلا خيرات يف نمب مالعإلا " -
1999 ،مزح نبا راد ،ينسحلا نيدلا رخف

راد ،راون ناملس زيزعلا دبع .د ،" ةيمالسإلا بوعشلا " -
1991 ،ةيبرعلا ةضهنلا

ةيملعلا بتكلا راد ، " ةطوطب نبا ةلحر " -

ملعلا راد ،يسلدنألا مساقلا وبأ ،" ممألا تاقبط " -
1963 ،نييالملل

باتكلا راد ،ةدايز الوقن .د ،" برعلا دنع تالحرلاو ةيفارغجلا " -
1962 ،ينانبللا

1978 ،ملقلا راد ،" ةمدقملا :نودلخ نبا " -

India and the Arab World
Retrospect and Prospects

Faisal Odeh Al-Rfou'h

Traditionally, friendly historical and cultural relations have existed between India and the Arab world which go back to the pre-Christian era. Both India and the Arab world flourished and have been the venue of ancient civilisations—the Indus Valley civilisation flourished in ancient India while the Nile Valley and the Mesopotamian civilisation thrived in the Arab World. Until the Roman military forays into the Arab world at the beginning of the Christian era, trade and commercial relations between the two sides had gathered momentum. The advent of Islam on Arab soil proved instrumental in transforming the Arab world from an age of *Jahiliya* or Ignorance to that of Enlightenment. By the seventh century A.D., the Arab conquerors had spread the message of Islam to various parts of the globe including India. Along with Islam, Arabic language, culture and literature were also introduced.

With much of the Arab world becoming part of the Ottoman Empire from the fourteenth century to the end of the First World War, interaction between India and the Arab world was minimal and confined to trade. In the wake of the collapse of the Ottoman Empire, most of the Arab Territories fell under the mandate of Britain and France. In the aftermath of the First World War the nationalist leaders in India who were spearheading the Indian freedom struggle against the British had identified India's freedom struggle with freedom struggles being waged against colonialism in other parts of the globe. India sympathized with the people of Palestine who were subjected to oppressive laws by the Mandatory Authority. Great Indian leaders like Mahatma Gandhi and Jawaharlal Nehru decried the Mandatory Authority's policies of discrimination and settling of Jewish populations in a clandestine manner and against the wishes of the native Palestinians.

During the period of British rule Indian leaders sympathized with the aspirations of the Arab people and were in full agreement with them on the colonial question. Nehru's deep interest in Asian resurgence and world affairs led to the establishment of personal contacts with Egyptian, Syrian, Iraqi and other Arab nationalist leaders. Fraternal delegations from Egypt, Syria and Palestine and some Arab countries usually attended Indian National Congress sessions in the pre-independence days.

Mahatma Gandhi, Jawaharlal Nehru and Maulana Azad evinced keen interest in the developments taking place in the Arab World. Gandhi was opposed to the idea of the establishment of a Jewish state in Palestine. He wrote, 'The cry for the National home for Jews does not make much appeal to me. Palestine belongs to Arabs in the same sense that England belongs to the English and France to the French. It is wrong to impose Jews on the Arabs.'[1] In an identical manner, Nehru also wrote that 'Palestine was an Arab country and Arab interests must prevail there.'[2] All these developments played a crucial role in shaping India's attitude towards the Arab world.

Throughout the period of the mandate, India continued to extend its sympathies and support to the people of Palestine. India also expressed its opposition to the UN proposal for the partitioning of Palestine in 1947. When the Jews unilaterally established the state of Israel in May 1948, India did not immediately accord recognition to the new state but expressed its solidarity and support for the Palestinian people.

When India hosted the first Asian Relations Conference at New Delhi in March 1947, Arab delegations participated in that conference. During the decade of the 1950s, India's foreign policy was galvanized to practical considerations due to its awareness of security requirements. In a world riven by Cold War rivalry between two power blocs, India was faced with challenges to its political and security interests in its relations with the Arab world. Anglo-American attempts to bring about military pacts to safeguard their oil and colonial interests in the region threatened to bring Cold War rivalry to India's doorsteps. The Arab nationalist leaders, who perceived such moves to be part of calculated Western tactics to prolong their military and political supremacy in the region, reacted in a hostile manner.

National self-interest as well as the desire to assist and contribute to the peaceful settlement of the crisis punctuated India's approach to the Suez crisis in 1956. The temporary closure of the Suez Canal adversely affected India's economic interests. Nehru told the Indian Parliament on 31 July 1956 that 'India was not a disinterested party but a principal user of the Suez canal and its economic life and development is not unaffected by the dispute, not to speak of worse developments, in regard to it.'[3] India was not critical of Nasser's move of nationalization of the Suez for it regarded Nasser's act as a sign of the weakening in domination of West Asia by the European Powers; Nehru, rather, hailed the move.

The Anglo-French and Israeli invasion of Egypt evoked a sharp reaction in India. Nehru publicly branded it as a case of 'clear naked aggression and reversion to the past colonial method'. He termed the Great Powers intervention as 'gross and brutal exercise of violence and armed might'[4] against weaker countries and remarked that it in fact challenged the conscience of the world.[5] India played a conciliatory and constructive role throughout the crisis. For India the major question was whether it was right and proper for the Great Powers to impose their will over small and weak countries.[6]

In the wake of the Arab-Israel war (June 1967), in which Israel managed to occupy Arab territories, India, while condemning the Israeli invasion, also called for the vacation of Israeli invasion and restoration of the Arab occupied territories. Prime Minister Indira Gandhi told the Indian Parliament:

> The world today faces a disastrous war in West Asia... and the situation becomes graver by the hour. If not stopped the war is likely to expand into a much wider one, drawing into its vortex other countries and developing perhaps into a World War... it is our solemn duty as a government to help in restoration of peace in the present perilous situation.[7]

India's policy during the 1967 Arab-Israeli war was based on the principled opposition to acquisition of land by force. It was critical of Israel for resorting to pre-emptive strikes and initiating the war. New Delhi wanted Israel to withdraw to the pre-June 1967 position so that progress could be made to resolve the crisis. India had made it explicitly clear that there could be no solution to the problem until Israel withdrew from occupied Arab territories in accordance with the provisions of the UN Security Council Resolution 242 (1967).

During the October 1973 Arab-Israel war India supported the Arab cause and declared that 'the cause of tension in the area is Israeli aggression and refusal to vacate territories occupied by armed forces. This intransigence on the part of Israel is clearly the basic cause leading to the outbreak of present hostilities'.[8] India further stated that the Arab cause was based on justice and demanded immediate implementation by Israel of UN Resolution 242. While reaffirming India's total sympathy with the Arab world, Prime Minister Indira Gandhi provided two reasons for the Indian attitude: first, India's old and solid relations with the Arabs required India to stand by its friends in times of travail; and second, Israel's refusal to vacate the Arab lands occupied by it in the 1967 war and its refusal to honour the UN resolution.

The change of government in New Delhi in no way affected India's policy towards the Arab world. Atal Behari Vajpayee, currently the prime minister of India, had become Foreign Minister under the Janta Party in 1977. In his first foreign policy statement in the Indian Parliament on 29 June 1977, Vajpayee said:

> With... the entire Arab world, we shall not only continue to seek to maintain old links but further strengthen our economic co-operation. We have assured the Arab world that we shall continue to lend our full support for a just settlement of the West Asian Problem based on UN Resolution which required the vacation of occupied territories.[9]

Apart from recognising the Palestine Liberation Organisation (as the sole legitimate representative of the people of Palestine) India also assured that the Arab people of Palestine who had been forcibly evicted from their hearths and homes must also be able to exercise their inalienable right to return to their homeland. India has extended its wholehearted support to all such attempts and measures which are designed to establish permanent, durable and lasting peace in West Asia. Such initiatives taken by either side have always elicited India's support.

India is heavily dependent on import of oil from the Arab Gulf countries. Oil occupies a prime strategic significance in India's process of rapid economic growth. Any untoward political development in West Asia resulting in the curtailment of oil supplies adversely affects the Indian economy. A peaceful and politically stable West Asia is conducive for India in economic, political and strategic terms. Apart from being a major source of oil supplies, West Asia is also strategically important for India because two main sea lanes of communication (SLOCs), the Suez Canal and the Straits of Hormuz, are situated in this region. The bulk of India's foreign trade—about 95 per cent—is seaborne and passes through the Suez Canal. In the eventuality of the closure of the Suez Canal, India's foreign trade is bound to be adversely affected. Besides, India is geographically proximate to Arab countries hence its security and strategic interests are closely linked to those of Arab countries.

The Arab world provides an immense market for Indian products. Currently, India's share in the total Arab foreign trade is almost marginal and it has deficit trade balance with some oil exporting Arab countries. India's middle level technology is suitable for some Arab countries because of its high quality and affordable price. India can explore the possibilities of augmenting bilateral trade with Arab countries by studying the market requirements, quality standard and negotiating the quantum and price mechanism. Oil producing Arab countries offer India ample opportunities to explore the possibilities of establishing joint ventures in fertilizers and petro-chemical industries.

In an era of globalisation and the World Trade Organization (WTO) regime, foreign direct investment (FDI) has assumed considerable significance. There is a vast potential for Arab investment in India and vice versa. The process of economic reforms initiated by India in 1991 has opened up its economy to FDI but the bulk of FDI pouring into India is from the USA and Europe. The flow of FDI from Arab Gulf countries has almost been negligible. There is a need for concerted efforts on the parts of both India and the Arab countries to explore the possibilities of augmenting the inflow of FDI on both sides.

Foreign remittances flowing into India from the overseas Indians working in Arab countries is an important source of foreign exchange for India. Hundreds of thousands of Indian workers are working in many countries, especially in the Arab Gulf countries. They have contributed to development on both sides; through their skills to the Arab countries and through their remittances to India.

Information technology in which India has made commendable strides is another potential area for enhancing cooperation between India and the Arab world. Most of the Arab counties are rapidly switching over to adapt information technology in order to harness this technology for accelerating the pace of economic development. India, with its technical know-how and software infrastructure, can help the Arab countries to embark on the superhighway to information technology. Finally, cementing the bonds of friendship between India and the Arab world is vital to re-establish durable and lasting peace in the world.

Notes

1. *Harijan*, 26 November 1938.
2. *The Hindu,* 17 December 1938
3. *The Times of India*, 1 August 1956
4. *India*, Lok Sabha Debates, 8 August 1956, Part V, vol. 7, no. 18 col. 2537
5. Ibid. 1 November 1956, Part II, Vol. 9, No. 4, col. 383
6. M.S. Rajan, *India in World Affairs,* Bombay, 1964, p. 146
7. *Foreign Affairs Record,* New Delhi, June 1967, p. 81
8. Ibid, October 1973, p. 357
9. A.B. Vajpayee, *New Dimensions of India's Foreign Policy,* Delhi: 1979, p. 85

Personal Reflections on Indo-Arab Relations

Rafiq Zakaria

I must, at the outset, make it clear that I am not an academic, though I have founded and I continue to manage more than a dozen colleges and institutes of higher learning, in different disciplines and professions in Mumbai and my old constituency of Aurangabad. I have been involved in the promotion and furtherance of Aurangabad. I have, of course, been involved in the promotion and furtherance of Indo-Arab relations ever since the time of India's independence and have written at length on it, and can, therefore, claim to be knowledgeable about the subject.

Indo-Arab relations are perhaps older than any other international contact that this country has had but my brief is not to go into the remote past. The greatest link in this relationship has, however, been the advent of Islam in India in the eighth century in the form of trade and commerce in the South and the Arab invasion of Sind. What happened thereafter is history; but let me tell you that, contrary to the impression that has been created by our historians, there is enough evidence to the effect that even the Prophet Muhammad was, though remotely, influenced by the thought process in India, This has been beautifully expressed by Allama Iqbal, the poet-philosopher of modern Islam:

Meer-aye Arab ko ayee thandee jahansay
Mera vatan wahi hai mera vatan wahi hai

The land from where came
cool breeze to the chief of the Arabs
That is any country, that is my country.

But there was in the last century a long lapse in this relationship, which occurred as a result of the intervention in both India and the Arab world by the colonial powers; this kept the Arabs and Indians apart for a long time.

This was explained by Jawaharlal Nehru, the first prime minister of free India, while inaugurating the Indo-Arab Society in Bombay on 7 October 1954; 1, as a young man, then had the privilege to found this society. Panditji [i.e. Jawaharlal Nehru] said that while India's relations with the Arab world went 'far back into the dawn of history', something happened three hundred years ago 'which rather snapped the bonds that tied us'. Some kinds of barrier—political and governmental — were erected between neighbours and contacts and exchange between them became difficult. As he explained, 'It was easier for us to meet in Berlin or Paris or in London than to meet in Asia.' That was the price that the countries in Asia had to pay for European domination; and as a result, they became, politically speaking, passive, quicscent and stagnant.

The advance of science and industrialisation, sea-ways and land-ways developed greatly and India became reconnected with her neighbours in the Arab world. Then came the development of the air-ways, which made mutual contacts easier and more frequent. Finally came independence and the whole pattern of things in India and the Arab world began to change. Both the peoples started picking up old threads, which had broken long years ago; the old connections were renewed. Also old memories, traditions and melodies were revived and there was, as if, a resumption of the old story afresh. The interim period of two to three hundred years of European domination was a kind of super-imposition, which, despite the fact that it came in our way for a moment, made us richer in certain common experiences. Though necessarily unpleasant, those experiences made us understand each other better and drew us closer together.

Apart from the historical background there was something eternal which tied us together. Nehru emphasized this, while approving the formation of the society. He characterized it as 'the embodiment of popular will'. He said:

> When I first heard of the formation of this Indo-Arab Society, the thought struck me as to why we have waited so long to start such a society. I welcome the idea, of

course, and even though we are rather late in having some such formal approach to this question of developing Indo-Arab relations, or strengthening them, nevertheless it was a good thing to begin; and so 1 gladly consented to be present here on this occasion.

Nehru had stressed the importance of this relationship even before the attainment of independence, when, as the Vice-President of the interim government, he spoke of the closeness of India with the Arab world at the Asian Relations Conference; he had convened it in New Delhi in April 1947. He asked the colonial powers to take serious note of the development and warned them that Indians, and other Asian and African nations, would no longer tolerate the disruption caused by them in their affairs.

Soon after India became free, the Dutch took 'police action' against the infant Republic of Indonesia; Nehru called the representatives of fifteen Asian governments in New Delhi in January 1949 and called upon the Dutch for an immediate halt to aggression, describing it as a 'flagrant breach of the U.N, Charter'. This also resulted in the formation of the Arab-Asian Group in the United Nations, consisting of Afghanistan, Burma, Egypt, Indonesia, Iran, Iraq, Lebanon, Pakistan, Saudi Arabia, Syria and Yemen. Later with the addition of some African countries, this group was enlarged and renamed the 'Asian-African Group'.

It was under this climate of unity that the new nations of Asia began their relationship; and since then it has grown in strength. Meanwhile, revolutionary changes took place in the Arab world, beginning with the revolution organised by young army officers under the charismatic leadership of General Nasser in Egypt, which not only ended the corrupt rule of King Farouk but also unleashed a new socio-political force, which changed the face of the classic land of the Pharaohs. India welcomed this change and her friendship with the new Egypt developed rapidly.

The visit of India's Prime Minister to Cairo in February 1955 was an event of great significance. The rise of Nasser, who spearheaded the revolution against the British-supported rule of Farouk, created a wave of liberation throughout the Arab world. Nehru welcomed it and by his visit to Cairo demonstrated India's solidarity with the resurgence of nationalism in Egypt. It also strengthened the bonds between the two countries. The joint communique of the two prime ministers, Nehru and Nasser, emphasized that there existed between them an 'identity of views... on major international issues' as also on 'the attainment of social and economic justice and the raising of the standard of living of their peoples'.

Two months later Nasser visited New Delhi. He had assumed complete control over the government in Egypt. The meeting of the two leaders of India and Egypt was of great significance. It was formalised by their signing the treaty of friendship which sent the right signal to all colonised peoples that in unity lay the prospect of prosperity for their teeming millions.

In his approach to international affairs Nasser was greatly influenced by Nehru; this was admitted by him in a press interview later. Nasser said:

> My visit to India proved a turning point in my political understanding. I learnt and realised that the only wise policy for us would be of positive neutrality and non-alignment. Coming back home I found out from the response it received from my people that it is the only possible policy which could get the broadest possible support from the Arabs as a whole.

This was in a way a reaffirmation of the approach towards the Arabs that Nehru, with the blessing of Mahatma Gandhi, had taken during the freedom struggle. They had established close contact with Nahas Pasha and the other leaders of the Wafed Party, who had pioneered the movement for Arab liberation. The Mahatma had openly declared India's support to the cause of the Palestinians.

From New Delhi Nehru and Nasser left together for the famous Afro-Asian Conference held at Bandung in Indonesia; there they were able to see more of each other and to come closer to one another. 'They conferred with Arab delegations, who assured them that they stood solidly by the policy of non-alignment which Nehru and Nasser, along with Sukarno of Indonesia had formulated. 'The game of power-politics,' Nehru declared, 'in which the small nations can be used as tools by the big powers must be stopped if the existing international tension is to come to an end.'

The Ten Principles of International Cooperation which were subscribed to by a larger group of nations, including China, gave further impetus to Afro-Asian cooperation. Their leaders met at Bandung and agreed upon the Five Principles, known as Panchsheel, which pronounced their adherence to mutual collaboration and adherence to non-alignment. The event proved a landmark in the history of the two continents—recently freed of Western domination.

Soon after the Bandung Conference, Nehru again visited Cairo in July 1955; talks took place between the two Prime Ministers covering, as their joint statement mentioned "a wide range of matters of mutual interest to the two countries, as well as larger problems of international interest and concern'. These were held in an atmosphere of frankness and cordiality, characteristic of the close and friendly relations between them; the two leaders declared 'their conviction that involvement in military pacts or alignment with great powers does not serve the cause of peace and indeed, often has the opposite effect'. Towards that end they clarified that 'general disarmament and the banning of the production and use of nuclear weapons is of basic importance'.

Meanwhile Nasser's popularity was on the increase not only in Egypt but also in the rest of the Arab world. We was being hailed by Arabs everywhere as the symbol of a new awakening. For India his friendship proved valuable and helped in creating a reservoir of goodwill for her among the Arabs. This was true not only of people in Syria, where the Egyptian leader was most popular, but also in such remote places as the Shekhdoms of Kuwait, Abu Dhabi and Qatar. I was invited by the late Amir to visit Kuwait, where I had several fruitful discussions with not only the Amir but also with many of his key advisors. Many of them had lived in Mumbai and had businesses in that city. Naturally they had the fondest memories of India and were keen to develop the best of relations with her. Similarly I was also privileged to visit Abu Dhabi and Dubai as the guest of their respective governments. In both places I found a lot of warmth for India and earnest to see that Indians and Arabs came closer to one another. Thousands of Indian families were settled in Dubai, carrying on flourishing businesses and they constituted a lasting link of friendships with the Arab subjects of the Emirate. Shaikh Zayed bin Sultan al-Nahayyan, President of UAE has testified to this fact:

'The relations between India and the UAE date back to the remote past, forged by geography into an intimate commercial and cultural bond ... After the discovery of oil and implementation of our development projects, Indian experts, engineers and administrators as well as a skilled workers helped in implementing our ambitious development policies. We are grateful to India for this contribution and value it highly.'

I was also fortunate to meet President Nasser on a number of occasions. He was more and more attracted to India. In the reception that we gave him in Mumbai on behalf of the Indo-Arab Society he spoke so warmly of his feelings for Indians that everyone in the gathering was deeply moved. He had some relatives in Mumbai, whom he met. He told me that this was one of his long cherished desires. He treated me with great affection and invited me to Egypt, where he spent several hours with me explaining his philosophy of uplifting the Arabs and uniting them under one umbrella. He had great admiration not only for Nehru but also for Gandhi, whose broad humanism had a deep impact on him. He felt that India and Egypt had a lot to contribute to ameliorate the condition of the poor and the downtrodden in Asia and Africa. I found him very human, patriotic to the core and utterly dedicated to the furtherance of Indo-Arab collaboration as a prelude to Afro-Asian advancement.

During this period India also developed a special relationship with several other Arab countries, which had obtained their freedom. Sudan, for instance, looked to Nehru for guidance and asked for India's efforts to rehabilitate their country. Several high-powered delegations came to India and asked for technical and other assistance. To the Sudanse, as their Finance Minister, Hamad Tawfik, put it: 'India represents the finest example of all-round development. Hence they were eager to learn from her.' In response to their request, India not only supplied Sudan with technical experts but also gave her judges and teachers. In May 1955 the Prime Minister of Sudan, Ismail el-Azhari, visited India and expressed his country's determination to be on the friendliest terms with us. A month later, the Prime Minister of Yemen, His Royal Highness Saif al-Islam paid an official visit to India and pleaded for technical aid so that it might be properly modernised. In consequence many Indian experts were loaned to the desert kingdom.

In November 1955 His Majesty King Saud came on a state visit to India and from the moment he stepped on Indian soil until his departure a month later he received a tumultuous and rousing reception everywhere; it gave a big boost to improving relations with the Muslim world as a whole, because Saudi Arabia has always occupied a special position among Muslims. At the banquet given in honour of the King by the Indo-Arab Society His Majesty paid a glowing tribute to India's leadership particularly for its just and fair treatment of Indian Muslims. In his capacity as the Guardian of Muslim Holy places, he expressed his gratitude to Pandit Nehru for his 'wise policy of affection and neighbourliness to all Indians, irrespective of creed' with the result that 'the huge Muslim minority is necessarily receiving the greater benefits of his wise and noble efforts.' His Majesty said that he was assured of this not only by the President and the Prime Minister and many other responsible Hindu leaders but also by 'all Muslim leaders whom I have met'.

Kind Saud's testimony had a profound effect on the Muslims of the Arab and Muslim worlds and gave a new meaning and content to India's effort to foster inter-communal harmony. Later when India's Prime Minister returned the visit by going to Riyadh in: September 1956 he was greeted by the Saudi Arabians as *Rasul as Salam* or the 'Messenger of Peace' and welcomed with tremendous enthusiasm there as the 'Friend of the Arabs'. It also showed that Nehru had captured the affection of not only the popular Arab leaders but also of their kings and princes, despite his ideological resortation about them.

As years rolled on, Nehru and Nasser came much closer to each other; they collaborated with President Tito of Yugoslavia at Brioni in July 1956, and reinforced their policy of non-alignment. To the leaders of the West, this declaration brought forebodings; *New York Times* warned them to be on 'guard against strange combination of forces that may be plausible on the surface but that could be sinister in their ultimate effect'. The immediate result of Brioni was the withdrawal by America and Britain of their offer to aid Egypt for the construction of the Aswan High Dam. Nasser hit back immediately by nationalising the Suez Canal Company. Justifying the Egyptian action Nehru blamed the US, and UK for their denial of help to Egypt and said, 'More than the decision, the way it was done hurt Egypt's pride and self-respect and disregarded a people's sentiments.' Shukr-al-Kuwatly, President of Syria, was impressed by 'the intimate knowledge that Nehru has of the problems of the Arabs, knowledge which has made him earn their respect. It has rarely been enjoyed by any other statesman in the world.' He told me when I met him in Damascus that in Nehru, Muslims in India had their best friend.

Nehru encouraged Nasser's counter-stroke of nationalising the Suez canal; Britain and France were naturally taken aback. They applied economic sanctions against Egypt, held a 24 Nation Conference in London; and sent the Menzies Mission to Cairo to persuade Nasser to restore the status quo. But Nasser remained adamant. Israel joined Britain and France and declared war on Egypt in October 1956 by invading Port Said. India came out openly on the side of Egypt and took a leading part in sponsoring the resolution in the United Nations which forced the aggressors to withdraw from Egypt. In his contribution to the *Study of Nehru*, which I edited and which was sponsored and published by *The Times of India*, Nasser made a special mention of Nehru's powerful support at that crucial hour. He quoted a message of support which Nehru had sent him; it stated:

> If colonialism succeeds in coming back to Egypt, it will reverse the entire course of history and return to every other country from which it had been forced to go. Therefore, ... colonialism should not be allowed to succeed in Egypt. Otherwise, it will signal a new and long fight for the whole of Asia and Africa.

Nasser was so moved by it that he wrote: 'What a quick comprehension of a complicated situation! And with what stimulating and brave words he conveyed it. It gave us courage and stirred us to fight back.' However, as a result of this support by Nehru, India suffered greatly in her relations with the West.

In the eyes of the Arab world, however, India's stock rose very high and Nehru came to be looked upon as the leader to whom oppressed peoples in Asia and Africa could turn to with confidence and hope in their hours of crisis. Only in Iraq, which was then under the iron heel of Nuri as-Said, the position was different. That country had become a part of the Baghdad Pact, which denounced the policy of non-alignment and entered into close military alliance with the West. Jordan remained united at first with Egypt but when President Eisenhower announced his doctrine of aid to the Middle East in order to build up America's friendship with the Arabs, King Husain gave in and joined Iraq against Egypt, forming the short-lived Arab Federation of Iraq and Jordan.

For his part Nasser took another great step to strengthen the forces of Arab nationalism and brought them under one Union; he united Egypt and Syria under one union, which was called the United Arab Republic. A new Constitution was promulgated which was approved by the people of both the countries. Under it Islam ceased to be a state religion and secularism become its basis. This was largely the result of Nehru's influence. It helped Nasser to project the progressive nature of Arab nationalism. For Nehru particularly, this was a matter of satisfaction. He publicly hailed Nasser not only as the symbol of the new movement, but as 'one of those men who gave history a new turn'.

Meanwhile popular resentment began to mount in Iraq and on 14 July 1958, its army revolted and put an end not only to the monarchy but also to the rule of Nuri es-Said. On gaining control the first thing it did was to recognise the United Arab Republic. Its leader Abdul Karim Kassim hailed Nasser's efforts at Arab unity and abrogated Iraq's union with Jordan. In Baghdad, on the day of the revolution, people danced with joy in the streets, carrying placards in Arabic describing Nehru as a 'saviour of the Arab people'. Furthermore, while

Pakistanis were warned by the army not to get out of their houses as there was great resentment against them, Indians were welcomed in the streets of Baghdad. Kassim, the leader of the revolt, hailed Nehru as the man who had 'a mind and determination which revealed the greatness of his spirit and the depth of his genius'. Later, when another military commander, Arif, overthrew Kassim, one of the first things he did was to visit India and express the new regime's solidarity with India and its desire to strengthen Iraq's ties with her. Soon thereafter a new Republic was proclaimed in Iraq and it sent one of its most prominent men, who had been jailed thrice by the deposed government of Nuri es-Said for his opposition to the Baghdad Pact, as ambassador to New Delhi. On his arrival in India the envoy declared, 'New Iraq feels that its relations with India have now become closer and stronger and it will endeavour to co-operate with India to the utmost.'

Similarly, India's relations with the Arab Maghreb, which consists of the countries of Tunisia, Morocco and Algeria, took a most friendly turn. More importantly, between the leaders of the National Liberation Front of Algeria and the Congress in India, who have had close contacts for many years, their relationship was further strengthened by exchanges in various fields. Even during their struggle against France, the Congress had given its full support to the Algerian nationalists. Later, free India also championed their cause in the United Nations. It was the wisdom and far-sightedness of Nehru, who saw to it that India did not fail to stand by the Arab freedom fighters in different countries. His policy annoyed the colonial powers but it helped greatly to further her ties with the Arabs everywhere.

After the passing away of Nehru in 1964, there was a sort of lull in Indo-Arab relations; his successor, Lal Bahadur Shastri, was no less committed to pursuing the same policy but his rule was short and the new prime minister was bogged down with the hostilities with Pakistan. He visited Cairo to attend the Non-Aligned Conference and what he felt was mentioned by him in the inaugural address which he delivered at the seminar on 'India and the Arab world', organised by the Indian Council for Cultural Relations in New Delhi on 15 February 1965:

> I really felt very happy to be in Cairo; I did not feel any difference between the people of Egypt and myself; there was a tremendous good feeling for India among the people. It was, I personally know, very difficult for me to pass through the streets because hundreds and thousands of people would collect around me, would try to come near me, to show their affection; but if I shook hands with them all, I would have been submerged in the crowds. I am not tall or stout enough to face this kind of reality. On all basic and important international policies, we agree.

Soon thereafter Shastri was faced with the Pakistani aggression; he was much distressed at the anti-Indian propaganda that Pakistan had unleashed, especially among the Arab and Muslim countries, aimed at showing that India was anti-Muslim, persecuting the Muslims and forcefully occupying Kashmir, with its prevalently Muslim population. I was then a Cabinet Minister in Maharashtra but Shastri sent me to New York as India's representative to the United Nations to refute these allegations. I was happy to rebut the diatribe against India by Z.A. Bhutto, the then Foreign Minister of Pakistan. In my reply to him I concentrated on presenting the real situation especially on Kashmir. On 15 October 1965, the General Assembly was in full session. I was fortunate in getting a most responsive audience; apart from Bhutto and the other members of his team, most of the Muslim representatives were also present. I spoke for about an hour. However a mild stir was created, especially among the delegates of the Muslim countries, when I referred rather cautiously to the danger that Indian Muslims would face in case Kashmir were to be taken over by Pakistan. I said:

> For the 50 million Muslims of India the very fact that at least one of the 16 states of the Indian Federation, namely, the State of Jammu and Kashmir, has a Muslim majority is a matter of deep satisfaction; they are determined not to allow any one to rob them of this satisfaction and in its defence, they will consider no sacrifice too great.

I declared in unequivocal terms on behalf of the 50 million Muslims of India to whom I have the privilege to belong that we shall fight to the last man any move to disturb the non-communal character of our Republic. The Pakistani delegate mocked at our cohesion. He even asked why should the Government of India not be able to take care of any such situation or why it should treat the Muslims of India as hostages in order to prevent a plebiscite being held in Kashmir? I told the Pakistanis that we have already had one terrible experience; we conceded partition, fondly believing that it would end all our troubles and difficulties, but we were sadly disillusioned; millions of our people had to undergo intolerable suffering. Our economic resources were stretched to the breaking point in order to rehabilitate the millions, who were uprooted by man's inhumanity to man; we lost our greatest man, Mahatma Gandhi; we faced enormous difficulties in our efforts to rebuild our society. Therefore India would not allow history to be repeated. I explained that India of 1965 is not the India of 1948; it is not prepared to swallow the communal poison again at the bidding of anyone.

There was no room for the revival of the two-nation theory, which is a blot on the history of mankind.

The speech had the desired effect; Bhutto shrieked and shouted that I was a traitor to the Muslim cause. The Saudi Arabian ambassador walked out in protest. But the other Muslim delegates were sympathetic; they were alarmed by what I had probated about the repercussions on Muslims in India. They did not want to jeopardize their position in India, however much they might have liked to support Pakistan. True, there were other considerations, which also weighed with them. They were not willing to antagonize India, which had stood by them in every crisis. Moreover, their countries had a flourishing trade with India which it was not in their respective national interests to disrupt. They were realistic enough not to be duped by Pakistan's slogan of 'Islam in danger'; they could not ignore the fate of more than 50 million Muslims — they number more than 120 million now. In his frustration, Bhutto had later stormed out of the Security Council, gesticulating and shouting, 'Indian dogs, go back.' Indians remained; Pakistanis had to go out.

One of the reasons, which I think prompted Shastri to send me to the United Nations, was a short poem of mine which I had recited while seconding the resolution on Kashmir at the meeting of the A.I.C.C. (All India Congress Committee) held in Bombay in 1964; it was the last meeting which Nehru had attended. Ten days later he died. He had also brought Shaikh Abdullah with him to the meeting. At my request the noted Indian-born English poet, Dom Moraes, who has won several international awards for his poetry, has translated it into English. The poem, which is as relevant today, is as follows:

कसम है खूने गांधी की
कसम खूने शहीदां की
कसम जनता के सपनो की
कसम मजदूरो देहकां की
ये मुमकिन हैं के सूरज का उभरना बंद हो जाए
समुंदर खुश्क हो जाएं, हिमाला दबके रह जाए
और ये भी मुमकिन है
बरसना छोड़दे अब्रे बहारां भी
चहकना छोड़ दे शाहे गुलिस्ता भी
गरजना छोड़दे शेरेए बयाबां भी
ये सब मुमकिन है, लेकिन ये कभी मुमकिन नहींः
कोई भी जम्मू–ओ–कश्मीर हमसे ले नहीं सकता
वतन की एकता को फ़िरसे धक्का दे नही सकता
ये दो कौमोंका नारा फिरसे जिंदा हो नही सकता
किसी कीमत पे बटवारा कभी भी हो नही सकता

By the blood of Gandhi and our martyrs
We swear this; and by all the aspirations
Of our people; and by the sweat and tears
Of the peasants and workers of our nation.

It is possible that the sun will not rise at all
And the oceans of the world will dry up,
Possible that the mighty Himalayas will fall
And that rain from the clouds will stop,
That the queen of birds will not sing any more
And the kingly lion will cease to roar.

All that is possible; but this is not:

None can take Jammu and Kashmir from us;
None dare strike at our unity a second time.
All talk of two nations is dead and buried.
We shall not be divided a second time.

Though this is, in a way, a diversion from the main theme of Indo-Arab relations, I have referred to Kashmir because it continues to be an issue, which, from time to time, at the instigation of Pakistan, threatens to spoil India's relation with the Arabs. Pakistan uses the Islamic link to misguide them; she often succeeds in getting the OIC to pass resolutions in support of her case for Kashmir. But these are just sops to satisfy Pakistan and not declarations of hostility against India. Arabs and Muslims are aware of the ground realities and none of them have ever taken any concrete step against India. The impact of India's leadership in the anti-colonial struggle, its mission; of broad humanism and the ideas of Gandhi and Nehru have been so strong among Arabs that India has been able to overcome all the storms that Pakistan has been engineering to spoil her relations with the Arab and Muslim world. In a recent article in *Asian Age* I have mentioned the dangerous consequences of tampering with the status of Kashmir. I explained in unequivocal terms:

> The valley of Kashmir, however picturesque, consists of 74 miles by 25 miles and accommodates not more than six million Muslims. As against it, in the rest of India there are 140 million Muslims, as many as in Pakistan. They are spread in every city, town and village of India. If any tampering with the status of Kashmir is done, the backlash will be horrendous. It may provoke another Bosnia.

I plead, therefore, with the intellectuals and representatives of the Muslim world to ponder seriously over what might happen in case Kashmir is given over to Pakistan; it will provoke the worst-communal carnage. Pakistan must not forget that it is the Indian Muslims whose forebears were in the vanguard of the struggle for the creation of Pakistan;

they should not be put in any jeopardy to appease President Musharraf who should, in the larger Muslim interest, shed Kashmir from his blood.

During the Janata Party regime there was not much warmth in India-Arab relations. Morarji Desai, as the prime minister, was more inclined to develop friendship with Israel. He had even invited its Defence Minister, Moshe Dayan, to India but kept his visit secret. He was afraid that any reverse of Arab policy, as pursued by Nehru and his successors, would not be liked by the people of India. His tenure of office was too short. He could not, therefore, reverse the pro-Arab policy of the Government of India and establish full diplomatic relations with Israel, which he had devoutedly wished. This was subsequently carried out by a Congress Government, headed by P.V. Narasimha Rao in 1992; by then the relations with the Arabs had considerably cooled down due to various developments in the international arena.

On the return of Indira Gandhi as the prime minister in 1980 the old friendly approach towards the Arab countries had been revived; but Indira Gandhi had different priorities and the Arabs did not occupy the same importance in her scheme of things as they did during the time of her father or even during her earlier rule. She was correct but not particularly warm towards them. The Arab world had also much changed and there were no Nassers to keep the ties as strong as they were during Nehru's times.

On the side of the Arabs also there was a definite cooling off in Indo-Arab relations after the death of Nasser; his hold also had begun to wane after the defeat of the Arabs against Israel in 1967. His successor, Anwar Saadat, came increasingly under American influence and was keen to come to a settlement with Israel, which he did. There were also two other reasons for it. One, the rising influence of King Faisal in the Arab world, who went all out to help Pakistan against India. And the success of the oil embargo by the oil producing countries, mostly Arab, which put enormous financial burden on the already shaky economy of India. Saadat's turning away from the Soviet Union and developing a closer relationship with America had also alienated him from India.

At the instance of Indira Gandhi I went to Cairo and had a long meeting with Saadat; but he was ambivalent. He had also, under King Faisal's pressure, tilted towards Pakistan. He used the Lahore Islamic Summit to project himself as the great defender of the faith. After the Summit he visited New Delhi and assured Indira Gandhi that there was no change in the Arab attitude to India; but it was more an expression of courtesy than of concern for India.

The break-up of Pakistan and the emergence of Bangladesh, with the military assistance of India, had also soured India's relations with the entire Arab and Muslim world. The Rabat incident of Organisation of Islamic Conference, where India was deliberately humiliated, was the nadir point of her relations with the Arabs. Since then a kind of strange barrier has been created between the Arab countries and India; even after the lapse of several decades it has not been removed. However, I cannot say that the foundation of that relation has really been weakened. For instance, after the assassination of Indira Gandhi, Colonel Muammar Al-Qadhafi said:

> The political and cultural relations between India and the Arab world are growing in strength, and this is bound to have great and positive effects in the common interests of the Arab and Indian peoples in achieving freedom, independence and final emancipation from the residues of the despised imperialism. In view of the friendly relations which existed between me and Mrs. Gandhi, I have to reiterate the deep rooted Indo-Libyan relations and their development in order to fulfil our common aspirations regarding the future of our struggle.

During the second phase of her rule (1980-84) Indira Gandhi became conscious of the lack of the earlier warmth in Indo-Arab relations. She tried to improve these, but I must admit it was in a half-hearted way. As her deputy leader, I had several discussions with her. I found her rather cautious; she did not want to upset Israel. The international situation had also gone through a dramatic transformation. Somehow she did not exhibit the same passion to cement the ties. Also, the Arabs were not particularly anxious to restore the position which had prevailed during the Nehru era; the chemistry on either side had almost disappeared. Each was looking more to its national interest, afraid to displease America, which was emerging as the sole superpower.

However, just a year before her assassination in 1984, Indira Gandhi was somewhat troubled by the continued deterioration in Indo-Arab relations. Her advisors came out with peculiar explanations; but she was not satisfied. She asked me to visit some of the Arab and Muslim countries as her Special Envoy and find out why the old warmth in our relationship with them had cooled off and how it could be improved. On my journey to West Asia as I travelled from one country to another I met not only the heads of state and government but a galaxy of other leaders, editors, intellectuals and even trade union executives. I tried to probe the Arab mind. It had meanwhile become too centred on its own national affairs in which India had ceased to be of much value. The Arabs had begun to align more towards the West than the East. Every one talked fondly of India and its democracy and of its rich civilisational heritage and struggle for liberation but showed little enthusiasm for bettering the ties with her. Only the aging President of Tunisia, Habib Bourguiba, who continued to be until the last a beacon light of emancipation and reform, was nostalgic about his friendship with Nehru and the historic bond of the Arabs with India. He complained that his daughter, despite several invitations to her, did not find time to visit him. In my report to the prime minister I urged her to respect the old man's heart-warming desire which she did by paying soon thereafter a visit to Tunisia.

I have given the background, in the light of what I had heard, seen and experienced in the long and chequered course of our relations with the Arab world, extending over the last fifty years. I have been frank enough to show how the earlier tide had been replaced by the ebb in that relationship. I will end my reflections with an Urdu couplet:

Gaya woh din ke ham sayyaad ko ilzaam daite they
Watan main in dino ahl-i-watan ki aazmaaish haiy

Translated into the English, it means: 'Gone are the days when we used to blame our persecutors/Now the time has come when each of us has to account/for what he is doing for his people.'

Enduring Relationships
Maritime Contacts in the Western Indian Ocean

HIMANSHU PRABHA RAY

The letter of my lord, the most illustrious elder, arrived... Please give Sus Siti and Kinbati [and Isha] and Ishaq the Banyan my best regards, and tell them of my longing for them. Inform them in my name that as for pepper, in this coming year its value, [that is] the price per bahar, will be thirty dinars, and more, and as for refurbished iron, a bahar will be [worth] not less than twenty dinars, and that the raqs [shining, glittering iron], which was in the city, is completely exhausted. [Tell them also] to despatch a ship from Mangalore, if they can, and to send in it any available pepper, iron, cubeb, and ginger; it should set out at the first opportunity for al-Dyyb [Diu], taking some coir [coconut fibre], fine aloes wood, mango [?], and coconuts, because all these are selling well.

'If they are equipping a ship in Aden, and they want me to take part, I will share [in it] with them. If there were a ship sailing from Mangalore this year, I would send them gold, sugar, raisins and [other] goods. Be sure to inform them of all this, and do not be remiss, for you take the place of a letter of mine to them.

These are excerpts from a letter of 11 September 1149 in Arabic written by Madmun bin Hasan bin Bundar, representative of the merchants and superintendent of the port of Aden.[1] Like his father, he was also a ship owner and the middleman between the Jews of the Mediterranean region and those that were active in India. The addressee of the letter was Abraham bin Perahya Ben Yiju, a learned Tunisian Jew who operated a brass factory on the Malabar Coast. The term *'banyan'* that is mentioned in this communication was the usual appellation for an Indian merchant at that time.

The letter is an obvious example of dependence among the trading communities of the Indian Ocean in the medieval period. Nor is this an isolated instance. Inscriptions in Arabic dating from A.D. 1218 to 1291 refer to traders and shippers from Arabia and Persia resident in the towns of Gujarat such as Cambay, Somnatha, Junagadh and Anhilavada (Desai 1960: 353-64). An epitaph from Cambay refers to a trader of betel-nuts and another who died by drowning, while a third one from Junagadh commemorates the erection of a mosque by the chief of ship-masters (ibid.).

The beginnings of these maritime networks across the western Indian Ocean date as early as the third millennium B.C. A triad of names that figures consistently in Mesopotamian texts includes those of Dilmun (the Bahrain archipelago), Magan (the Oman Peninsula) and Melukkha (identified with the Harappan settlements). An early reference appears in the boast by Sargon of Akkad (2334-2279 B.C.) stating that:

> The ships from Meluhha
> the ships from Magan
> the ships from Dilmun
> he made tie-up alongside
> the quay of Akkad.

Thus it is evident that to present a chronological history of maritime contacts in the western Indian Ocean, particularly between West Asia and India, is an enormous enterprise and one that would require at least a volume.[2] Archaeological excavations in West Asia in the last few decades have provided valuable information on early sites in the Persian Gulf and the southern coast of the Arabian peninsula. This data has yet to be incorporated in the study and teaching of maritime history, which has generally been discussed in India with reference to external inputs such as Mesopotamian contacts, Roman trade or early Islamic conquests. In contrast, there has been little deliberation on the different knowledge traditions in the region and how these ideas were transformed or adapted by receiving societies. Similarly, there has been inadequate discussion regarding the agents of change, and the centrality of the state in the cultural life of ancient societies has generally been assumed on the basis of present analogies.

The objective of this presentation is to highlight the diversity and range of contacts in the ancient period and the fact that many of these continue well into the present. It should also be stressed that within the limited space provided by this paper, we can do no more than underscore the variety of networks and the diversity of communities that were involved in seafaring and maritime activity between West Asia and India in the ancient period. These ranged from contacts between boat-building and seafaring groups along the littoral to merchant groups involved in the exchange and trade of a range of commodities, and travel by religious functionaries.

BOAT BUILDING AND CARGO CARRYING

Boats in the Indian Ocean in antiquity were marked by a diversity as complex as at present, though it was the stitched or sewn tradition that was distinctive and has hence merited detailed descriptions in accounts of travellers to the region. These sewn boats were undoubtedly the cargo carriers of antiquity, and though they shared some common elements, there were several regional variations.[3] A common feature of the sewn boats of the Indian Ocean was the use of coir-rope for stitching (Chittick 1980: 301). As coconut palm plantations were restricted to certain parts of the Indian Ocean littoral, coir-rope would have been one of the commodities in demand along the boat-building settlements of the coast. Coconut is referred to as *nargil* in Arabic, derived through Persian from Prakrit *nārgil*. Elsewhere it is termed *al-jawz al-Hindi* by the Arabs, which translates into 'the Indian nut'. There are several references to rigging materials in early European records (Qaisar 1982: 22), especially to cordage and cables made of coir, which were as strong as the hemp ropes used by the Europeans, the only difference between the two being that the coir had to be stored in salt water to retain its strength. Even at present coir required for the *beden* constructed at Hafun in Somalia is brought from further south, probably Kenya or Zanzibar. Similarly, timber for planking is said to come from Mombasa and Tanzania via Mogadishu and from India via Mukalla or Aden.

Perhaps the earliest reference to the import of timber dates to the fourth century B.C. The Greek author Theophrastus writes that in the island of Tylos (i.e. Bahrain) off the Arabian coast they say that there is a kind of wood of which they build their ships, and that in sea water this is almost proof against decay (*History of Plants*, Book V, chapter 4). As there is no such durable wood in the Persian Gulf, this in all certainty refers to the import of teak from the Indian subcontinent. Somewhat later in the first century A.D. the *Periplus Maris Erythraei* (section 36) again mentions the import of rafters and beams into Oman, a fact repeated in the medieval period by Ibn-Jubayr (p.71).

The construction of sewn boats involved a laborious process, as is evident from the reconstruction of 'Sohar' undertaken by Tim Severin and his team. It required a special quality of coconut rope made from coconut husks retted in seawater and rolled by hand. For a nominal hull length of 24.5 metres, fifteen hundred bundles of coconut string equal to 640 kilometres of rope were used (Severin 1991: 40). In the context of the *mtepe* of the east African coast, such vessels lasted three or four years and had to be totally re-sewn every year (Lydekker 1991). The reason for the preference of sewn construction has generally been given as their resilience to take the shock of striking the shore as well as withstanding the pounding of the surf better.

These cargo carriers travelled to the distant centres of the Indian Ocean depending on the remunerative freights offered and returned to their home ports for overhauling during the southwest monsoon. Often boats of the same type and build were given different names on account of the nationality of the owner. Divergences were insignificant and primarily in terms of the ornamentation The *sambuk*, though of Arab origin, continues to be constructed in boat-building yards on the west coast of India, an important centre being at Beypore, south of Calicut (Wiebeck 1987: 96).[4]

The three-masted *baghla* as a ship-type became extinct sometime in the 1960s, but was known earlier for its large cargo-carrying capacity of approximately 300 to 400 tonnes. Its enormous sail required a crew of 40 to 50 men to manoeuvre it and it carried a boat on its main deck, as also another on the after-deck (ibid.: 95) The *patemara* was the traditional cargo carrier of Karnataka and of a large part of the west coast. It had a thatched cabin in the aft part and underneath the deck a cooking galley was provided for. The capacity of these vessels ranged from 30 to 300 tons and they used from one to five sails depending on the size of the craft (Rajamanickam and Swamy 1991: 69). In contrast to other types of vessels that generally use triangular sails, cargo carriers used lateen sails on the main and mizzen masts (Hornell 1970: 197).

It is significant that this trade, generally referred to as dhow trade, continues between the Persian Gulf and Gujarat, though the nature of vessels has changed. The term 'dhow' is of Swahili origin and there is a range of mechanised dhows from 80 to 1000 tons freight capacity that ply on the route. Small-scale traders find these more economical for transporting their cargoes than larger container vessels. This arrangement also works to the advantage of the owners of the vessels, as they do not get delayed in foreign ports till all the cargoes are collected (Shahani 1997: 15). The ports for this trade include Hai Bunder in Mumbai and Mandavi and Mundra in Kutch to Hamriya Dock in Dubai and Bandar Abbas in Iran (ibid.).

These cargo carriers formed the foundation of trading ventures between West Asia and India. Merchants and traders in some cases certainly owned ships and water-craft, but they neither manned nor sailed these. More often, however, goods and cargoes were entrusted to the captain of the vessel who was then responsible for their sale and profit. Though it is difficult to get precise information on ownership of vessels from ancient sources, early Buddhist texts do make a distinction between owners of vessels, sea-traders and the crew manning the watercraft. Merchants who earned a living by maritime trade or *jalapathakammikena* are referred to in the *Jātakas*, while the Sanskrit grammarian Panini makes a distinction between merchants who owned two vessels (*dvināvadhana*) or who sailed with five ships (*pañcanāvapriya*) (Agrawala 1953: 155). In contrast, members of the crew responsible for manning a big ship or *mahānāva* included a captain (*śāsaka*), a pilot (*niryāmaka*), a manipulator of the cutter and ropes and a bailer of water (*utsecaka*, see *Arthaśāstra*, II.28.13). The *Jātaka* mentions a *niyyamakajetthaka* (Book XI: no. 463) and includes amongst the crew oarsmen (*Jātakamālā*: XIV) and sailors (*kammakāra*, Book I: no.31) who worked the sails while the ships sailed in the open sea where the coast was no longer visible (*Jātaka*, Book XVI: no.518).

TRADE AND EXCHANGE

The commodities involved in maritime trade in the western Indian Ocean may be divided into various broad categories such as aromatics, medicines, dyes and spices; foodstuffs, wood and textiles; gems and ornaments; metals; and plant and animal products. These categories find mention in a range of textual sources from the first century A.D. *Periplus Maris Erythraei* (Casson 1989: 39-44) to the Geniza documents of the eleventh to thirteenth centuries, Chinese accounts and medieval Arab writings (Tampoe 1989: 131-53).

Textiles were a major commodity involved in the Indian Ocean trade and included a wide range from coarse cottons to fine silks. Furniture in Asia consisted mostly of various types of carpets, cushions, canopies and draperies—all of these being produced by the textile industry. It is not surprising then that the first European accounts of life in Arab and Asian ports invariably mention the presence of trading craft that carried large quantities of textiles. On account of their non-permanent nature, textiles seldom survive in the archaeological records, unless preserved in especially favourable conditions, such as, for example, in the dry deserts of Central Asia.

In recent years there have been attempts to date by radiocarbon methods textile collections in museums, for example the Newberry Collection at the Ashmolean Museum, Oxford, and to study the designs and patterns for information on the clientele, as also the origin of the textiles in question. These analyses are revealing for historical studies on trade and also the inter-linkages with religion. For example, several specimens in the Newberry collection bear close stylistic similarity with the eleventh century painted wooden book covers of early Jaina manuscripts (Barnes 1990). Similarly while the cloths travelling to Southeast Asia were stored or ceremonially displayed as signs of wealth, those that went to Egypt were transformed by stitching into garments, seat-covers or cushions.

The Ashmolean houses more than 1,200 textile fragments collected in Egypt and forming part of the western Indian Ocean trade. The series of radiocarbon dates ranging from the eleventh to the fifteenth centuries for the Ashmolean collection available since 1996 has further enhanced its value (Barnes 1997). While textiles with similar or at times identical designs as the Ashmolean specimens have been reported from Indonesia, often bearing Dutch East India Company (VOC) stamps, it is significant that one of the large pieces acquired from Sulawesi has been radiocarbon dated to 1440, plus/minus 40 years (ibid.). How then does one explain the find of Indian textiles from Gujarat at two ends of the Indian Ocean network? Thus rethinking on the nature of transoceanic trade in the region is imperative. How does this trade muster regional and local communities of craftsmen and traders? Was this trade controlled by the state and hence directed towards satisfying the requirements of the elite? To what extent can one talk of the autonomy of the producer or the craftsman?

The charter of Visnusena dated to A.D. 592 from Lohata in the Gujarat-Kathiawar region provides a detailed list of seventy-two trade regulations or customary laws to be followed by the community of merchants (*vaniggrama*) established in the region. The charter assures protection to them and endorses their continued functioning (*Epigraphia Indica*, 30: 163-81). Some of the regulations are of great interest to this study. For example, it is specified that merchants staying away for a year were not required to pay an entrance fee on their return. Other clauses specify duties that were to be paid. A boat full of household vessels (*bhāṇḍa-bhṛta-vahitrasya*) had to pay 12 silver coins, but if the vessels were for a religious purpose then it was only one and a quarter silver coin. In the case of a boat carrying paddy, it was half this amount. Other commodities mentioned as being carried on boats included dried ginger sticks and bamboo (ibid.).

Indigo or *nīla* is mentioned as one of the items exported from areas such as Gujarat and the charter of Visnusena mentions a tax on the pressing of the indigo dye (ibid.: 172). It is significant that in the Geniza papers indigo figures as one of the items of trade from India westward to Egypt handled by the business house of Ibn 'Awkal in the period from A.D. 980 to 1030 (Stillman 1973: 15-88). One of the three varieties mentioned includes Sindani indigo—Sindan/Sandan being identified with the Konkan coast of the subcontinent.

Gold, silver and copper were the main traded metals, exchanged both as currency and bullion. Though sources of copper and lead are available in the subcontinent, the *Periplus* refers to the import of copper, tin and lead to Kane (section 28), Barygaza (section 49) and Muziris (section 56) on the west coast. This is repeated in the Geniza documents, which refer to trade in metals from south India and regular export of iron and steel, brass and bronze vessels. In return, copper, tin and bronze vessels were imported into the south where new ones were created and old ones repaired.

These commodities were exchanged through a complex diversity of transactions including gifts, barter and trade. There are several references in the *Periplus* to presents given to the elite, for example, wine and grain in considerable quantity imported into the region of the Barbaroi in east Africa was 'not for trade but as an expenditure for the good will of the Barbaroi' (section 17). Muza offered a good roadstead for mooring and a market for a wide variety of merchandise. To the king and governor were given horses and pack mules, gold-ware, embossed silverware and expensive clothing (section 24). Similarly, in the region of Barygaza or Bharuch on the west coast of India, for the king were imported slave musicians, beautiful girls as concubines, fine wine, expensive clothing with no adornment, and choice unguents (section 49).

This practice is alluded to in the later period as well when the governor of Sohar sent a variety of gifts to the Caliph in A.D. 917 to solicit his help against the Qarmathians. These included a talking myna bird from India, several monkeys from Indonesia, and an ant as large as a cat from Africa and a number of giant serpents. 'These exotic gifts clearly made a great impression on contemporaries since different items are recorded by no fewer than four independent writers' (Williamson 1974: 87).

In addition to these gifts, the elite constantly endeavoured to control trade. The *Periplus* refers to a customs officer and a centurion being despatched to the harbour of Leuke Kome on the east coast of the Red Sea (section 19). The island of Socotra at the mouth of the Red Sea was under the control of the king of the frankincense-bearing land who had leased it out and the island was hence under guard (section 31). Somewhat later in the text there is reference to the harbour of Moscha Limen in the region of Omana where frankincense was guarded by some power of the gods. 'Neither covertly or overtly can frankincense be loaded aboard a ship without royal permission; if even a grain is lifted aboard, the ship cannot sail, since it is against the god's will' (section 32).

Similarly, the Sanskrit text, the *Arthaśāstra* of Kautilya dated to the early centuries of the Christian Era, refers to several measures to ensure the control of the state. The sale of goods at their place of manufacture was banned and a *śulka* or duty was collected at the city-gates (II.16.18-24). Similarly, traders had to pay duty at ports as well and when travelling by the king's ships had to pay hire charges for the voyage (II.28.4). Kautilya praises frontier officers (*antapāla*) for maintaining trade routes and bemoans profiteering by traders who co-operated with each other in order to raise or lower prices, making substantial profit (VIII.4.35). He also emphasizes the role of the forest tribes or *āṭavikas* and a trader travelling outside the country is asked to establish contact with them along the way (II.16.21). Kautilya's statement that the *āṭavikas* 'staying in their own territory, are many in number and brave, fight openly, rob and strike areas, being like kings' (VIII.4.41-3) has been taken to indicate that the forest tribes and their leaders presented some sort of political power (Scharfe 1993: 184). In additon to the state machinery, there are references to traders with caravans who were afforded protection when they stayed in villages (IV.13.7-12).

Contrary to the picture presented in the *Arthaśāstra*, the *Jātaka*, containing stories relating to the past lives of the Buddha, describe an economy that was only marginally under state control and one which involved commercial transactions at different levels governed by the nature of the commodity handled (Ray 1986: 107-8). Thus, for articles of royal consumption it was the king who decided the price. The Tandulanali Jataka (Book I: no.5) narrates the story of the Bodhisattva who was a valuer (*agghakāraka*) of the king of Varanasi. He used to value horses, elephants, jewels and gold and paid to the owners of the goods the proper price as he had fixed it. Two other *Jatakas* (Book II: no.158; Book III: no. 254) refer to horse dealers of the north country (*uttarapathaka assavaṇijā*) who used to transport horses to Varanasi for sale. Commodities for the consumption of city dwellers, however, were transported and traded by merchants in caravans. The Bodhisattva was born in a *saṭṭhavāhakula* in Varanasi and used to journey to the east and to the west with 500 carts driven by oxen. The roads were rough, wares were bartered and haggling over prices was difficult work (Book I: no.1.) Thus it is evident that the nature of control exerted by the state or ruling elite depended on the nature of the commodity traded. Though it was customary to present a gift to the ruler or his representative in order to establish contacts, trading activity was largely in private hands.

Archaeologically, there is both quantitative and qualitative expansion of the city in the latter half of the first millennium B.C. in north India with a corresponding increase in trade networks. This increase was sustained by demands for a range of commodities from urban dwellers, including for imported and imitation goods. The efflorescence of an urban milieu resulted in the expansion of new styles and the emergence of the *nāgaraka* or urbanite of Vatsyayana's *Kāmasūtra*. The *nāgaraka* was exhorted to reside in a city or town, to pay attention to his appearance and to participate in social gatherings and popular festivities (*Kāmasūtra*, B.N. Basu, trs., Calcutta 1944: 47-53). It was this evolution of the urban lifestyle from the middle of the first millennium B.C. onwards that fuelled the demand for a wide range of commodities and styles, which were then sustained by the extensive trade networks and communication channels.

In the Persian Gulf ed-Dur, a large archaeological site on the west coast of the Oman peninsula has provided crucial data for this maritime connection.[5] The site has been identified with Omana, mentioned in the *Periplus* as exporting pearls, purple clothing, wine, dates, gold and slaves to India (section 36). Ed-dur was on the shipment route to Charax at the head of the Persian Gulf and from there via the overland route to Palmyra.[6]

THE MARITIME NETWORK

The Sasanians ruled lran and adjacent countries from A.D. 226 to 651 and were active participants in the trade of the Indian Ocean. Information about this trade is provided largely by written sources that attest a convincing record of expansion, beginning in the fourth century. The Nestorian annals refer to trade with India and Sri Lanka during the reign of Yazdigird I (399-421) while Tabari reports that his successor, Bahram V (421-438), married an Indian princess and received as a dowry the port of Daibal in the Indus delta, together with the adjacent parts of Sind and Makran (Whitehouse 1996: 344).

Archaeological excavations conducted at Siraf in the Persian Gulf indicate its beginnings in the Sasanian period when a fort was located at the site. Roughly square on plan, the south side contained a monumental entrance flanked by hollow semi-circular towers (ibid.: 341). On the basis of the ceramic evidence, Tampoe (1989: 99) has argued that the fort was largely military in character, while the settlement at Bushire provided the base for commercial activities. This conclusion has, however, been debated by Whitehouse (1996: 342) who contends that in addition to military functions, Sasanian Siraf was also a commercial port as evident from imported objects at the site.

After a break in settlement, Siraf re-emerged as a major centre around A.D. 700. The total dimension of Islamic Siraf within the defensive walls was 250 hectares, with the mosque and the bazaar forming the main functional areas. Sohar, situated close to the mouth of the Gulf on the coast of Oman, reached its greatest size in the tenth century A.D., occupying 73 hectares with a defence wall protecting it on the seaward side (Williamson 1974: 88). These two sites in the Persian Gulf participated in a regional trade network in the ninth to eleventh centuries A.D. extending to settlements in the Indus delta, such as Banbhore, several centres along the west coast of India to Mantai on the north coast of Sri Lanka.

Banbhore, located on the Makran coast, has been identified with the port of Daybul, which was given as dowry to the Sasanian king Bahram V in the fifth century A.D. Like Siraf and Mantai, Banbhore is located on a barren coast and the resources for supporting an urban centre were largely generated by participation in the trading network. Archaelogical excavations at the site have revealed a fortified city enclosing 167 hectares in the early Islamic period, with an inner residential and commercial area and an industrial sector outside the defences. The nucleus of the port was a mosque—one of the earliest in the region—with two Kufic inscriptions dated to A.D. 727 and 907 (Tampoe 1989: 107).

Chinese records refer to Persian or 'Possu' merchants from the fourth to twelfth centuries A.D., but it is only from the ninth century onwards that the Persians initiated regular sailing to Southeast Asia and China. Siraf formed a major port for this purpose. Judging from the numismatic evidence at Siraf, the recovery of the Gulf region began around A.D. 700 in the mid-Umayyad period, with the circulation of some quantity of Umayyad coins at Siraf. The skeletal coin evidence from the site points to contacts as far-flung as the Byzantine world and southern Spain, indicating a grafting of this very early Islamic trade onto the framework of trading contacts of the Byzantine-Sasanian world (ibid.: 101).

The earliest references to Muslim merchants engaged in long-distance trade occur in an Omani text by Al-Rahil dated to the ninth century. These refer to Al-Qasim, a learned Ibadi Sheikh involved in the aloes wood trade with China. The second merchant, Maymun, lived in Basrah and was related to two Ibadi Imams. Though in the literary sources the focus is on luxury goods, the archaeological data indicates trade in subsistence items and bulk commodities. In additon, there are references to a large number of artisans at Siraf including shipwrights, weavers, metalworkers, jewellers and potters (Whitehouse 1970: 143). The peripatetic nature of this enterprise is well-portrayed by Istakhri's description of a merchant of Siraf:

> The men of Siraf and the surrounding coast travel so much that it happens that some of them stay away on the sea all their lives. I was told of a man of Siraf who was so accustomed to the sea that for nearly forty years he did not leave his ship. When he came to land he sent his associates ashore to look after his business in all the towns, and he crossed over from his boat to another, when the vessel was damaged and needed to be repaired (Kervran 1983: 22).

Sohar was the base of a cosmopolitan merchant community that included Jews engaged in commerce, money-lending and the manufacture of baked brick. Persian traders sailing from the Gulf to India and China regularly halted at Sohar and Persian was one of the accepted languages for business. In addition were the enterprising Omani Arabs.

There are several references to small peripatetic merchants who travelled vast distances and traded in a variety of goods. Thirteenth century accounts of a merchant at Qais describe him as wishing 'to carry Persian saffron to China where I understand that it has a high price, and then take the dishes from China to Greece, Greek brocade to India, Indian steel to Aleppo, glass of Aleppo to Yemen, and the striped material of Yemen to Persia' (Kervran 1983: 22).

The somewhat later Geniza documents indicate inter-linkages between merchant groups from different regions and distinctions on the basis of the scope of operations and organisation of trading activity. For example, the distinction between retailers and wholesalers is well developed. Many of the retailers were trading artisans who marketed their own products. The term '*tajir*' was used for big merchants who traded in a wide variety of goods. They were divided into three categories: one who stored large quantities to sell when the price was high; one who transported goods from one country to another; and one who sent shipments abroad (Tampoe 1989: 126). One such merchant was Nahray bin-Nissim, a wholesale merchant mentioned in 250 of the Geniza documents (Goitein 1967: 149-50, 155).

One of the characteristic features of maritime trade from the ninth-tenth centuries onwards was the location of markets in fortified settlements along the Indian Ocean littoral, as also in the interior. Rules governing the payment of taxes and regulating the functioning of the markets were often inscribed on copper plates and provide useful insights into the organisation of the trade network. The Quilon copper plates of Sthanu Ravi (*Travancore Archaeological Series*, II, 9) are significant in connection with trading rights granted to the church. A market was located within the precincts of the fortified settlement at the port of Quilon, while the church was situated outside the fortification wall (Abraham 1988: 110).

Along the Konkan coast, there are references to the fortified market centre of Balipattana. The Kharepatan plates of Rattaraja dated to A.D. 1008 list out gifts to the temple of

Avvesvara built by Rattaraja's father and situated inside the fortifications. These included a *gadyāṇa* (a measure) of gold from every vessel coming from foreign lands and a *dharaṇa* (also a measure) of gold from those coming from the coast, except those from Chaul and Chandrapura. Also located within the fortifications were settlements of female attendants, oilmen, gardeners, potters and washer men, as also some land (Mirashi 1977: 185).

FOREIGNERS AND TRADE

The mobility of the merchants enabled them to migrate and shift their areas of operation to newer regions and ports. For example, the merchants of Siraf and Sohar shifted to the ports of Qais and other regions after the decline of trade in the upper Gulf (Yajima 1977). This mobility also meant that merchants were often stationed on foreign shores and there are several references in literature and inscriptions to groups categorised as outsiders. On account of the complexity of economic transactions in the ancient period, determining ethnic identities and national affiliations is a task fraught with difficulties.

From the first century B.C. to the second century A.D. while many of the Arabs of the eastern Mediterranean regions were Roman subjects or Roman citizens, others lived beyond the frontiers of the Empire and included groups such as Nabataeans, Palmyrenes, Sabaeans, and so on. In the Indian context, references to *yavanas* are ubiquitous in Sanskrit and Tamil sources and refer to a range of non-local groups from West Asia (Ray 1988).

At the same time there are references to foreigners in-charge of provinces in the subcontinent, especially in Gujarat and the Konkan. The Junagadh inscription of Rudradaman, recounting the history of the Sudarsana lake, states that it was created by the *vaiśya* Pusyagupta during the reign of Chandragupta Maurya and endowed with conduits by *yavana-rāja* Tusaspha on behalf of Asoka (*Epigraphia Indica*, 8: 36-49).

The grammarian Panini, a resident of Salatura in the vicinity of Taxila, states in his *Aṣṭādhyāyī* that the feminine form of *yavana* is *yavnāni* (4.1.49). This latter, according to

Katyayana, denoted Greek writing (Varttika 3 on Panini 4.1.49) and is further paraphrased by Patanjali in the middle of the second century B.C. Panini also associated the *yavanas* with the *kambojas* and described them as having shaven heads (Panini's *Ganapāṭha* 178 on 2.1.72: *yavanamuṇḍa* and *kambojamuṇḍa*). *Yavanas* were regarded in the law books as degenerate Ksatriyas (Manu X.43-44; *Mahābhārata,* śantiparva XII.200). *Milindapañha* (p.1) *'atthi Yonakanam nānāpuṭabhedanam Sagalanāmā nagaram...'* In the Gargi Samhita a work on astrology has a section named the 'Yuga Purāṇa', which contains some historical information, including the story of the attack on Saketa and Pataliputra in which the *yavanas* took part (Jayaswal 1928). The association with the northwest continues in the Viṣṇu Purāṇa dated to the latter half of the first millennium A.D. which refers to the *yavanas* as living in the west of the country (*The Vishnu Purana: A System of Hindu Mythology and Tradition*, H. H. Wilson, trs; Calcutta, 1972 (reprint) 11,3: 141-4). Thus many of the early references to the *yavanas* indicate Greeks settled in the northwest, though this is not the pattern elsewhere in the subcontinent (Ray 1988).

The *Daśakumāracarita* of Dandin refers to a ship in which *yavanas* travelled across the Bay of Bengal as being under the command of the captain called Ramesu (*Rameṣunāmne nāvikanāyakāya*: 155)—clearly a Sanskritic name of non-*yavana* origin. Another problem is the inadequacy of the literary sources themselves to distinguish between different ethnic identities, as in the case of allusions to Romans, Arabs, Indians and Ethiopians in Greek accounts.

This debate notwithstanding, there are several instances of foreign settlers being taxed by local polities in the early medieval period. The evidence from the subcontinent indicates the presence of non-Indian merchants such as the Tajikas and the Turuskas in different areas. 'Turuṣkadaṇḍa' is a term that occurs commmonly in the Gahadavala inscriptions of the Ganga basin and has been taken by several writers to mean a tax on Turkish settlers (Avasthy and Ghosh 1936: 171; Gopal 1965: 116-8).

A *yona* (*yavana*)-rāja of Sanjayata or Sanjan located on the north Konkan coast is mentioned in an inscription from

Nagarjunakonda dated to the fourth century A.D.(*Epigraphia Indica*, 34: 197-203). The Chinchani copper plates mention that the entire *maṇḍala* of Samyana (Sanjan) was made over by the Rastrakuta rulers Krsna II (878-915) and Indra III (915-927) to Sugatipa Madhumati (Muhammad) of the Tajika community. The latter conquered the chiefs of all the harbours (*velākūla*) of the neighbourhood on behalf of his master and placed his own officials in them (*Epigraphia Indica*, 32: 45-60). He established free ferry service at two streams and also a feeding-house at Samyana. In addition he created an endowment for repairs to the *matha* at the site as also for offering worship (*naivedya*) to the goddess Dasami (ibid.). A somewhat later grant of the eleventh century refers to the region as being under the rule of Chamundaraja, many of whose officials bear names of Arabic origin (ibid.: 61-9). A little later, relations between the ruling elite and the *yavanas* seem to have soured. The Kharepatan plates of Anantadeva I dated to A.D. 1095 refer to Anantapala driving out the vile *yavanas* who had devastated the Konkan region (Mirashi 1977: 115-20).

BUDDHISM AND MARITIME ACTIVITY

Thus the participation of several groups from West Asia in the maritime networks is evident, but what is the nature of participation by communities from within South Asia? In this regard the attitude of Buddhism towards seafaring activity is extraordinary, though it is not to be suggested that adherents of Buddhism dominated maritime activity in the ancient period. Instead there are references to a range of communities involved, owing affiliation to a variety of religions, such as Hinduism and Jainism. The approach of Buddhism in adopting the notion of a saviour from the dangers encountered at sea was unlike that of its contemporary religions (Ray 1994: 153-4). Perhaps the earliest representaion of a seafarer in distress is to be seen on a second century B.C. medallion from Bharhut, which shows a gigantic sea-monster threatening to swallow a boat (Cunningham 1879, plate 34). On the basis of the inscription the merchant has been identified as Vasugupta who was saved in his moment of peril by meditating on the Buddha.

Chronologically, the next depiction is at Mathura, (Cunningham 1871-72: 20-1) where the Bodhisattva in the form of a horse saves some ship-wrecked sailors from a group of hungry *yakṣīs* or demonesses. Various versions of the story occur in the *Jataka* and in *Mahāvastu* and it is said to allude to the pseudo-historical legend of Prince Vijaya's conquest of Sri Lanka (Schlingloff 1988: 256). The legend is represented in cave XVII at Ajanta, whereas the painting in cave II depicts the Buddhist monk Purna flying down to save his shipwrecked brother, Darukarnin, the owner of the vessel.

A related development was the emergence of the cult of the Boddhisattva Avalokitesvara as a saviour of mariners and travellers in distress. This has generally been associated with Mahayana and the *Saddharma-puṇḍarika-sūtra* (chapter XXIV), though an enumeration of dangers of travel is to be found in earlier texts as well, such as the *Anguttara Nikāya* (*'Kessivagga'* 119-20; vol. 2: 121) and the *Divyāvadāna* (92: 25-8). The cult was prevalent at the time that the Chinese pilgrim Fa Hsien came to India in the fourth century, though the first sculptural representations of the litany can be dated no earlier than the fifth century A.D. (Ray 1994: chapter 5). This theme is to be found in the Buddhist caves of Ajanta, Aurangabad, Ellora and Badami, though nowhere is the composition so elabroate and the treatment so elegant as in cave 90 at Kanheri (Mitra 1980: 165). For the first time around the sixth to eighth centuries A.D. in the rock cut sanctuaries at Ellora, the function of the Avalokitesvara as the saviour from the eight perils is delegated to the goddess Tara (ibid.: 185). This theme occurs prominently in the monastic establishment at Ratnagiri in Orissa. A standing image of *aṣṭamahābhaya* Tara dated to the eighth century A.D. is shown flanked by scenes of the eight perils depicted in two vertical rows of four panels each (Mitra 1983: 444-5). A second standing image is dated somewhat later to the eleventh century on the basis of a fragmentary inscription and graphically portrays the *jalārṇava-bhaya* or fear of drowning in a sinking boat (ibid.: 428).

CHRISTIAN COMMUNITIES

The spread of Christianity beyond Palestine into Arabia, the Persian Gulf and further east is a subject still inadequately known and researched, though archaeological data for the presence of Christian churches and cemeteries is gradually emerging. In the fourth to seventh centuries A.D. several tribal groupings in the regions now known as Jordan, Syria and Iraq are known to have adopted Christianity (Langfeldt 1994: 53). Christian presence is known in Hijaz and in southwest Arabia there was a strong Christian enclave in Najran. Christian monasteries were located on the caravan routes in western Arabia and functioned as caravanserais.

Sasanian records refer to six villages governed by them around Bahrain and these have also been identified as the sites of bishoprics in the eastern dioceses of the Nestorian church (Beaucamp and Robin 1983). A study of the subdivisions within the Nestorian church indicates that after A.D. 420, the seat of the patriarch who ordained all the bishops of Asia was at Ctesiphon and that this included the island of Socotra and the bishopric of south India (Sachau 1916). But from A.D. 554 to 790 the metropolitan of Persis separated his diocese from the patriarch and he ordained the bishops of the region. The Bible was translated into Persian—a language which was also adopted for conducting church services in place of Syriac, as had been the case in the church of Mesopotamia.

These developments are reflected in the occurrence of a set of six Pahlavi inscriptions written on Christian stone crosses found in south India.

> These are stone panels with the relief of a cross in the Nestorian manner with a three-stepped base and floral petals under a colonnade of Indian style with makara capitals, and with the inscription on the margin. One panel is preserved in the church of St. Thomas near Madras, the others in the province of Kerala in the churches of Kottayam, Murrucira, Katamaram and Alangad (Gropp 1991: 85).

It has been argued that of the six Pahlavi inscriptions, it is the Mylapore epigraph that preserves the original text. The remaining five are copies made in the sixteenth century by the Portuguese who discovered the record during excavations of the site for the construction of the new church of St. Thomas. About 1,580 copies were made and transported to the Kerala churches.

Eleventh century Pahlavi inscriptions from cave 90 at the Buddhist monastic complex at Kanheri on the west coast provide a record of further visits by Persians. In contrast to the other inscriptions at the site, these do not mention donations but seem to have been inscribed with the objective of documenting visits of *hamdinikan* or co-religionists listed by name (Gokhale 1991: 142-7).

In Kerala, the copper-plate grant from the year 849 recording the grant of several rights in the reign of King Sthanu Ravi to the Tarisapalli church built by Maruvan Sapir Iso, bears witness signatures in Arabic, Pahlavi and Hebrew. The copperplates were discovered in the town of Quilon and some of the names of the witnesses using Pahlavi script are distinctly Christian. It is then evident that a Christian community was settled in Kerala and Tamil Nadu from about A.D. 600 to the ninth century and that this community used the Persian or Pahlavi language (Gropp 1991: 86).

PILGRIMAGE AND PILGRIMS

'Merchants, craftsmen, and scholars alike would combine journeys undertaken in their personal interests with pilgrimages to holy places. The Muslim pilgrimage, of course, far outstripped in importance those of the other two religions'

(Goitein 1967: 55).

In addition to religious centres such as Mecca and Medina, the sacred topography of Islam accepted journeys to local shrines of important holy figures. Most of the pilgrim routes passed through inhospitable terrain and necessitated the development of facilities, while pilgrims from East Africa and India arrived by the sea route. There has, however, not been adequate research on the investigation of the sea routes involved (Petersen 1994: 47-56).

Archaeological excavations in the Indus basin have provided evidence for the early spread of Islam in the region dating from the eighth century onwards. The vestiges of a mosque survive at the site of Banbhore on the Indus coast comprising an open courtyard and two gateways, one each on the east and north. It had a flat roof supported by wooden columns and no *mihrab*. During the four centuries of its use, it was repaired thrice, as is evident from an Arabic inscription dated A.D. 906. A second mosque, rectangular in plan, is known from Mansurah located in the vast fertile plains of central Sindh on an old course of the river Indus. The city was founded around A.D. 730-732, at the same time that the smaller settlement of Biro Bham developed on the bank of a channel of the river Indus (Mughal 1992: 267-85).

Archaeological explorations in the Indus delta, especially on the island locally known as 'Jaki Bandar' and referred to as 'Lahori Bandar' in ancient maps has revealed a fortress, neighbouring mosques as well as numerous pottery workshops dated between the thirteenth/fourteenth to the seventeenth centuries A.D. Local fishermen regularly travel to the island to visit the tomb of a saint at some distance from the fortress and one that has been erected from the debris of grey blocks of sculpture. Under this architectural complex more ancient ruins have been identified dating to the ninth-tenth centuries A.D. while still earlier pre-Islamic remains are visible under the present sea level. Many other sites are to be seen in the vicinity indicating ancient anchorage and early centres, which continued into the Islamic and later periods (Kervran 1996: 48-9).

In one of the letters of the *India Book*, a merchant visiting India informs his family in Old Cairo that he would visit the holy places in Iraq on his way back and accordingly asks his brother to delay his wedding (Goitein 1967: 185). Thus a combination of trade and pilgrimage need not necessarily imply a clash of interests. In a recent study, however, Pearson emphasizes that there was no co-relation between the sea trade to Jeddah and the *haji* as these were based on two different calendars and often took place at different times. There were two major markets in the Hejaz at this time: one, a routine commercial market in Jeddah and other Red Sea ports; and the other was the fair in Mecca associated with the congregation of pilgrims at the time of the *haji*. Ships sailing from Surat and other ports on the west coast of India set sail in March and April for the Red Sea and returned in September and October, the total journey time being about twenty-five days. For a variety of reasons, cargoes had to be trans-shipped at the Red Sea ports either into smaller vessels or onto caravans for the overland routes. Though historically there has been a shift in the ports of trans-shipment, the general pattern has remained unchanged. While this trade in the Red Sea involved wealthy cargoes, it was totally dependent on the monsoon winds. In contrast, the date of the *haji* was decided in accordance with the lunar calendar and it was seldom that the two coincided.[7]

CONCLUSION

From this overview it is evident that several networks overlapped in the western Indian Ocean in the ancient period and brought together interest groups ranging from boat-building communities to religious functionaries and traders. We have not been able to discuss many other relevant topics in this paper, such as the diverse knowledge traditions, incense trade and its myriad manifestations including for ritual purposes, or the artisans involved in textile production. Is this encounter to be termed an example of globalisation or world systems in antiquity? Maybe not, since the data does not suggest coalescing of the various nodes, such as political, economic and religious as in the case of the modern states. Instead, in most cases these networks transcended national boundaries and functioned as somewhat autonomous traditions.

This then has implications for the study and research on ancient history in the region, which in most cases has emphasized national histories, rather than issues of cultural transformation within a wider Indian Ocean sphere. Nor does the teaching of Ancient Indian History take into account the movements of maritime communities and cultures in the ancient period and the emergence of their distinctive identities. Perhaps it is time to redress the situation and to incorporate more wide-based issues in the teaching and research of the history and culture of the Indian Ocean in antiquity. This is essential if we are to build on the enduring relationship that has marked interaction between West Asia and the Indian subcontinent in the early period.

Notes

1. The forty-two India letters of the Cairo Genizah provide significant information on the modes of transactions between partners albeit of different religious affiliations, such as Jews or Muslims. The term 'geniza' in medieval Hebrew designates a repository of discarded writing and these eleventh to thirteenth century documents discovered in Cairo are a valuable source for an understanding of the medieval Indian Ocean trade.
2. Some of these issues are discussed in a study by the author titled *Archaeology of Seafaring in Ancient South Asia,* Cambridge World Archaeology series, 2003 (in press).
3. For example, the pattern of sewing is one of the attributes that the flat-bottomed plank-built *madel paruwa* of Sri Lanka shares with the *beden* of Somalia, the *sambuq* of Oman, the *mtepe* of Kenya and the *masula* of the Tamil coast (Kentley and Gunaratne 1987: 41) One major difference is that the South Asian examples, such as the *paruwa* and the *masula*, do not employ tree-nails, which seems to be the practice in the western Indian Ocean. These are distinctive in other ways as well, and are the only known types of flat-bottomed stitched boats in the Indian Ocean.
4. Thus the *baghla* and the *gunjo* are the Arab forms of the Indian *kotia*, the Arab *bum* the counterpart of the Indian *dhangi* and *nauri*, with the Indian *batel* representing the Arab *sambuk* (Hornell 1970: 197).
5. In the first century A.D. ed-Dur has provided data for fishing and pearling activity with fish accounting for the largest portion of the faunal inventory followed by shellfish. A bell-shaped lead weight identical to the stone weights used by pearl divers was found in a house. The recovery of large pearl oyster shells in graves at ed-Dur also suggests that the pearl was a highly valued commodity (Potts 1997: 92-3).
6. Further support for this hypothesis comes from the finds of fifteen Characene coins at ed-Dur and the fact that 40 per cent of the diagnostic pottery at the site has Characene analogies. The site dates to the first century A.D. and 147 objects of glass recovered from archaeological excavations reached the site between 25 B.C. and A.D. 75. Chemical analyses have confirmed the Roman origin of the glass. Forty per cent of the samples were made by casting and 57 per cent of the cast vessels were ribbed bowls, while 43

per cent were made of mosaic glass. Of the 59 per cent samples made by inflation, 70.1 per cent were of blown glass. It is significant that a majority of the vessels were used for eating and 48.4 per cent were flat or shallow vessels, 26 per cent were small bottles, jars and boxes, perhaps for storing and/or transporting cosmetic or medicinal perparations. This recent data on the shapes of the vesses challenges the parameters of the earlier debate centred on luxuries or prestige items required by the state (Whitehouse 2000: 87-128.

7. 'What is most clear in all this is that very little of this trade had anything to do with religion or specifically with the *hajj*. The sea trade simply could not fit with the times of the *hajj*. Land trade could, but given the way so many goods travelled part of the way by sea, much land trade also was circumscribed by the monsoon, and was timed to reach a particular port at the time when ships could also reach it on the relevant monsoon. The exceptions were the pilgrim caravans, which of necessity were governed by the lunar calendar. The economic role of these was small' (Pearson 1994: 165).

References

Abraham, M. 1988, *Two Medieval Merchant Guilds of South India*, New Delhi.

Agrawala, V.S. 1953, *India as known to Panini*, University of Lucknow.

Avasthy, R.S. and A.K. Ghosh, 1938, 'References to Muhammadans in Sanskrit Inscriptions in Northern India-AD 730 to 1320', *Journal of Indian History*, 15: 161-84, 16: 24-26.

Barnes, R. 1990, 'Indian Trade Cloth in Egypt: the Newberry Collection', *Textiles in Trade*, Proceedings of the Textile Society of America Biennial Symposium, September 14-16, Washington, DC: 178-91.

— 1997 *Indian Block-printed Textiles in Egypt*, Oxford: Clarendon Press.

Beaucamp, J. and Ch. Robin. 1983, 'L'eveche Nestorian de Masmahig dans I' archipel d'al Bahrain', in D.T., Potts, ed. *Dilmun*, *Berliner Beitraege zum Vorderen Orient*, 2: 171-87.

Casson, L. 1989, *The Periplus Maris Erythraei*, Princeton.

Chittick, H.N. 1980, 'Sewn boats in the western Indian Ocean and a survival in Somalia', *The International Journal of Nautical Archaeology and Underwater Exploration*, 9 (4): 297-304.

Cunningham, A. 1871-2, *Annual Report*, *Archaeological Survey of India*, 3: 13-46.

— 1879, *The Stupa of Bharhut*, London.

Desai, Z.A. 1960, 'Muslims in the Thirteenth century Gujarat as known from the Arabic Inscriptions', *Journal of the Oriental Institute*, 10: 353-64.

Goitein, S.D. 1967, *A Mediterranean Society*, I, University of California Press.

Gokhale, S. 1991, *Kanheri Inscriptions*, Deccan College Post-Graduate Research Institute.

Gopal, L. 1965, *The Economic Life of Northern India*, New Delhi.

Gropp, G. 1991, 'Christian Maritime Trade of Sasanian Age in the Persian Gulf', K. Schipmann, A. Herling, and J.F. Salles, eds. *Golf-Archaeologie, Buch am Erlbach*: Verlag Marie L. Leidorf: 83-88.

Hornell, J. 1970, *Water Transport*, Newton Abbott.

Hourani, G.F., 1963/1995, *Arab Seafaring in the Indian Ocean in Ancient and Early Medieval Times*, Beirut.

Jayaswal, K.P. 1928, 'Historical Data in the Gargi Samhita and the Brahmin Empire', *Journal of the Bihar and Orissa Research Society*, 14: 410-1.

Kentley, E. and Rohan Gunaratne. 1987, 'The Madel Paruwa — a sewn boat with chine strakes', *International Journal of Nautical Archaeology*, 16 (1): 35-48.

Kervran M. 1983, 'Famous Merchants of the Arabian Gulf in the Middle Ages', *Dilmun*, Journal of the Bahrain Historical and Archaeological Society, 11.

— 1996, 'Indian Ceramics in Southern Iran and Eastern Arabia: Repertory, Classification and Chronology', H.P. Ray, and J.F. Salles, eds. *Tradition and Archaeology: Early Maritime Contacts in the Indian Ocean*, New Delhi: 37-58.

Langfeldt, J.A. 1994, 'Recently discovered early Christian monuments in Northeastern Arabia', *Arabian Archaeology and Epigraphy*, 5: 32-60.

Lydekker, C.J.W. 1919, 'The 'mtepe' dhau of the Bajun islands', *Man*, 19.

Mirashi, V.V. 1977, *Corpus Inscriptionum Indicarum, 6, The Inscriptions of the Silaharas*, New Delhi.

Mitra, D. 1980, *Buddhist Monuments*, Calcutta.

— 1983, *Ratnagiri* (1958-61), Memoirs of the Archaeological Survey of India, 80 (2), New Delhi.

Mughal, M.R. 1992, 'Early Muslim Cities in Sindh and Patterns of International Trade', *Islamic Studies*, 31 (3): 267-86.

Pearson, M.N. 1994, *Pious Passengers: the Hajj in Earlier Times*, New Delhi.

Petersen, A. 1994, 'The archaeology of the Syrian and Iraqi Hajj routes', *World Archaeology*, 26, 1: 47-56.

Potts, D.T. 1997. 'The Roman Relationship with the Persicus sinus from the Rise of Spasinou Charax (127 BC) to the Reign of Shapur II (AD 309-379)', Susan E. Alcock, ed. *The Early Roman Empire in the East*, Oxford: Oxbow Monograph 95: 92-3.

Qaisar, A.J. 1982, *The Indian Response to European Technology and Culture*, Delhi.

Rajamanickam, G.V. and Swamy, L.N. 1991, *Maritime History of South India*, unpublished report, Tamil University.

Ray, H.P. 1986, *Monastery and Guild: Commerce under the Satavahanas*, Oxford University Press.

— 1988, 'The Yavana presence in ancient India', *Journal of the Economic and Social History of the Orient*, 31: 311-325.

— 1994 (reissued as Oxford India Paperbacks in 1999), *The Winds of Change: Buddhism and the Maritime Links of Early South Asia*, Oxford University Press.

— forthcoming, *India and the Indian Ocean: The Formative Period*, Cambridge University Press.

Sachau, E. 1916, *Vom Christentum in der Persis*, Sitzungsberichte Preuss. Akad. Wiss: 958-980.

Scharfe, H. 1993, *Investigations in Kautalya's Manual of Political Science*, Wiesbaden.

Schlingloff, H.D. 1988. *Studies in the Ajanta Painting*, Delhi: Ajanta Publications.

Severin, T. 1991, *The Sindbad Voyage*, Arrow Books.

Shahani, L. 1997, Ethnoarchaeology of Harappan Sea Trade: A Preliminary Study, *Man and Environment*, 22 (1): 9-18.

Stillman, Norman A. 1973, 'The Eleventh Century Merchant House of Ibn 'Awkal' (A Geniza Study)', *Journal of the Economic and Social History of the Orient*, 16: 15-88.

Tampoe, M. 1989, *Maritime Trade between China and the West*, BAR International Series 555.

Whitehouse, D. 1970, Siraf: A medieval port on the Persian Gulf, *World Archaeology*, 2 (2): 141-57.

— 1996, 'Sasanian Maritime Activity', in J. Reade, ed. *The Indian Ocean in Antiquity*, London: 339-49.

— 2000 'Ancient Glass from ed-Dur', *Arabian Archaeology and Epigraphy*, 11 (1), May: 87-128.

Wiebeck, E. 1987, *Indische Boote und Schiffe*, Rostock.

Williamson, A. 1974, 'Sohar and the Sea Trade of Oman in the tenth century A.D', *Proceedings of the Seminar for Arabian Studies*, 4.

Yajima, H. 1977, Maritime Activities of the Arab Gulf People and the Indian Ocean World in the Eleventh and Twelfth Centuries', *Journal of Asian and African Studies*, no. 14.

Cultural Implications of Trades between South Asia, the Gulf, and Mesopotamia in the Bronze Age

SHEREEN RATNAGAR

Between 2600 and 1800 B.C., there were movements of goods like stones, wood, metal, shell and crafted objects between South Asia, Baluchistan, southern Iran, Oman, Bahrain, Kuwait, and Iraq, mainly by sea. In those days, as surviving literary evidence from Mesopotamia reveals, the regions involved in intercultural movements of goods were known as 'Meluhha' (South Asia), 'Magan' (Oman, Makran of Baluchistan, south-eastern Iran), 'Dilmun' (Bahrain to Kuwait, and the coast of the Eastern Province), 'Elam' (south-western Iran), and 'Sumer' (southern Iraq).

Archaeologists refer to this period as the Bronze Age, meaning an age when (some of) the tools of production were made of metal: copper and bronze (alloying either tin, arsenic, or lead with copper). These metals (unlike iron) are scarce on the face of the earth, so a technology based on their regular utilization would have entailed the organisation of trade (in contrast with incidental or sporadic, down-the-line exchanges) and the development of metallurgical technology (hence specialists whose lore and skills were not shared by all). Individual farmer households would not have been able to make their own (metal) tools, as they had done in the neolithic and chalcolithic stages. So there was a division of labour between families, sometimes between regions (suppliers of raw materials as against processors of materials). As handicrafts developed, in some cases it became efficient for them to be clustered in urban centres: early urban professions were often interdependent, say, bronze casters/potters, seal cutters on bronze casters. Urban centres, in turn, could emerge when ruling elites took effective control of collective labour, sponsored the search for ores, supported metallurgists and other specialists with material and basic requirements like charcoal, and, in their role as theocratic rulers and temple builders or managers of cults, often became the points around which developed sub-cultures that consumed the best of crafted items and exotic things.

Let us make a rapid survey of the trading cultures and their goods. Wool and woolen textiles, barley, edible oil, bitumen and silver went out from Sumer, the silver being an item not produced there but acquired from Anatolia in the northwest. Sumer had no stone or metal resources of its own. Its date palms and riverside poplars did not produce wood of the quality required for fine furniture, roof beams, or boats. But it had the highest levels of agricultural production in that area, due to the fertility of soils and easy irrigation from gravity flow canals. Not only were there prolific harvests of barley and wheat, there were also especially large herds of sheep (producers of fine wool) and goats at the edges of the cultivation. Subsistence wealth also derived from river fish. With this basic economic advantage, the Mesopotamian landscape saw the early emergence of the largest cities (which were 400 ha, 200 ha in extent) of our area. It is not surprising, then, that this region was the net consumer of traded wealth. Bahrain, in contrast, saw cultivation only along the north and west coast because of the prevalence of subsoil artesian water; pearls were procured from the shallow sea in the vicinity of Bahrain. Its main trade centre was probably located at the site of Qala'at al Bahrain, approximately 30 ha in extent.

Marble/calcite vases were exported from Shahr-i Sokhta in Seistan (Iran) in the inland delta of the Helman river. Here was a region of high agricultural potential, the dense vegetation growth around the inland *hamun* also providing pasture for livestock, and a habitat for a great variety of birds. From the arid peninsula of Oman, with only a few arable *wadis* growing dates and some barley, where more secure subsistence was to be had from herding goats (later camels), were procured not only a hard, glossy black stone called diorite, used extensively in Sumerian monumental sculpture, but also copper. With over a hundred sources of copper ore, Oman was the land par excellence of copper for Sumer and at least sometimes for South Asia. Meanwhile, at a small settlement today called Tepe Yahya, in southeast Iran near Kerman, were carved vessels of a soft dark green/grey stone called chlorite and, it appears, sent as far west as Sumer and Elam (the latter under heavy cultural influence—and often political domination—from Sumer, and yet developing its own system of writing) and as far east as Mohenjo-daro.

Other than Sumer and Elam, the other literate society of those times in our 'world' was South Asia, home of the Harappa civilization spread over the plains of the Indus and its tributaries, and in the drier peninsulas of Kutch and Kathiawad. Here was the trading culture with the widest geographic spread, having established its settlements not only in the foothills of the Punjab and in arid Makran, but also below the lapis quarries of the Kokcha river of north-eastern Afghanistan. Such a wide dispersal meant that the Harappa civilization (Meluhha) could access fine high altitude woods, copper from northern Rajasthan, carnelian from Gujarat, gold from Badakhshan and Punjab, and lapis lazuli from Badakhshan, sea shells, as well as several other exotic materials. Here were to be found the best boat building woods; cuneiform tablets from Sumer speak of Meluhha woods and of wood coming by sea via Dilmun. Meluhha ships appear to have been of a specific type or form. Harappan seals have been found at many Sumerian cities and also Susa, in Oman, and in Bahrain, while a jar impressed with a Harappan seal occurs at Tepe Yahya.

The Harappan system of weights appears to have been used in Bahrain, with Sumerians referring to it as the system of Dilmun. Many curiosities and finally crafted items of Harappan origin have been found abroad (shankh shells, long carnelian beads, decorated carnelian beads, etc.). A Mesopotamian seal is inscribed with the name and official title of a translator of the Meluhha language. We are, thus, justified in inferring that the Harappa civilization played the role of major seafarer and supplier of goods, whereas Sumer was the most populous and prosperous consumer.

What was the cultural or social fallout of maritime trade between such contrasting regions and cultures? Did the poorer countries gain anything by supplying copper or pearls to the richer ones? Did they progress technologically or economically, as we are told poorer countries will, today, as a result of globalisation? Is there a causal connection between the collapse of this trade and the end of the Harappan civilisation, its cities, writing system, bronze technology, seals, and weight system? This is the overall problem of my current research. The answer cannot possibly be given here, but three interesting social aspects will be touched.

From one perspective it may be said that there was great commonality of culture across this trading region. In all the concerned cultures, the crops and animals that supplied food and energy belonged to the same species, except for humped cattle unique to South Asia, and the marginal role of the Bactrian camel, and some minor millets in use in Kutch and Kathiawad. So too, the sinking of wells appears to have been a technique known to the Harappans, Sumerians, and Dilmunites in Bahrain. Most of the trading cultures used stone weights, each its own shape and system, and most cultures had a characteristic form of seal. Across this world, people learnt to make faience, a synthetic substance that substituted for coloured stones like lapis and turquoise, although the details of the technology varied according to the culture. Although no monkeys live west of Baluchistan, we find small stone figurines of monkeys, obviously of Indian origin, in Sumerian towns, at Susa, and in Bahrain. Perhaps Harappan sailors took pet monkeys abroad with them, and these were a fascination for the people of western Asia. So too, bones, and a unique instance of the dung of an infant, indicated that the two-humped Bactrian camel had been introduced at Shahr-i Sokhta and in the Harappan world (not that it became a subject of figurative art in the latter, or survived after the Harappan period).

In many ways, and at more than one level, this was 'one world', and yet if we explore other aspects of the daily lives of ordinary people, we find striking differences. Mesopotamian town workshops employed thousands of men and women for the production of fine cloth from sheep's wool in huge quantity, but at Shahr-i Sokhta surviving fragments of fabric have, on analysis, been found to have been made of goat and camel hair. In Bahrain and Oman, on the other hand, patches of cloth and string that have survived at archaeological sites have been identified as linen, made from the fibre of flax/

hemp. The fourth tradition is found in the Harappan world, where cotton thread and cloth have been found. So each culture area seems to have had its own technology and modes of clothing.

Not surprisingly, material culture requiring specialist production also shows some sharp technological barriers. Carnelian is one of the hardest of the bronze age stones; long and shiny red carnelian beads and shorter carnelian beads decorated in white designs were made at Harappan sites, but not elsewhere, not even in Sumer. But by far the most remarkable technological contrasts in production outside the domestic unit lies in metallurgy. Copper is a relatively soft metal, not a particular advance on stone except that it can give an artifact of almost any required shape. Arsenic, tin, and lead alloyed with copper give harder materials, and tin-bronze is clearly the most efficacious of these alloys where sculpture and tools and weapons are concerned. The Harappan sites have yielded artifacts in pure copper and also the three alloys. In Mesopotamia and Elam, arsenic-alloying appears to have gradually given way to the preferable tin alloy during our period. But at Shahr-i Sokhta and Yahya, and in Bahrain, tin alloying is practically non-existent. Most significant of all, Oman has produced very few tin-bronze artifacts of the third millennium—so the largest producer of copper could not develop a level of metallurgy comparable to that of South Asia and Sumer, even though (judging by the extraneous pottery, seals, weights, and beads found in the peninsula) it provided copper for these two areas.

When we look into the ways in which foreign lands are written of in the cuneiform tablets of Sumer, the great consuming country with the largest cities, we find that there was no great knowledge of the world outside. An early ruler of Lagash, around 2600 B.C., set up inscriptions in many places boasting that 'boats of Dilmun brought cargoes of wood from far-off mountains'. Dilmun was obviously not a producer of fine wood, and the origin of wood is only a distant place, without a name! Similarly, ivory was quite extensively used in Sumer, for inlay work, containers, and ornaments. Its only source could have been South Asia. But in the Sumerian texts is most often Dilmun which is said to be the source. (Trade secrets are one possible explanation for this.)

Considering that the Sumerians were not the best sailors, did they have any knowledge of the land of Meluhha? In lexical and economic texts, Meluhha is mentioned as the source of many kinds of wood and stone, and is a land of seafarers, with large boats. But there is only one text—a myth—in which Meluhha is described at any length. This myth describes how Enki, a deity of the netherworld, fashioned the universe. After finishing his work, he blessed his creations, Sumer, Meluhha, and other lands. Meluhha here is said to be a black land, with big highland trees, whose fine wood is for the thrones of the palace. Its bulls are large. Its bird is one whose call fills the palace of the king. That is to say, Meluhha was for the Mesopotamian literati a distant land, only vaguely known. No extant cuneiform literature refers to its forests or greenery, to the startling brickwork of its cities, or to its intrepid sailors.

It is all the more remarkable, therefore, that evidence exists for the spread of cults across our region. Carved chlorite vessels of Tepe Yahya and the Eastern Province of Arabia, and later of Oman, have been found by the hundreds in Sumer and at Susa, in Kuwait, Bahrain, southeast Iran, and also Mohenjo-daro. These are superbly carved, with geometric designs and also snakes, animals, and mythological beings. The quality of these makes us ask if these bowls were exchanged only amongst elites, but there are too many of them to make this the obvious explanation. The imagery and symbolism they embody makes us ask if they could have been used in a cult. Moreover, a cuneiform tablet actually characterizes chlorite stone and its cosmic destiny as intended for the craftsmen to be 'worked' [carved?] to carry [temple?] offerings. And one such carved bowl from Kuwait carries an inscription of the name of a god. By 'cult' I mean a religious phenomenon free of an organisation or hierarchy and official priesthood. Cults often involve centres of pilgrimage to which flow people and their offerings. People leave these centres with blessings and sometimes material items. By definition, cults attract people from diverse communities, classes, and cultures. So regional cults in the bronze age may well have provided the frameworks for travel, the exchange of goods, and the dispersal of myths, techniques, and social values.

Lack of precise knowledge about the world outside was not tantamount, at least in the case of Sumer, to an absence of cosmopolitan values. An emotive poem describes the fall of the city of Akkad, and highlights its desolation by contrasts with word sketches of the city in its prime. When Akkad flourished, we are told, its patron goddess was working restlessly so that the city would be prosperous and its people would 'eat splendid food, rejoice, and throng the places of celebration'; so that 'acquaintances would dine together' and, quite significantly, 'foreigners would cruise about like unusual birds in the sky and ...monkeys, mighty elephants, water buffalo and exotic animals would jostle each other in the public squares....' The buffalo is not a Mesopotamian animal. Corroborating this poem are about half a dozen seals of the Akkad period that actually depict the water buffalo.

What comes across in bronze age material culture, imagery, and written words across our world, then, is the pride people took in the cosmopolitan cultures of cities, all the more remarkable in our times when doors are closing and chauvinism has become a weapon of political mobilization.

Arabian Gulf During the British Era

The Impact of India

ABDULLA ELMADANI

The relationship between India and the Gulf region is well rooted in history. It stretches back to ancient times. Based on the artifacts like embellished pottery and seashells recovered from the Harappa Valley in north India and those belonging to the Dilmun civilisation of Bahrain or Magan civilisation of Oman, some archaeologists suggest that Indo-Gulf interactions can be traced to the third millennium B.C.

On the other hand, Sumerian and Acadian versions indicate that the valley of Mesopotamia had profound commercial ties with the Indus civilisation which flourished from about 2500 to 1500 B.C. or little earlier. One of the three ancient trade routes between India and Europe went through the strait of Hormuz across the Gulf, Mesopotamia and Aleppo. Because of its central location on this route, in addition to its capability to provide transit traders and sailors with food and water, the Gulf region became a farourable middle-point for the trans-shipment of Indian merchandise to Mesopotamia and further. This led gradually to a greater involvement on the part of the Gulf inhabitants in trade with India. What supports such a conclusions, and additionally proves the stationing of some Indians in the Gulf for the purpose of conducting trade in those ancient days, are the many seals discovered in Bahrain. These seals bear typical Indus Valley designs and characters and some of them are prism-shaped like the ones of the ancient Harappas. It is possible that along with these trade relations some socio-cultural exhanges occurred as, according to archaeological evidence, there was resemblance between a number of methods used in certain activities (such as fishing, boat construction, measuring, and weighing) in both civilisations.

Long before the advent of Islam, India and Indian commodities were known to the tribes of Arabia and were admired by them to the extent that they called their daughters 'Hind'; the Arabic name for India. Moreover, Arabian poems written in the pre-Islamic era (or *Jahiliyah*) contain many words praising or referring to Indian swords, silk, musk, and amber. For example, the word *muhannad*, which means 'from *Hind*', was repeatedly used in these poems as one of the many Arabic names for sword. The fact that many words of Indo-European stock were used in the Quranic versions and in ancient Arabian poetry, the two most important sources of Arabic philology, is in itself evidence of the long process of social and commercial intercourse that must have taken place between India and West Asia in the centuries immediately preceding Islam.

In the pre-Islamic era a large number of Indians migrated to different parts of the Gulf coast, either to establish businesses, seek employment with Arab traders, or just to escape instability at home. Among the seven Indian groups that migrated to Arabia and settled down in Bahrain, Oman, and Ubulla (Basra) at this period were the Zuth (known in India as Jats), the Bayasira, and the Siabja. Thus at the time of the advent of Islam, there were many Indian settlers in Arabia who were involved in various activities.

The rise of Islam in the seventh century A.D. was significant for Indo-Arab commercial interactions, particularly in the aftermath of the Arab conquest of Mesopotamia and Persia and the transference of the capital city of the Arab/ Islamic Empire from Mecca to Damascus and later to Baghbad. The political unification of Arabia, Egypt, Iraq, Syria, Iran, and North Africa, and the emergence of new cities along with the growth of old urban centres, created an enormously powerful zone of economic consumption and widened the demand for Indian commodities. These developments stimulated both caravan and maritime trade in the Gulf region. As a result, commercial ties between Arabia and India grew tangibly in terms of both the composition and volume of goods imported from India.

Until the Muslim conquest of India in A.D. 711 much of Indo-Gulf interactions had been mainly confined to trade exchange. But with the inclusion of Sind and part of Gujarat into the Arab/Islamic empire, the two regions became politicallv linked, a development which paved the way for greater contacts and, therefore, strong socio-cultural relations.

Commercial and other forms of exchange between Arabia and India continued until the great setback in the sixteenth century caused by the emergence of Portugal as a dominant sea power in the Gulf and in the Indian Ocean. With the emergence of the Portuguese, Arabia's merchants were deprived of their influence in the Indian Ocean and of their share of Indian and Oriental goods. Their rulers in Hormuz, Muscat, and Bahrain were suppressed and forced to pay annual tributes to the Portuguese. Their mercantile activity in the Gulf and Indian Ocean became subjected to trade licenses and taxes. In Goa, the Indians of Arab origin known as 'Navayats' were excluded from office and deprived of their control over the import and re-export of Arabian and Persian horses which were needed in the cavalry (the backbone of the Hindu armies in those days). However with both the regions, India and the Gulf, getting politically and administratively linked under the British from the late nineteenth century up to the mid-twentieth century, Indo-Gulf relations entered a new era. Until India's independence in 1947, all decisions regarding the fate of the Gulf region and its political and economic affairs have been taken in India and implemented by India's British authorities. The Gulf's dependency on India became, therefore, strong in almost every field as its chiefs and people were not allowed to venture further than India. Talking about the Gulf's Indian connection in the British era, Rosemarie Zahlan said:

> The Indian rupee was the currency in circulation... Indian stamps were overmarked 'Kuwait' and 'Bahrain.' The Arabic dialect of the coastal areas contained many Urdu words, and the political officers stationed there....were members of the British government of India who had been trained for service in India. They applied British Indian regulations throughout the Gulf states.[1]

The above lines, however, show only some features of the connection but not all. Indo-Gulf relations during the first half of the twentieth century were so varied, multi-faceted and of significant impact on the Gulf region that further elaboration is needed. This paper, therefore, is an attempt to illustrate the role played by India and Indians in the Gulf's political, economic, and socio-cultural life during that period.

India and the Gulf Pearling Industry

In the pre-oil days, one of the principal sources of livehood in the Gulf was pearl fishing and trade. A large segment of the population in Kuwait, Qatar, Bahrain, the Trucial Sheikhdoms, and the eastern coast of Saudi Arabia was involved in this activity. In those days, Indian merchants, known in the Gulf by the name '*banyan*' came to the region to conduct deals with their local counterparts. Some of these Indians were stationed permanently in the Gulf for this purpose. The Gulf's merchants also travelled regularly to Bombay to market their pearls, as well as to seek loans for the expansion of their pearl-diving operations. Their vessels on return journeys were loaded with an assortment of staple foodstuffs and materials of Indian origin. Some of these merchants chose to settle there, investing their pearl revenues in real estate and other economic activities. Among them were Albassam and Algosaibi from Saudi Arabia, Alebrahim and Aljina'i from Kuwait, Alzayani and Alurrayed from Bahrain, and Almidf'a and Alsayegh from the Trucial Sheikhdoms.

In India, the Gulf pearls were bought, pierced, polished, manufactured into jewellery and re-exported to Europe or sold to Indian Maharajas, bringing both Arab and Indian merchants immense wealth.

It is necessary here to state that the Indian role in the Gulf pearling industry was confined to such activities as purchasing, providing loans, and participating in the construction and ownership of the vessels. There was no actual involvement of the Indians in pearl-diving operations, probably due to Bahrain's refusal to grant them permission to compete with the local divers, fearing the outbreak of hostilities between the Arabs and Indians should it decide otherwise. However, this must not lead to the conclusion that the Indians never tried to get involved in the pearl-diving process. There were a number of occasions in which Indian merchants got permission from the local chiefs to practice pearl-diving, but were interrupted by the British political Resident.[2]

The Gulf's Commercial Dependency

Throughout the nineteenth century and until the immediate post-oil discovery years, India was not only the main market for Gulf pearls but also the Gulf's major supplier of all sorts of merchandise. There are statistical tables dating back to 1873 that prove India's dominant position in Bahrain's imports. The value of Indian exports to Bahrain in that year (1873) was 1,167, 375 rupees or more than a third of total imports.[3] India continued to be the biggest exporting country to Bahrain and probably to other Gulf emirates until the early 1930s. For example, Indian goods constituted 72.47 per cent of the total imports of Bahrain in 1929/1930.[4]

Annual trade reports in the era under discussion evidently show that Gulf imports from India increased or decreased, in range and volume, in accordance with the rise or decline of pearl prices. What facilitated the conduct of business between the two regions was the existence of a common means of payment, the Indian rupee. In fact, dependency of the Gulf merchants on the Indian market for the sale of their pearls contributed to the emergence of the Indian rupee as the major currency in circulation in the Gulf. This continued until 1959 when the Indian government, under economic pressures caused by continuous smuggling of gold into its territories against obtaining Indian rupees, issued the 'Gulf rupee' as a special currency for use in the Gulf states. The Gulf rupee, which was at parity with the Indian currency, remained the official means of payment in these states until they issued their own currencies around the mid-1960s.

Enriching the Gulf's Merchant Houses

It was through establishing business with India or in India at this time that many of today's prominent merchant families in the Gulf made the first portions of their great wealth. The business histories of these families reveal interesting stories about their early modest beginnings and the role of the Indian connection in their riches.

In Kuwait, for example, the head of Alghanim business empire began his business, which has vastly developed in the last four decades under his sons and grandsons, by plying the Basra-Bombay route, selling Iraqi dates to the Indians and buying from India food, cloth, and timber on return to Kuwait.

The wealth of some of the most prominent Saudi merchant families like Alireza and Algosaibi, was basically attributed to their decisions in the late nineteenth and early twentieth centuries to establish purçhasing offices in Bombay and Calcutta through which they sold pearls and exported an assortment of Indian commodities to Jeddah, Bahrain, and Alahsa. Establishing such offices did not only give them a foothold in the Indian commodities market and advantage over other Arab merchants, whose contact with India was confined to occasional visits, but also gave them opportunities to win contracts to represent Indian companies in the Gulf such as the Bombay and Persia Steam Navigation Company which held a monopoly over the pilgrim traffic between India and Arabia.

In Bahrain, Yusuf Kanoo, the founder of Kanoo business empire, started as a banker with offices in both Bahrain and Bombay:

> [Those] merchants who went to Bombay to arrange the sale of their pearls in October and November could leave their money with Yusuf in India and make their drawings a few months later from his Bahrain office. Those who ran food and timber-importing businesses would pay into their accounts in Bahrain and make their drawing in India, either from Yusuf's own offices or from various Bombay merchants with whom Yusuf held accounts.[5]

Similarly, merchant families in the Trucial Sheikdoms made their early fortunes through import-export relations with India. However, the wealth of a number of them basically came from smuggling big quantities of gold into India, an activity also practised by other Gulf merchants but to a lesser degree. These merchants, particularly from Dubai, exploited the relative geographic proximity of their coasts to the Indian shores, and the need by India's huge population for gold as an essential part of every bride's dowry, to conduct this practice and to make immense fortunes. Connected to this, another illegal trade was run by them, particularly from the immediate post-oil discovery years until the 1960s; the use of the pearling and gold smuggling boats on return journeys in smuggling

Indian young men, eager to obtain jobs and earn money, into the Gulfs states.

Gulf Merchants' Activities in India

The activity of the Gulf merchants, who settled in India or who were stationed there was not only restricted to marketing pearls or capturing business opportunities. In addition, they were very active in India's social and cultural life, observing political developments in the Indian sub-continent, establishing contact with Indian intellectuals, particularly the leaders of the Muslim community, and trying to educate themselves. Not only that, but some of the wealthiest among them constructed mosques, schools, and clubs in India to serve Muslim Indians as well as the Arab community. The Hijazi merchant, Muhammed Zainal Alireza for example, built a number of schools in Bombay, Bahrain and Dubai including the famous Alfalah school in Bombay (1931) for teaching Arabic language, Islamic studies, and other subjects,[6] while the Kuwaiti Alebrahim contributed to the building of schools in both Kuwait and Bombay.[7]

They also generously assisted and looked after the Arab intellectuals and reformers who happened to be passing through Bombay or those who were deported to India for their anti-British activity.

In brief, their multi-faceted activities brought them into contact with British officials and Indian elites and traders, taught them English and Hindi, and introduced them to new ways of business and life, all of which had a significant impact on the socio-cultural development of the Gulf and constituted the nucleus of a consciousness movement in Bahrain, Kuwait, and the Trucial Emirates.

India's Impact on the Gulf Reform Movements

Demands for administrative and legal reform and the improvement of some of the traditions and laws related to the pearling industry and labour conditions began in Bahrain in the early 1920s. These demands continued throughout the 1930s and 1940s and expanded to include the call for a greater role in the running of domestic issues and for the reduction of the British Political Agent's responsibilities, gaining much of their momentum from political developments in India.

Major Dickson, the British Political Agent in Bahrain in the 1920s, stated in a report that one of the sources of instability in the Island was the effect of efforts by the Muslim Indians to revive the notion of Islamic Caliphate.[8] In letters exchanged between the British Agent in Bahrain, Major Clive Daly, and his masters in the Gulf and in Bombay, India's struggle for democracy was mentioned as one of the influencing factors responsible for the anti-British movement in Bahrain.[9]

When the British struck against Bahrain's reform movement in 1923, two of its prominent leaders, Abdulwahab Alzayani and Ahmed Bin Lahij, were arrested and sent into exile to Bombay. In India, they received the support and sympathy of many Indians including the Indian National Congress's leaders. And when Alzayani took his case to judicial authorities of British India, his lawyer and defender was the man who later became the founder of Pakistan, Mohammed Ali Jinnah.

The impact of the Indian national movement on the Gulf reform movements was significant as the Gulf merchants who settled in India were in touch with their people at home, supplying them with the news of political developments in India and elsewhere. The letters exchanged between them and their colleagues and friends at home contain interesting discussions and exchanges of views regarding these developments and the proper ways to incorporate the experience of other nations into their own struggle for reform and freedom. What probably made the Gulf merchants and reformers keenly observe India's experience was the fact that their efforts were directed against the same colonial power, and the fact that the Indians supported their case. The Indian National Congress passed, as early as 1928, a resolution expressing its sympathy with all Arabs in their struggle for freedom.[10]

India's Contribution to the Gulf's Cultural Renaissance

India acted during the early years of the twentieth century as a channel through which the latest news of political and cultural developments in the main centres of the Arab world flowed into the Gulf. In those days, the Gulf region had no direct contacts with these centres as a result of the British policy of isolating the region from the mainstream of Arab cultural developments. The Gulf merchants and reformers stationed at the time in India responded by capturing news of these developments from magazines published in Egypt, Iraq, and Lebanon, to which they had regular subscriptions, and sending them to the Gulf to be passed around. They were very observant and anxious to make their people at home aware of these developments. They were also very interested in learning from the relatively open Indian society, and in transferring new ideas to their own society.

Influenced by India's cultural life and its varied phenomena, these merchants undertook the transfer of some of these phenomena to the Gulf. The emergence in Bahrain of the Iqbal Awal Club in 1913 and the Literary Club in 1923, for example, was basically attributed to the effort and support of these reformist merchants.

Indian has also a role in the very beginnings of the press and publishing activity in the Gulf. For example, the appearance of Bahrain's first newspaper, *Albahrain*, in 1939 would not have been possible without the printing presses brought from Bombay by its publisher and editor, Abdulla Alzayed. Alzayed, a pearl merchant, reformer and poet, himself owed much of his fortune and experience to India where he had lived in exile for two years.

Prior to the 1930s, all official and unofficial written materials in the Gulf were sent for printing to presses in India. It is no surprise, therefore, to know that the printing and publishing of some of the very first Gulf books took place in Bombay. Among these books are *Ukud Aljawaher* (1918) and *Tuhfat Alnasik* (1925) which are believed to be the first and the second printed books in Saudi Arabia.[11] The first map defining the locations of pearl fisheries in the Gulf was also printed in Bombay in 1914.

Additionally, India was until the post-Second World War years the only favourable destination of the Gulf people for learning English and obtaining advanced education. Many Gulf families, including the Royal Families of Bahrain and Oman, chose Indian schools, such as Aligarh College, for their sons. As a result, many of those who led the socio-cultural renaissance in the Gulf in the early twentieth century owed their knowledge, experience, and prominence to India. Among these were: Khalid Alfaraj, Bahrain's most remembered poet and reformer; Ibrahim Alurrayed, a well-known Bombay-born Bahraini poet and literate; Said Alnooman, who played a remarkable role in the cultural movement in Sharjah as early as 1910; and many other names.

India and the Early Modernization Process in the Gulf

In order to have a firm hold on the region, the British colonial authorities began as early as the first decade of the twentieth century to introduce a series of administrative measures under the guise of reforms, with much concentration of Bahrain. These measures included the re-organisation of the customs department, establishment of postal and banking services, and imposition of the civil, commercial, and criminal codes of India. In all these reforms, and those introduced in the post-oil discovery years in the municipality, in the communication, health and agricultural sectors, the British largely depended on the Indians to fill most of the white-collar positions. For example, the very first directors or organisers of customs, post, and passport departments in Bahrain were Indians. So were the heads of the first medical clinic in 1925, and the very first doctors, nurses, midwives, banks and customs' senior clerks, and agricultural advisers. Similarly, the Indians were among the first to organise or run medical, postal, and banking services in Qatar, Kuwait, Dubai, and Sharjah.

On the other hand, the discovery of oil in the Gulf in the 1930s and lack of qualified personnel and labourers among the Gulf natives made the British look again towards India for the import of the needed skills. Even in Saudi Arabia, clerical, technical, and other positions created as a result of the development of the oil industry and related sectors in the 1940s and 1950s were partly filled by employees from India. The number of these newcomers increased gradually in accordance with the developments in the industry itself. For examle, statistical records show that their number in Bahrain doubled between 1936 and 1937, making them 14 per cent of the total Bahrainis employed by the oil company.[12] This percentage jumped in 1938 to about 26.5 although the actual number of the Indian employees slightly decreased.[13]

Along with the economic prosperity caused by the production of oil, the well-established Indian merchant communities in the Gulf expanded, taking the lead in meeting the growing demands by the Gulf inhabitants for modern consumer merchandise from Europe. This led to the emergence of a number of wealthy Indian commercial houses. In a confidential report on the richest among Bahrain's merchants in the 1930s, six out of thirteen names were Indian.[14]

Simultaneously, the Gulf States witnessed the emergence of new Indian communities consisting of all those who were attracted by the region's economic prosperity and who came legally or illegally to work as shopkeepers, cooks, tailors, barbers, drivers, and domestic servants, or to provide other services traditionally avoided by the natives.

To sum up, the role played by the Indians in the early modernisation of the Gulf region was varied. However, it must be remembered that it was this role which caused much grievance among the Gulf natives and ultimately led to strikes and disturbances in Bahrain in the 1930s and 1940s. The Bahrainis were enraged by the import of Indians to occupy governmental positions and jobs in the Bahrain Oil Company, by the protection and privileges extended to them by the British, and by the better wages and conditions they enjoyed. Because some of these Indians were involved in running the colonial administration, they were regarded as British agents whose assignments were to reinforce and prolong the British presence in the region. However, despite these tense relations between the Bahrainis and Indians, there are no records showing that they developed at any time into violence as the struggle was of a social and economic nature and did not stem from racial hostility. Probably what contributed to the avoidance of violent clashes was the fact that the Indians, in general, confined themselves to earning money rather that getting involved in the politics and domestic affairs of the Gulf countries.

India's Impact on the Gulf's Socio-Cultural Life

As mentioned earlier, India's impact on the Gulf's socio-cultural life has been observed since the old days. However, with both regions being linked under one colonial rule, greater and more varied interaction between the two nations took place and consequently such an impact became noticeably stronger.

The first to be noticed, in this context, is the Indian impact on the spoken dialects in the Gulf's coastal towns. Tens of words of Indian origin entered these dialects and became widely used in everyday conversations. These words related to jobs held by the Indians, products imported from India, modern merchandise and items introduced by the Indians, financial methods associated with the use of the Indian rupee, and tools and methods used in the pearl-diving and maritime trade.

Other aspects of the Indian socio-cultural influence include the entrance of many traditional Indian dishes into the Gulf cuisine, the adoption of Indian artistic designs in the formation of gold and silver and in embroidering clothes, the use of a number of musical instruments similar to those used by the Indian musicians, and the adoption of 'Wizar'[15] as an essential part of menswear in many parts of the Gulf. Also affected by the Indian culture, arts, and traditions were the interior decoration of houses and rooms; material, colours, and designs of women's costume; the types of jewellery worn by females in Oman and the southern Gulf; and the rhythmic pattern of music.

Long and continuous intermixture led also to frequent mentioning of India and Indians in the Gulf's traditional poetry, proverbs, sailors' songs, children's games, anthems, and tales.

The Indian Presence in the Gulf

With British hegemony over in the Gulf states, the position of the Indian merchants in the region was reinforced. The number of these merchants increased, and their activities stretched to include businesses other than those related to the pearling industry.

Among the factors leading to this new situation was the protection which the Indian merchants came to enjoy under British rule in the Gulf due to the fact that they were considered to be British subjects. In all treaties conducted between the British Indian Authorities and the Gulf

Principalities there were articles asserting such protection and privileges. Prior to these treaties, Indian merchants faced insecurity which restricted their existence in large numbers in the region. Their businesses and commercial vessels were, on many occasions, victims of domestic instabilities in Oman, Qatar, Bahrain, and the Trucial Sheikhdoms or victims of tribal wars between the ruler of these states. On other occasions, they were victims of the struggle for dominance by such forces as the Wahhabis, the Ottomans, and the Persians.

In must be asserted here that Britain's striving to protect the Indians in the Gulf was not because of its preference for them. It stemmed from the perception that such policy would assist the reinforcement of Britain's position and give it an excuse to interfere in the Gulf's domestic affairs. What further encouraged Britain to adopt this policy was the readiness on the part of some Indians to serve British interests in the Gulf by representing British commercial firms or running some of the colonial departments.

Through a maximum exploitation of the protection and facilities extended to them by the British, and by employing their position as money-lenders to the ruling families in Oman, Bahrain, and the Trucial Principalities, the Indians could establish themselves firmly and dominate a large segment of business in the region.

The oldest and strongest Indian merchant communities in the Gulf were in Muscat and Matrah where a wide range of business was, and still is, dominated by the Luwatias; members of an Indian Muslim sect from near Bombay, many of whom crossed to Oman some 200 years ago. Outside Oman, the largest of these communities were in Bahrain and Dubai, and the smallest were in Kuwait and Qatar. The reason given for the modest Indian influence in the latter was the resistance shown by their rulers to any prominent Indian role in businesses as these rulers themselves were merchants and feared competition. For example, the ruler of Kuwait attempted in the 1930s to exclude all Indians from his state and, as a result, he entered into a dispute with the British Political Agent.[16] However, one must not underestimate here the fact that, unlike the Kuwaitis, the natives of Oman, Bahrain, and the Trucial Sheikhdoms were in those days reluctant to be involved in any business other than pearl trading, giving the Indians plenty of opportunity for commercial dominance.

It is interesting to note that some Indian merchants, probably from Bahrain, extended into the coast of Alahsa in the period prior to the rule of Alsaud. According to Lorimer, a small Indian community involved in the import of general merchandise from India and the export of dates settled in Qatif as early as 1864. And when its members began to withdraw under the pressure of high taxation and harassment caused by the ruling Ottoman Authorities, Bahrain's Indian merchants used their money and influence between 1880-1903 to convince the British to establish an agency in Alahsa for the purpose of protecting their brothers there.[17]

Finally, there were many Indians who succeeded in establishing strong business communities in Hijaz using the pilgrimage access. Many of today's prosperous merchants in Mecca and Madina are of Indian descent whose ancestors came on the pilgrimage and stayed on rather than returning to India.

Conclusion

The relationship between India and the Gulf region goes back to the pre-history days. There is definite archaeological evidence of contacts between the ancient civilisations of the two regions since the third millennium B.C. These contacts included demographic movements, commercial intercourse and probably cultural communications.

The Gulf has acted for centuries as a bridge connecting India with the rest of the world on the west. History, culture, and religion have all contributed to strengthening the ties created by the factor of geography.

With the advent of Islam and its expansion beyond the Arabian Peninsula, Indo-Gulf contacts deepened. And with the inclusion of part of India into the Arab/Islamic Empire, the relationship branched out into fields other than commerce. The mediaeval period is identified by many scholars as a golden age of Indo-Arab relations as it witnessed enormous fruitful exchanges in different fields.

However, with the British dominance over the Indian subcontinent and the Gulf, the latter became politically, economically, and administratively linked to India. Its fate and entire affairs were decided in Bombay by the British Indian Authorities. As a result, the Gulf's dependence on India increased significantly to cover almost every sector. This led to greater commercial exchanges, demographic movements, and socio-cultural communications, all of which had remarkable impact on all aspects of life in the Gulf.

These long, intimate, and multi-form historical relations between the two nations must, therefore, constitute the basis on which present and future cooperation is planned. In other words, the legacy of the past in the case of India and the Gulf must be employed today in shaping certain, if not all, foreign policy decisions of each side towards the other as this legacy does not contain such irritant factors as territorial dispute, ethnic hostility, or political competition.

Notes

1. Rosemarie Said Zahlan, *The Making of the Modern Gulf States*, Unwin Hyman: London, 1989, p. 13.
2. See Mohammed Mitwali, *Howdh Alkhaleej Alarabi* (The Arabian Gulf Basin), Maktabat Alanglo, Cairo, 1981, Part 2, p. 181.
3. Ali Aba Hussain, 'Historical Relations between Bahrain and India', *Alwatheekah* (Bahrain), no. 17, July 1990, p. 217
4. Mohammad Al-Rumaihi, *Kadhaya Altaghier Alsiyasi Wa Alijtimai Fi Albahrain* (Issues of political and Social Change in Bahrain 1920-1970), Alwahdah: Kuwait, 1976, pp. 101-102.
5. Michael Field, *The Merchants, The Big Business Families of Saudi Arabia and the Gulf States*, The Overlook Press: New York, second printing 1985, p. 268.
6. Muhammad Ahmad Al-Shatry, *Muhammad Ali Zainal*, Dar Alshuruq: Jeddah, 1977, p. 61.
7. Saif M. Al-Shamlan, *Tarikh Alghous Ala Alulu Fi Alkuwait Wa Alkhaleej Alarabi* (History of Pearl-Diving in Kuwait and the Arabian Gulf), Kuwait, 1978, Part 2, p. 253.
8. See Mohammad Al-Rumaihi, op. cit., p. 275.
9. Ibid., p. 286.
10. Ajay N. Jha, *India's Economic Diplomacy in the Gulf*, ABC Publishing House: New Delhi, 1988, p. 84.
11. *Asharq Al-Awsat* (London), 13 March 1999.
12. See I.O.R. R/15/6/536 Persian Gulf Administration Report 1936,

and I.O.R. R/15/6/537 Persian Gulf Administration Report 1937.

13. See I.O.R. R/15/718 Report for year 1938.
14. See I.O.R. R/15/2/1362 Confidential C.T.B. No. 17 and No. 18, Enquiries reports about trading companies in Bahrain, 14 July 1936-16 June 1941.
15. Wizar is a length of printed cotton material wrapped around the lower part of the body.
16. See I.O.R. R/15/5/201 Exclusion of Prosperous Indians from Kuwait, 16 July 1936 - 16 November 1939.
17. See J.G. Lorimer, *Gazetteer of the Persian Gulf*, IIB, Historical, Part 3, p. 1449, pp. 1474-1476, and pp. 1492-1495.

India and West Asia Relations
The Changing Economic Matrix

GIRIJESH PANT

India-West Asia relations have been critically influenced by the economic imperatives of the times. History testifies to it, be it the Mudarabah trade of the sixteenth and seventeenth centuries or the British East India Company of the nineteenth century. The fact that the Indian currency was legal tender till the Trucial States became independent, further underlines the intensity of economic factors shaping the mutual relations. With the Cold War replacing Pax-Britannica and defining the parameters of interaction along the bipolar trajectory, the ties between India and the West Asian countries too got shaped accordingly. The political-security concern articulated in the Non-Alignment doctrine became the major factor in shaping interaction between the newly independent countries of Asia, Africa and Latin America. The Nasser-Nehru elan symbolised the new and dominant mood of the relationship. However as the countries started defining their national interest along the Cold War divide, India and the West Asian countries started moving apart.

The Cold War economy designed by the Bretton Woods regime induced the economic relations on what in popular parlance was known as the North-South axis. Consequently, while the old basis of interaction between India and West Asia lost its relevance, there was no new economic rationale or the complementarity to take over from the old commercial ties. The West Asian economies, tied to the American aid regime, got locked to the American market. India on the contrary opted for an autonomous development regime—'the non capitalist path'. Its foreign economic relations were influenced by the imperatives of the domestic market. In their respective search for developmental resources India and West Asia had nothing much to offer to each other. Consequently their mutual economic interaction was at the lowest as reflected in trade turnover or investment flows. It was in the seventies and the following years that a new dynamics emerged which led to a revival and revitalisation of the old economic ties with a new substance. West Asia has emerged as India's extended neighbourhood. As outlined above it is not only the geographic proximity but also the intensity of interaction from historical times till today that define the dynamics of mutual relations. Developments in West Asia impinge on India as well as on South Asia. Similarly, India and South Asia are very much visible in West Asia. The present paper provides an overview of the changing economic matrix which has been shaping the ties between India and West Asia since the seventies.

The seventies mark the beginning of a new phase in India-West Asia relations, which emerged as a consequence of the converging impact of the changes in the Bretton Wood-based world economy, the West Asian regional economy and in the Indian economy. In 1971, the American dollar started losing its shine when it was delinked from gold, indicating the beginning of internationalisation of finance. The global divide between North and South reached its peak, at least in its rhetoric, as epitomised in Cancun. The OPEC decision to chart an independent course in 1973 was seen as a defiance of the West-defined oil regime and the rise of commodity power in the form of cartels, giving a new identity to the region. It needs to be underlined that oil shifted the regional gravity in favour of the Persian Gulf as against the Mediterranean. Iran, Iraq and Saudi Arabia gained new clout, crowding out Egypt, Turkey and Syria from the regional theater. India's emergence as regional power after the division of Pakistan in 1971 gave it a new confidence to reassess its role in the extended neighbourhood. Its increasing need for oil from external sources and the construction boom in the Gulf provided a new rationale for interaction between India and West Asia. In the emerging relationship it was not the spice but the industrial and civil contracts that provided the lead. It needs to be underlined that in West Asia in general, and the Persian Gulf in particular, India bagged some of its prestigious overseas projects against the competitive bidding of the Western companies. The project exports in the seventies provided the needed breakthrough for Indian engineering goods by creating a market. The Indian turnkey projects, both civil and engineering, created an altogether new basis for relationships which today get manifested in a multidimensional profile. Of these only the four leading dimensions of India-West relations are elaborated in this paper.

The Energy Ties

The growing energy-intensity of the Indian economy made it imperative to augment domestic supplies with external sources. In 1970-71 India imported 12,767 thousand tonnes of oil but by the end of the decade, its import touched the figure of 23,537 thousand tonnes, registering a jump by 100 per cent. The growing reliance on external supplies made India look for assured sources of oil supply. It was natural that the oil-rich Persian Gulf region became the leading supplier. It can be argued that with every additional increase in oil import tonnage, the significance of the region enhanced in India's development process. This was revealed in the nineties when, as a fallout of the Iraqi invasion of Kuwait, India had to mortgage its gold to meet the Balance of Payment obligations. Oil imports accounted for more than 78 per cent of total imports. This added strategic dimension to the emerging energy ties, bringing into debate India's energy security concerns. With India going for a market-led economy, the orientation of its energy policy too changed. It is no more inward looking. As the Hydrocarbon Vision 2025 clearly spells out, India will be exploring overseas sources to meet its growing demand, which is likely to be met by external sources to the tune of 70 per cent.

> By 2005, Indian oil demand is expected to reach 2.8 million BPD (barrels per day), representing a growth of 6.0 percent to 6.5 percent annually from 2001. This will reach 3.6 million-BPD by 2010, with middle and light distillates balancing out lower fuel oil growth rates. Natural gas demand will surge with 7.5 million metric tonnes of LNG per year to be imported by 2005. Crude oil imports are expected to meet 70 percent of domestic consumption by 2005.

What needs to be underlined here is that the Indian surge in demand is taking place at a time when the Western demand for oil is not growing. It is Asia, and that too India and China, that are going to be the leading destination for oil and gas. Estimates suggest that demand in Asia has grown from 14 million barrels per day in 1990 to more than 20 million barrels in 2000. And of the 9 million barrels per day net increase in world oil demand over the decade, Asia accounted for 7 million barrels per day.

The centrality of West Asia in India's oil imports can be seen from the fact that Saudi Arabia, Kuwait, Iran and UAE account for more than 75 per cent of oil import. Among other countries from the region are Iraq, Bahrain, Egypt, Yemen and Qatar. From the perspective of the Gulf supplier still depending on oil and gas revenue, the emerging Indian market has critical importance. Though China is a more robust market than India but in the Chinese matrix, logistically, Central Asia is the preferred region. For the Gulf region the South Asia market has the potential of that critical mass that could be the source of assured demand over a long-term perspective. One of the major energy issues facing South Asian nations today are having to keep up with rapidly rising energy demands and beginning to promote cross-border energy trade. South Asia thus is faced with the challenges of diversifying traditional energy supply sources (and expanding the use of indigenous energy resources), promoting additional foreign investment for energy infrastructure development, improving energy efficiency, reforming and privatizing energy sectors, and expanding regional energy trade and investment. The centrality of the Indian market could be seen by the fact that no South Asian project of regional size could be commercially feasible unless along with the Indian market. This has been demonstrated by the Iran-Pak pipeline project. Iran is keen that the project be extended to India to maximise gains.

In the market-based economic regime, the energy ties are not limited to trading in hydrocarbons. India has of late opened its oil and gas sector to the private sector. It now permits 100 per cent FDI investment and ownership into refineries, besides exploration and production. Marketing of certain products like lubes, LPG and commercial/industrial kerosene has also been opened up. According to Indian government sources, 'Saudi Aramco and Shell came to us last year and said they wanted retailing rights in India for petroleum products. We welcome the move as long as they clear the entry barriers—Rs 20 billion investment and operate an oil refinery or produce 3 million tonnes per year'. India is the emerging market for petroleum products. To meet the growing demand for petro products, it is proposed to enhance the refinery capacity more than three times from the current 112 mt to 358 mt four or five years hence.

Reportedly, Saudi Aramco, National lranian Oil Company (NIOC) and Abu Dhabi National Oil Company (ADNOC) have shown a keen interest in picking up a stake in the east India refinery of the Indian Oil Corporation (IOC). The companies are understood to have initiated discussions with IOC to take a 26 per cent equity stake in the project to be built in Paradip in Orissa State. The three West Asian oil majors have also started discussions with the promoters of Mangalore Refinery and Petrochemical Ltd (MRPL) to take up a stake in that project. Foreign oil companies have shown more interest in retail marketing of petro-products in India as it is seen to be a more profitable business segment. Saudi Aramco has also presented a proposal to the Indian Ministry of Petroleum and Natural Gas for buying out the retail outlets of any of the three Indian public sector oil companies, IOC, HPCL and BPCL. Recently, a Memorandum of Understanding has been signed between Indian Oil Corporation and Kuwait Petroleum Corporation for setting up a joint venture refinery in Orissa.

Clearly, the new synergy has given the energy-based relations a new strategic dimension. This is particularly true with natural gas, which is said to be the fuel of the future with its eco-friendly attributes. The surging demand for natural gas is 7.5 million metric tons of LNG per year to be imported by 2005, which is going to be from West Asia. Trade in natural gas is not the same as trade in oil. Gas needs a dedicated market, it has to be routed through pipelines; therefore it demands strategic understanding.

LNG ventures from Qatar, Oman, Abu Dhabi, and Yemen are exploring the possibility of supplying the import terminals proposed along India's West Coast and East Coast. Receiving facilities are being promoted in the western coastal state of Gujarat, Maharashtra and Kerala as well as in Tamil Nadu.

Geography gives producers in the West Asia region a competitive advantage over long haul ventures in Southeast Asia and Australia. According to a British Gas estimate, it costs some 40 cents/mn BTU to ship LNG from Qatar to Gujarat. The equivalent figure for Oman, which is situated outside the strait of Hormuz, is just 35 cent/mn BTU. This compares favourably with shipping cost of some 95 cents/mn BTU from Australia's Northwest shelf, 91 cents/mn BTU from Indonesia's Bontang and 68 cent/mn BTU from Malaysia. The freight advantage applies only to import sites located along the country's west coast. The high stakes in the Indian market are well recognised by the gas suppliers from the Gulf. This precisely is the reason why the multi-billion dollar Dolphine project has the Indian market in its clientele list The growing mutual stakes in the energy market has elevated its relevance and significance from being merely a trading venture to investment in the evolving India-West Asia relations.

Indian Community: Expatriates to Entrepreneurs

The Indian community in West Asia has been a dynamic component of India-West Asia interactive processes. What is significant is that it has been evolving over time. In the earlier years the Indian community in the region comprised traders and financiers. Not very large in number, Indian merchants had a significant presence in the local market. Some of them like Chibaldas Advani Bhojraj, popularly known as Bhoja, have even become legendary names. Widely regarded as the patriarch of the Indian business community, he came in the early 1920s to Dalma Island, then a center of business, as a pearl merchant and a general trader. He later moved to Abu Dhabi and set up Souq Al Banyan. 'Such was his standing in the community that the British Political agent in Abu Dhabi would seek his assistance in matters relating to the Indian community.' Born and raised in Sindh he was proud of his UAE passport. It was the ruling family, which came to his rescue when he needed help. Shaikh Khalifa bin Zayed granted a piece of land and two villas built at his own expense to bail him out of trouble. Similarly, in Oman the oldest Indian family has been settled there since the last eight generations. One estimate says that around 600-700 Indians have been given Omani nationality.

A totally new dimension was added to the profile of the Indian community in the region after the advent of oil. The construction boom of the seventies and expansion of the regional economy created unprecedented demands for manpower which could be met only by importing workers. The expatriates thus emerged as a distinct factor of production, exceeding even the size of the local workforce. India became one of the leading sources of manpower supply to the region. The growing volume of Indian workers crowded out the traders and fanciers, changing the very profile as a bulk of them were unskilled or semi-skilled. It was a transition in the profile of the Indian community from being simply People of Indian origin to expatriates or NRIs.

The current estimates are that there are 3.5 million Indians engaged in different categories of economic activities. Of the three million plus about 70 per cent are semi-skilled or unskilled, 20 per cent are white collar employees including families and 10 per cent are professionals including families. The largest number are in Saudi Arabia (about 1.5 million) followed by UAE (1.2 million). In Oman their number is estimated at 336,000, in Kuwait at 260,000, in Bahrain at 140,000 and in Qatar at 1,20,000. About 60 per cent of the Indian workforce hails from Kerala. Indian nationals in the Gulf remit US$4 billion a year. Their contribution gained prominence in 1991 when, following the Gulf War and the subsequent oil price hike, the Indian balance of payments was in the red and it could be sustained only by the remittances from the Gulf. More recently, following Pokhran II, when the State Bank of India floated Resurgent India Bonds to the extent of Rs.17,000 crores, the Gulf NRIs contributed 40 per cent to it. Similarly, to the State Bank of India's Millennium Deposit scheme, NRIs contributed about US$6 billion out of which more then 50 per cent came from the Gulf, and 90 per cent from the UAE.

A new structural shift in the Gulf labour market in the late nineties has affected the demand for expats. The growing concern for local demographics (foreigners outnumbering locals by 4-1 and the increasing pressure for the restructuring of the Gulf economy) is restraining the flow of expatriates. The Gulf governments are actively engaged in correcting what is called labour market distortions by attempting to bring in demographic balance. Sociologists reportedly have warned of a 'demographic crisis.' They apprehend 'that the imbalance in the population might change the ethnic characteristics of the nation. And, if the situation is not redressed urgently, there will be instability in society.' Consequently new economic and legal regimes are being conceived to encourage the participation of the local work force replacing the expats. Inevitably, this will have a bearing on Indian workers going to the region. Though the numbers have not declined perceptibly, the growth is definitely checked. What is significant is that despite the apprehension of reverse migration, 'the trend has not been reflected in the country's outstanding NRI deposits, which have invariably grown throughout the nineties. NRI deposits which totalled $13, 721 million in 1991 grew steadily to $21,301 millions in 1999 and further to $22,880 million on February 2000.

However, despite the efforts of the local governments to reduce the dependence on expats, their critical role remains and cannot be wished away. These changes have affected the demand for middle level expats, especially in the service sector.

The Indians in the Gulf are responding to these changes. They see in the liberalisation process of the Gulf economies a new role for them. The portfolio of Gulf Indians is changing. A distinct class of new generation Indian entrepreneurs is emerging. For instance, Manu Chabaria in UAE, with a $ 1.5 billion business empire could be cited as a case in point. His company Jumbo Electronics is said to be a trend-setter in the electronic market in the region. 'In fact in the UAE Jumbo had been a synonym for Sony just as Sony had become a bye word for electronics.' What is important is that in tune with the economic plans of Dubai the company is promoting industries and services in strategic areas identified by the government.

The point that needs attention is that Indians like the Chabarias might have begun with sugar trading but are showing all the attributes of a modern corporate sector to grow regionally and globally in correspondence with the needs and aspirations of the local economy. Ram Buxani, Bavaraghuthu Raghuram Shetty, Yousuf Ali are a few more names of this genre. New Medical Centre Hospital, the largest private hospital in Abu Dhabi, is run by an Indian entrepreneur hailing from Udipi in Karnataka who came here in 1972 and presides over a group of companies engaged in the health sector. Similarly, if Buxani is actively engaged in harnessing the economic clout of his tribe as chairman of Overseas Indian Economic Forum, Yousuf Ali's dream came true when Air India took off from Cochin International Airport (CIAL) at Nedem linking Cochin with the Gulf. The Rs. 3.25 billion CIAL project was launched by a non-resident Keralite under the leadership of Yousuf in 1994. It was started with the contribution by 15 friends of one million each. Subsequently it was transformed into a public limited company converting assets into shares. The Kerala government supported the venture by taking 51 per cent of the share.

An interesting development has been the increase in associational activities of the Indian community. These associations are true representatives of India's composite culture. They are not only formed on professional interests but also culture and religion. In the UAE if there are associations like Indian Business and Professional Group and Indian Social Centre, there also is the Indian Islamic Centre and Tamil Sangam. In Oman there were as many as twenty-five Indian Associations till 1994 when the government banned all expatriate associations except one, Social Club. But the Social Club has seven regional language wings like Hindi, Marathi, Bengali, Tamil, Malayam, Gujarati and Punjabi.

Significantly, a new pattern of interaction is emerging between the overseas Indians and their motherland. The agenda of the civil society of Indians in the Gulf countries is not limited to merely protecting the interests of the community; on the contrary its contribution lies in creating a cultural ambience which has given a new boost to Indian identity. Indian Association Dubai celebrates Navratra every year by organising cultural meets including all night Garba and Dandya dances in which more than 10,000 people participate. In the weekend the number goes up to 12,000. Besides they have been engaged in mobilising resources for international causes in tune with the policy of the Gulf countries; for example, last year they collected 189,000 dhirams for the Palestinian cause and the African drought.

The growing strength of civil society has given the Indian community a new confidence to play a high profile role in meeting the needs of their home country, be it in moments of crisis or for new projects. During the Kargil war and the Gujarat earthquake the Indians from the Gulf wholeheartedly contributed to the cause. It is in recognition of their new role that besides the Indian government, the chief ministers of different states like Andhra Pradesh, Kerala, Goa, and so on have been visiting the Gulf region and soliciting support for various projects, like airports or Narmada. During his visit to Dubai, a former Narmada minister, Jay Narayan Vyas, while emphasizing that the Narmada dam was the only answer for 'thirsty Gujarat' in the days to come, solicited the support of the fraternity settled in the UAE to come forward and invest money for the noble cause. The NRIs on their part are engaging in new areas of goodwill and philanthropy, like felicitating six welfare activists in Gujarat. A group of NRI reportedly started a college for Muslim women in a Muslim majority city, Dindugal, in Tamilnadu. It will be offering higher education to about 500 students with hostel facilities for one hundred and fifty. It is expected to cost Rs 300 million.

These illustrations are given here to underline the changing perception of the role that the NRIs are expected to play not merely as sender of remittances but as partners in development. Though Indians in the region have yet to acquire the clout to influence India-West Asia relations like the Indians in the USA, the process that has begun of transition of Indians from expats to entrepreneurs is decidedly going to provide a new and vital dynamism to India-West Asia relations in coming years.

Participation in Development Projects

If it was the construction boom of the seventies that rejuvenated the age old commercial relations between India and West Asia, it can safely be said that the future of this relationship is going to be dictated by the IT (Information Technology) revolution and human resource development. West Asia is only a $3.5 billion market for India, accounting for less than 12 per cent of the total Indian exports of $33 billion. The commodity composition of Indian exports has been dominated by traditional items like tea, coffee, spices, tobacco, rice, etc. Clearly, Indian exports to the region have yet to grow in volume to reflect their potential. In recent years the trend however is changing. It is expected that the service sector will be transforming the face of trade transactions between India and the region and software will be the trendsetter. In 1996-97 India exported software worth $50 million to the Gulf countries.

West Asia is rated highly as a potential market for India. In participating in the global knowledge regime, the West Asian region is faced with the handicap of inadequately developed infrastructure including human resources. The region in fact is faced with the challenge of preparing their bulging population to the skill requirements of the new economy. India's expertise in the field of IT is well recognised internationally. India enjoys a comparative advantage. It is expected that IT exports are going to be the lead sector. According to the National Association of Software and Services Companies (NASSCOM), software exports worth Rs 1,359 million ($30.2 million) from India to the Gulf states in 1998-1999 increased by nearly a third to Rs 2,124 million the following year. A NASSCOM survey has indicated that annual IT exports to this region could exceed Rs 10 billion over the next two to three years.

The Gulf region, or for that matter the entire West Asian region, is engaged in the transition towards the WTO regime. In restructuring the economy initiatives are being taken to move beyond the hydrocarbon economy. The coming up of Free Trade Zones are indicative of this trend. The Gulf countries in particular are developing service centres. A visible trend is that the corporate sector is moving hardware location to the Gulf. In view of escalating infrastructure costs in Europe, the better logistic facilities, minimal customs and red tape and good infrastructure of the region it is expected that the region will attract big corporate houses. The Sharjah Free Zone has attracted big names and today it is servicing more than 510 companies. The Sharjah Free Zone is examining the possibility of developing an Internet Park to create better infrastructure for IT companies intending to set up units in the area. With India supplying software, the region is witnessing a kind of IT resurgence. Indian companies see the presence in the region of countries like the United Arab Emirates to access markets outside India, for instance, Africa and the Gulf countries.

Dubai Internet City (DIC) is emerging as the hub in which the presence of many Indian companies will offer a tremendous opportunity for this IT relationship to grow, with an eye on the Gulf and other world markets, especially given the advantage of the region's infrastructure and easy flight connections to most countries. Several Indian IT companies which have registered in the City are expected to commence operations from this month on. ICICI Infotech International Inc, for example, has tied up with the Emirates Bank Group to set up Tricolour Infotech International Inc., at DIC. Around twenty Indian IT companies concentrating on offshore software development, strategic alliances, on-site services and joint ventures have launched operations in the Gulf area over the past two years. With a view to giving a push to trade relations between Oman and India, especially in the fields of electronics and information technology, an MoU on cooperation was signed between the Oman Centre for Investment, Promotion and Export Development (OCIPED) and India's Electronics and Computer Software Export Promotion Council (ECSEPC). The council has been invited by the newly set up Economic Development Board (EDB) of Bahrain to sign a memorandum of understanding in the IT sector. Similarly the Joint Commission in its meeting at Cairo had on agenda steps to strengthen economic relations and cooperation in the field of information and technology.

With Indian corporate houses going for overseas market following the end of the regulated regime, the investment flows are becoming visible. In Egypt, India ranks as the twelfth largest investor, with 32 projects valued at $330 million. Among them are the joing ventures, like Alexandria Carbon Black Company, set up by Grasim India Limited with TRENCO and ATC as Egyptian partners, and another between ESSEL of India and Mashoor Pack of Egypt for manufacturing laminated toothpaste tubes for the use of Proctor and Gamble in Egypt. Dabur India Ltd., has started production of its herbal hair oils and other cosmetic products in a fully-owned facility at Ramadan Industrial City.

From Bargaining to Collectively Building

With the unfolding of the globalisation process, the patterns of co-operation are getting redefined. The emerging paradigm shows significant discontinuities from the past, transforming the existing structures. It may be noticed that the increased pace and magnitude of factor flows, particularly information, capital, technology and to some extent labour, i.e. skilled professionals, is taking place across territories, on a global domain, not necessarily on national terms. In fact these transactions have created a new space for exchange and interaction, apparently setting a process of dissolution of national economies and creating new spatial dimensions articulated as the rise of 'Region State'. The boundaries of the region state are not imposed by political fiat. They are drawn by the deft but invisible hands of the global market for goods and services. The new economy is recasting and mapping out its own space and it is here that the processes of interaction and exchange are more visible than in the traditional economic space. The cyber economy, for instance, has emerged beyond the national territories, demanding its own norms and regime, which need not necessarily be compatible with the prevailing regime. Thus international transactions are no more confined to two nations but spread among global corporates. Hence, quite often flows and interactive processes are transacted in a space beyond the governance of the nation-state. Transactions are concluded even if the state does not grant visiting visa, and trade alliances can be forged without government clearance. The stocks regime can be manipulated from a distance, creating catastrophe, e.g. the Asian flue.

The non-governable transactions have posed opportunities but challenges as well. The band of interactive processes is much widened and at multiple tiers. In other words, with the world economy increasingly becoming globalised, regional interactions are going to be more extended and intense, defying geographical and political boundaries. This is not to argue that national concerns will disappear but to suggest that the pace and nature of regional transactions are going to be decisively influenced by the globalising forces. For instance, the proposed Indian-Iran gas pipeline project cannot materialise without the financial support of global corporate consortiums. Further, these transactions are going to be rooted at a structural level, be it in the sphere of economy, politics, strategy or civilisation.

The relations between India and the West Asian region are also going to evolve via the dynamics of these structural changes. In the coming years the region has to accelerate the pace and give a direction to restructuring of its economy, as the date of joining the WTO regime comes closer. Certainly, hydrocarbons will continue to remain the principal source of global energy and the region the major source of global supply but the hydrocarbon-based regime can no more be sustained. The state-society and the state-economy relations have to be renegotiated and possibly redefined. The national agenda thus will have to address the issues related to institutional changes like creating legal, financial, commercial systems based on well-defined rules, the mechanisms for eliminating subjective interventions and procedures for their redressal. The new rationale for India-West Asia relations is going to be derived from these trends. The extended space has expanded the common space of interaction between India and the region. In this common space there are common challenges and common opportunities. What is required is a vision to identify these challenges and transform them into opportunity.

The common vision that India and the West Asian countries need to develop is with reference to the threat of erosion of their local sovereignty and identity in its different manifestations, including the economic one. The threat needs to be negotiated by collective endeavors, not so much to bargain for better terms as much as to build sustainable economic, legal and social regimes. The backlash of globalisation including terrorism underlines that the local systems have not been able to sustain the restructuring process initiated under the market-led reforms. West Asia is highly vulnerable on this account. The nation-building project in West Asia is indeed lagging behind. It will not be wrong to say that in a comparative perspective, West Asian countries face greater asymmetry in negotiating the challenges of institutional transformation. The process of graduation from unproductive to productive entrepreneur-ship or from rentier to production-based economy demands a new kind of interaction with the external world. The countries of the region, though engaged in the implementation of stabilisation and structural adjustment programmes at different levels, are facing the problem of incompatibility hence reservation and resistance. The Indian experience in the last decade of gradual reforms is rich enough to provide inputs for the West Asian transition process.

Conclusion

Located in a globalising world economy, India and the West Asian countries cannot escape its impact on their mutual relations. Globalisation represents that stage of capitalist development where the evolutionary imperatives of capitalism require expansion of world markets beyond manufacturing. It may be recalled that until the Tokyo Round the aims of the industrialised countries were basically to facilitate and accommodate new production in existing or new sectors and lines within the industrialised world. Trade liberalisation measures were designed to further the intra-industry trade among themselves. Their more or less equal technological and other capabilities and production of goods resulted in intense product differentiation and intra-industry trade as well as intra-firm trade. It was in the Uruguay Round that new issues, namely, services and agriculture, and intellectual property rights were added to the global trade agenda.

The Uruguay Round of negotiations lasted from 1986 to 1994 and paved the way for the transformation of GATT to WTO. The globalising world economy is imposing its nature. It is devising a rule-based regime where rules favour the rule makers. And the rules are going to govern the very creativity of mankind by patenting it. Decidedly, it is posing many serious questions whose implications are lasting in nature and are not yet comprehended. It is therefore imperative that the rules of the global economic regime which are going to impact India-West Asia relations are suitably modified. It may be mentioned that India was among the very few countries that resisted the skewed nature of rules at the Doha meet of WTO. But it could not go beyond a point because of inadequate support. Ironically the West Asian countries are not very active participants in the WTO debate, except countries like Egypt, though they face its adverse consequences, including the issue of food security. The point being made here is that India-West Asia relations need to be visualised as a strategic option for effective participation in the emerging world order. Though terrorism has clouded the agenda, it cannot be ignored that geo-economics will remain the prime mover of relations among the countries in the twenty-first century. India-West Asia relations are no exception to this. It is the emerging expanse of economic interaction that is going to provide new openings for a political and strategic dimension to the relations.

Population Dynamics in West Asia and North Africa

PRAKASH C. JAIN

In spite of the fact there has been unprecedented economic development in West Asia and North Africa (WANA) during the past few decades, it still remains one of the fastest growing regions in the world. This perhaps suggests that the patriarchal social structure in most Muslim countries of West Asia has not significantly changed over the years, and it continues to influence their population dynamics. The nature, causes and consequences of the demographic transition, which is by no means uniform across the countries of the region, are analysed here in the political economy framework.

The total population of the twenty countries of West Asia and North Africa considered here was estimated at about 345 million in 1995 and about 380 million in 2001. The most populous country in the region in 1995 was Iran (64.1 million) closely followed by Turkey (61.1 million) and Egypt (57.8 million). These three countries alone accounted for over half of the total population of the WANA region. There were four countries in the 10-20 million range: Iraq (20.1), Saudi Arabia (19.0), Yemen (15.3), and Syria 14.1). The remainder countries were under 10 million, with four of them having 2 million or less population (Table 1).[1]

Except Israel, the WANA countries are predominantly Muslim consisting of about one quarter of the world's total Muslim population. Substantial non-Muslim populations, however, can be found in Egypt, Israel, Lebanon and Cyprus. Again, with the exception of the two largest countries of the region, Turkey and Iran as well as Israel and Cyprus, the majority of WANA countries are Arab. The largest Arab countries, namely Egypt, Algeria and Morocco, are located in North Africa rather than the fertile crescent or the Arabian peninsula. On the whole, West Asia and North Africa combine to form a relatively homogeneous cultural area dominated by Islam.

Table 1 : **Basic Demographic and Socio-Economic Indicators, 1995**

Country	*Populatin (million) mid-1995*	*Area (thousands of Sq. Km.)*	*G.N.P. per capita Dollar*	*Life expect-ancy (Years)*	*Adult illiteracy (Per cent)*
Iran	64.1	1,648	2,490	68	28
Turkey	61.1	779	2,780	67	18
Egypt	57.8	1,001	790	63	49
Algeria	28.0	2,382	1,600	70	38
Morocco	26.6	447	1,110	65	56
Iraq	20.1	438	-	66	42
Saudi Arabia	19.0	2,150	7,050	70	37
Yemen	15.3	528	260	53	62
Syria	14.1	185	1,120	68	36
Tunisia	9.0	164	1,820	69	33
Israel	5.5	21	15,920	77	-
Libya	5.4	1,760	-	65	36
Jordan	4.2	89	1,510	70	13
Lebanon	4.0	10	2,660	68	8
U.A.E.	2.5	84	17,400	75	21
Oman	2.2	212	4,820	70	-
Kuwait	1.7	18	17,390	76	21
Cyprus	0.74	9	8,020	78	-
Bahrain	0.58	1	1,840	72	15
Qatar	0.65	11	11,600	72	21
Total/Average	343.3	11,937	-	-	-

Source : World Bank, *World Development Report 1997*, pp. 214, 215 and 248.

Demographic and socio-economic indicators present a striking profile of the region. Thanks to the oil wealth some of the smaller Gulf states like the U.A.E., Kuwait and Qatar are extremely rich. On the contrary, Yemen is the poorest country, in the region. Egypt, the most populous Arab country, is certainly better than Yemen in terms of the GNP per capita. Altough a majority of the WANA countries are middle-income economies, they still have at least a quarter to one-third of their populations below the poverty line, and this situation is likely to persist for quite some time.[2]

Just as there are great economic disparities among the WANA countries, so also there are disparities in the levels of urbanisation and education. On the whole, by 1990 about 53 per cent people of the region were living in urban areas. The level of urbanisation is therefore high by Third World standards.

A similar argument can be made about the level of primary education which is nearly universal in most of these countries except in Saudi Arabia and Morocco. 'Secondary enrolment is much lower. On average about one-half of the age groups are enrolled in secondary schools.'[3] In spite of almost universal primary schools enrolment, however, the level of illiteracy, especially among women, is considerably high. In terms of another vital indicator, i.e. life expectancy, all the countries except Yemen score high. On the whole, in terms of the socio-economic indicators discussed above, the WANA countries appear to be better off than most countires in Asia and Africa. Ironically, this 'development' does not reflect in the fertility rate of the region which is considerably high.

DEMOGRAPHIC PROFILE

Fertility and Mortality

One of the most significant demogrphic characteristics of the WANA region is the slow decline of fertility levels since at least the early 1950s. This is so in spite of the fact that in most of the countries there has been noticeable socio-economic development and consequently the mortality rates have fallen rapidly during the last two decades. Data regarding these trends for the year 1965, 1990 and 2000 (projections) are presented in Table 2. These data suggest that crude birth rates are generally high throughout the region, with eight countries having a crude birth rate in excess of forty. Yemen (53) tops the list with the highest crude birth rate and the highest crude death rate, which can be explained by the fact that Yemen is the poorest and the least developed country of the region. Iran's high birth rate until the mid-1990s can be explained by the negative impact of the Islamic Revolution of 1979 on the status of Iranian women as well as on the family welfare programmes. The eight-year long Iran-Iraq war was

Table 2 : **Fertility and Mortality in West Asia and North Africa**

Country	*Crude Birth Rate (per 1000 popl.)*		*Crude Death Rate (per 1000 popl.)*		*Total Fertility Rate*		
	1965	*1990*	*1965*	*1990*	*1965*	*1990*	*2000*
Algeria	50	36	18	8	7.4	5.1	3.7
Egypt	43	31	19	10	6.8	4.0	3.1
Iran	46	45	18	9	7.1	6.2	5.6
Iraq	49	42	18	8	7.2	6.2	5.1
Israel	26	22	6	6	3.8	2.8	2.3
Jordan	53	43	21	6	8.0	6.3	5.6
Kuwait	48	25	7	3	7.4	6.7	5.8
Libya	49	43	17	8	7.4	6.7	5.8
Morocco	49	35	18	9	7.1	4.5	3.4
Oman	50	44	24	6	7.2	7.0	5.9
Saudi Arabia	48	43	20	7	7.3	7.0	5.9
Syria	48	44	16	7	7.7	6.5	5.4
Tunisia	44	28	16	7	7.0	3.6	2.7
Turkey	41	28	15	7	5.7	3.5	2.7
U.A.E.	41	22	14	4	6.8	4.6	3.6
Yemen	49	53	27	18	7.0	7.7	7.5

Source : World Bank, *World Development Report, 1992*, pp. 270-271.

also a contributory factor in maintaining a high birth rate in both Iran and Iraq as the two countries reportedlly not only stopped all family welfare programmes but also exhorted the people to produce more children. Crude birth rates in the case of the small Gulf states (Bahrain, Qatar, Kuwait and the U.A.E.) are low but the figures are misleading as they are 'biased downwards by their large migrant worker populations'.[4] Taking nationals alone, birth rates in these countries are also above 40 per thousand. Since the oil-boom days these countries have followed pro-natalist policies which include schemes of substantial family allowances, free education and health services.

Since 1950 there has been a three-fold increase in the population of the West Asia and North Africa region. The region's current population growth rate is a little less than 3 per cent per annum, which is the second highest in the world after sub-Saharan Africa. The current population growth rate implies that there will be about 663 million people by the year 2025. From the data in Table 3, we can see that the hypothetical size of the stationary population of West Asia and North Africa is estimated at 1, 340 million which might be a reality sometime during the middle of the 21st century.

The persistence of high fertility rate in the context of the Islamic countries in general and the WANA countries in particular has been explained by three major approaches: (I) The Islamic hypothesis, (ii) the status of women hypothesis, and (iiii) political economy approach.

The Islamic Hypothesis

It is argued that Islam is not only a philosophical doctrine but also a way of life which is strictly observed by its followers, and as such it gives rise to some behavioural correlates which eventually affect fertility. It is suggested that 'Islam does not share the ascetic ideals of other religions, has a generally positive attitude towards sexual enjoyment within marriage, and encourages all believers to marry.'[5] Therefore, patterns of marriage, polygamy and divorce are considered important factors affecting fertility. The major issues that emerge in this context are whether early and multiple marriages and frequent divorces create conditions that are conducive to high fertility. As we shall see below, empirical, evidence does not support much of this explanation.

To begin with, the Islamic societies are not monolithic; they operate in diverse regional, economic, social and political contexts. These contexts invariably influence the three behavioural correlates discussed above. For example, contrary to popular belief, the practice of early marriage is not universal in Islamic countries. Studies suggest that on an average only about one young woman out of three is married before her nineteenth birthday. As the data (see Table 4) indicate there is considerable variation in age of marriage across the WANA countries.

Table 3 : **WANA : Population Growth and Projections**

Country	Average annual growth of population (per cent)			Population (millions)			Hypothetical size of stationary population (million)
	1965-80	1980-90	1989-2000	1990	2000	2025	
Turkey	2.4	2.4	1.9	56	68	91	120
Iran	3.1	3.6	3.4	56	78	166	492
Egypt	2.1	2.4	1.8	52	62	86	120
Algeria	3.1	3.0	2.8	25	33	52	78
Morocco	2.5	2.6	2.4	25	32	47	70
Iraq	3.4	3.6	3.4	19	26	48	85
Saudi Arabia	4.6	4.7	3.7	15	21	43	89
Syria	3.4	3.6	3.6	12	18	35	66
Yemen	2.3	3.1	3.7	11	16	37	110
Tunisia	2.1	2.3	1.9	8	10	14	36
Israel	2.8	1.8	3.3	5	6	8	10
Libya	4.3	4.1	3.6	5	6	14	36
Jordan	4.3	3.7	3.8	3	5	10	28
Lebanon	1.7	-	-	-	-	-	-
Kuwait	7.1	4.4	2.9	2	3	4	5
U.A.E.	16.5	4.3	2.2	2	2	3	3
Oman	3.6	4.7	3.9	2	2	5	10
Total/Average	-	-	-	298	388	663	1,340

Source : World Bank, *World Development Report 1992*, pp. 268-269.

Table 4 : **Percentage of Women Married at least once, Selected Countries, 1980**

Country	Age: 15-19 Years	Age: 20-24 Years
Egypt	21.8	61.1
Iran	34.3	78.6
Iraq	33.0	67.2
Israel	7.5	54.1
Kuwait	29.2	71.0
Libya	39.6	88.0
Tunisia	10.6	54.4
Turkey	21.7	72.9
U.A.E.	56.5	87.8
United States	8.0	46.6

Source : *UN Demographic Yearbook*, 1982, pp. 496-501.

The level of polygyny also differs from society to society, from as low as 1 or 2 per cent in Damascus or Cairo to probably no more than 10 per cent in some other Arab countries.[6] A Study of pologyny among Arabs concludes that polygyny is practiced by a comparatively small minority of Arab Muslim men, i.e. probably by no more than 12 per cent, and in most instances nearer five per cent.[7] Moreover, polygamous marriages are not necessarily more fertile than monogamous marriages.[8] Thus the alleged importance of the polygyny factor in high fertility can easily be dismissed.

The frequency of divorce also varies widely in the WANA countries. Studies suggest that the proportion of divorce within 20 years of marriage ranges from a low of 4-6 per cent in Jorban, Syria and Tunisia to 11 per cent in Egypt and 20 per cent in Morocco. "This wide range of divorce levels indicates that divorce is not readily linked with religion."[9]

Women's Status Hypothesis

This hypothesis is based on a fairly well researched finding that the socio-economic status of women is a critical determinant of fertility rates. In the case of the WANA countries it is argued that women enjoy a comparatively lower socio-economic status which is thought to be derived from Islam on the one hand and 'patriarchal' social structure on the other. The status of women in Muslim societies is an extremely controversial issue and one must recognise the different and contradictory ways in which the term is defined. Nevertheless, in operative terms this means restricted access to education and modern employment. Given the fact that in the WANA region female literacy levels have been considerably low and that there is absence of non-farm, non-household job opportunities for most women, the women's status hypothesis appears to have some merit. Already in some Arab countries we find increasing evidence of low fertility largely because of improvements in female education, employment opportunities and an increase in the age of marriage which reduces the traditionally large age difference between spouses.[10] Contrary to the situation in the 1960s and 1970s, in the 1980s the life expectancy for women has been higher than for men by at least two years. In spite of all this, however, the fertililty rate continues to be high in the WANA countries and there is no satisfactory explanation for this phenomenon as yet. Therefore, one may be tempted to agree with the view that 'studies of women's status and fertility outcomes in the Arab countries have not always yielded the expected inverse association between education, employment, and fertility... and have in fact emphasized the need for better measures of both "patriarchy" and women's status.'[11]

Political Economy Approach

Some demographers have recently begun to argue that Islam and women's status hypotheses provide only a partial explanation of health and fertility behaviour. The subordinate status of women is not so much a function of Islam as that of the peasant way of life. 'The importance of family life, the social and economic pressures to bear sons, and the strict control of women's sexuality are found in most peasant societies, whether Muslims or non-Muslim.[12] As most of the West Asian societies are in the process of development and change, issues like status of women and national identity are truly problematic. Related issues, such as whether or not the governments should promote family planning and to what extent, reflect dilemmas of national development in these societies. Viewed from this perspective, the way in which political elites articulate their ideology of development in relation to Islam is a crucial determinant of differences in the status of women.[13]

In more concrete terms, state policy towards such issues as family planning and education, employment and equal status for women is crucial in affecting fertility levels. Although Islam is not opposed to family planning as such, only a few WANA countries have vigorously pursued family planning

Table 5 : **Health and Family Planning Indicators In Arab Countries**

Countries	Per cent of women using contra-ception	Per cent of births attended by medical personnel	Number of per-sons per physician	Per cent of one-year old immu-nized	Per cent popl. having access to health care
	(1)	(2)	(3)	(4)	(5)
Algeria	36	85	2,340	65	88
Bahrain	-	98	-	89	100
Egypt	38	24	770	87	-
Iraq	14	50	1,740	86	93
Jordan	26	75	1,120	98	97
Kuwait	35	99	640	69	100
Lebanon	35	88	540	91	-
Libya	15	76	690	62	-
Morocco	36	26	4,760	61	70
Oman	-	60	1,700	88	91
Qatar	-	90	-	80	-
Saudi Arabia	15	78	740	89	97
Syria	20	37	1,260	58	76
Tunisia	50	60	2,150	91	90
U.A.E.	31	96	1,020	71	90
Yemen, YAR	1	12	6,010	29	35
Yemen, PDRY (South)	15	10	4,370	35	30

(a) Per cent of one-year-olds who are immunized against poliomyelitis, diptheria, pertussis, and tetanus.

(b) Per cent of the population that can reach appropriate health services by local transportation in no more than one hour.

Source: Carla M. Obermeyer, 1992, p. 41.

programmes and the results, have also not been disappointing. In Tunisia, for example, largely due to these programmes, the percentage of teenage women who were married fell from 43 per cent in 1956 to only 6 per cent in 1975. Similar, although less dramatic, decline occurred in Egypt and Turkey.[14]

In terms of state policy towards family planning programmes the WANA countries can be divided into three categories: (1) pro-natalist regimes, i.e. countries which want to increase their populations and hence are not very enthusiastic about family planning programmes (this comprises all GCC countries, Iraq and Iran until recently); (2) countries that are vigorously pursuing family planning programmes with varying results (Israel, Tunisia, Morocco, Egypt, Turkey, Yemen); and (3) countires that have no stated population policy. Data indicating use of contraception among women and their health and family planning indicators are presented in Table 5. Whereas many countries in the region have achieved low to moderate success in various programmes, Yemen appears to be seriously lagging behind.

Age Structure

Age structure is an important population characteristic which is largely a function of a certain pattern of birth and death rates. The greater the number of births in relation to deaths, the younger the population. In other words, there is a close relationship between a population's natural rate of increase and its age structure. Populations which increase at a rate of more than 1.5 per cent over a given period have a 'young' structure because of the high proportion of people under 15 years of age.[15] With a population growth rate of 3 per cent per annum, the WANA countries obviously present a very young population profile as shown in Table 6. Some of the salient features of this profile are discussed here.

1. (a) Except a few countries (notably the U.A.E. and Israel) a majority of the WANA countries have 40-45 per cent of their populations in the 0-14 age group and 50-55 per cent in the 15-64 age group. If we raise the upper limit of the young cohort to 19 or 20 years,

Table 6 : **Age Structure of Population (per cent) in West Asian and North African Countries, 1990**

Countries	*Age Structure of Population (per cent)*		
	0-14 Years	*15-64 Years*	*65+*
Algeria	43.6	52.7	3.7
Egypt	39.2	46.6	4.2
Iran	44.4	52.6	3.0
Iraq	46.5	50.8	2.7
Israel	31.2	59.9	8.9
Jordan	45.4	52.1	2.5
Kuwait	35.6	63.0	1.4
Libya	46.0	51.6	2.4
Morocco	40.8	55.6	3.6
Oman	46.3	51.3	2.4
Saudi Arabia	45.5	51.0	2.6
Syria	48.2	49.1	2.7
Tunisia	37.8	58.1	4.1
Turkey	34.4	60.9	4.3
U.A.E.	30.8	67.5	1.7
Yemen	48.7	48.2	2.7

Source : World Bank, *World Development Report, 1992*, pp. 268-269.

which is much more realistic in the context of the developing countries, then most of the WANA countries would easily claim 50 per cent or more of their populations as 'young'. Such a large proportion of young population requires a considerable amount of state investment in order to provide them facilities regarding nutrition, health, hygiene, general welfare and schooling. Investment at such a large scale is often beyond the capacity of most of the developing countries, and this in turn results in a high infant death rate, malnutrition, and illiteracy. In the WANA region only a few oil-rich Gulf states are an exception to this trend, and even these states find it difficult to support full state welfarism; (b) A larger proportion of younger population in a country leads to problems of unemployment of underemployment as the developing economies are not in a position to absorb the ever increasing numbers of young adults joining the labour market; (c) The WANA countries show a relatively high dependency ration (i.e. the ratio of the population under 15 years and over 64 years to the population aged 15-64), which is around 1 to 1.

2. Israel has the largest proportion of older people in its population that any other WANA country.
3. Some of the Gulf states as well as Israel have relatively higher proportions of populations in the 15-64 age group by WANA standards. This might be due to the larger proportion of immigrants who generally belong to this age group.

Urbanisation

Urbanisation is an important characteristic of population distribution in modern times. Urbanisation may variously be defined as (i) growth in the number of people living in urban areas, (ii) growth in the proportion of people living in urban areas, (iii) growth in the number of urban centres, (iv) socio-economic progress involving an increase in urban life, (v) the physical expansion of urban land use, or (vi) combinations of the above. Any one of the five processes (i to v) may occur independently without corresponding change in the other four.[16]

In most of the developing countries, thanks to the increased pace of rural-urban migration, the urban population growth is much faster than the rural population growth. Urbanisation also often outpaces social and economic development. Consequently, it may impose a heavy financial burden on the government for providing education, health facilities, houses, transport and public utilities, and may create unemployment problems and other social disturbances. Additionally, uncontrolled urban growth often causes problems of congestion and environmental pollution, which detrimentally affects the quality of life in urban areas. The West Asian countries are no exception. As already pointed out, the WANA region as a whole is one of the most urbanised regions of the Third World. About 53 per cent of its total population lives in urban areas (Table 7). In this sense the region is more urbanised than China, India, Southeast Asia, or Sub-Saharan Africa.

Table 7 : **Urbanisation in West Asia and North Africa, 1965-1990**

	Urban Population				
	As a percentage of total population		Average/annual growth rate (per cent)		
Country	1965	1980	1990	1965-80	1980-90
Kuwait	78	88	96	8.2	5.0
Israel	81	89	92	3.5	2.1
Qatar	-	-	89	-	-
Lebanon	50	76	83	4.5	-
Bahrain			83	-	-
Saudi Arabia	39	67	77	8.5	6.3
Iraq	51	72	71	5.3	4.4
U.A.E.	41	60	77	23.7	3.9
Libya	26	88	70	9.8	6.3
Turkey	34	47	61	4.1	5.9
Jordan	-	-	61	-	4.1
Iran	37	50	57	5.2	5.0
Tunisia	40	52	54	4.0	2.9
Algeria	38	44	52	3.9	4.8
Syria	40	50	50	4.5	4.4
Morocco	32	41	48	4.3	4.3
Egypt	41	45	47	2.7	3.1
Yemen	11	23	29	6.6	6.9
Oman	4	4	11	7.5	8.6

Source : World Bank, *World Development Report, 1992*, pp. 278-79.

There are wide disparities in the levels of urbanisation in the WANA countries. Thus all the Gulf states (except Oman) along with Israel, Lebanon, Iraq and Libya show a high degree of urbanisation (ranging between 70 per cent to 96 per cent). Turkey, Jordan, Iran, Tunisia, Algeria, Syria, Morocco and Egypt can be regarded as moderately urbanised (47 per cent - 61 per cent), whereas Yemen (29 per cent) and Oman (11 per cent) are the least urbanised West Asian countries. Irrespective of the levels of urbanisation, one of the most noteworthy features of urban growth in the WANA countries is its overwhelming concentration in large cities, and particularly in the capital cities. In Table 8 we have data regarding the proportion of population in cities of 'one million plus' and in the capital cities. The highest urban concentration is found in smaller countries like Libya, Syria, Kuwait and Israel. The urban population is also concentrated in Egypt. The WANA region supports about two dozen 'one million plus' cities including Cairo, Tehran, Istanbul, Alexandria, Baghdad, Basra, Casablanca, Ankara, Izmir, Algiers, Beirut, Damascus, Amman, Tunis, Tel Aviv, Rabat, Riyadh and Jeddah. As in most Third World countries, in the WANA countries too rural-urban migration has been the single most important factor contributing to the process of urbanisation.

INTERNATIONAL MIGRATION: INDIANS IN WEST ASIA

Apart from internal migration in each country, there has been considerable international migration from both within and outside the WANA region. Two factors have particularly accelerated the inward international migration into the area: (i) the creation of the state of Israel, and (ii) the oil price hike which brought unprecedented prosperity to the GCC countries. In this section, we focus on Indian migration into the GCC countries as well as Israel.

1. *GCC Countries*. India has had trade and cultural relations with the Persian Gulf region since antiquity. However, there is evidence of Indian settlement in the region since the sixteenth century. Small communities of Indian traders called *baniyans* existed in present-day Iraq, Iran, Oman, Yemen, and Saudi Arabia in the seventeenth and eighteenth centuries. When the region came under British influence in the nineteenth century, Indian merchant communities flourished in a number of towns of the Gulf countries. The Indians served as bankers, importers and exporters, custom farmers, agents for local merchants, government contractors, financiers, etc.

All these merchant communities however dwindled after the Second World War and more decisively after the independence of the Gulf countries for various reasons. Moreover, at the same time the emergence of Gulf countries as oil-producing and exporting economies and the consequent demand for labour changed the size and complexion of the Indian and other expatriate communities in the region. With the increase in oil prices in the mid-seventies Indians began

Table 8 : **Urban Concentration in Select West Asian and North African Countries, 1990**

Country	Population of Cities of one million or more (as a percentage of)		Population in capital city as a percentage of	
	Urban	Total	Urban	Total
Libya	65	45	-	-
Syria	60	30	32	17
Kuwait	55	53	53	50
Egypt	52	24	37	17
Israel	45	41	12	11
Iran	41	23	21	12
Jordan	38	26	53	32
Tunisia	37	20	37	20
Morocco	36	17	9	4
Turkey	35	22	8	5
Saudi Arabia	29	23	17	13
Iraq	29	21	30	21
Algeria	23	12	23	12
Yemen	-	-	11	3
Oman	-	-	41	4

Data for Jordan cover the East Bank only.
Source : World Bank, *World Development Report, 1992*, pp. 278-279.

to immigrate in large numbers into the Gulf countries for a variety of jobs, and this upward trend has been continuing since then. Currently there are about 3.5 million Indian expatriates in the six GCC countries. Indians constitute about one-third of the total expatriate population and 10 per cent of the total GCC population. The largest number of Indians live in Saudi Arabia (1.6 million), followed by the U.A.E. (1.1 million), Oman (400,000) and Kuwait (200,000).[17]

2. *Israel*. Outside the Persian Gulf region, Israel hosts the only permanently-settled Indian community in WANA. Following the creation of Israel in 1948, over 25,000 Indian Jews had migrated to Israel until 1987. Very well settled in their new home-land, Jews of Indian origin today number around 70,000.

WEST ASIAN DIASPORAS

The ethnic composition of WANA populations is dominated by the Arabs. Of the current 380 million WANA population, about 200 million are Arabs, 60 million Turks, 45 million Persians, 25 million Kurds, 4 million Jews and the remaining population includes groups like Copts, Berbers, Armenians, etc. Against this backdrop we will briefly discuss here only the major West Asian ethnic diasporas, that is, the Jewish, Arab, Turkish, Iranian and Kurdish.[18]

For about 2000 years the Jews had been living in diaspora and without a homeland until of course the establishment of Israel in 1948 which is presently inhabited by about 4.0 million Jews. About 8.5 million Jews are living in diaspora mainly in the U.S., France, Ukraine, Canada, Argentina, Brazil, South Africa, Russia and the U.K.

Arab diasporas can be discussed in three distinct categories: (I) Palestinian, (ii) Syrian/Lebanese, and (iii) North African. The Palestinian diaspora was the creation of Israel and the subsequent displacement of the Palestinians. Currently there are about 7.0 million Palestinians whose geographic distribution is as follows: West Bank and Gaza 30 per cent, Israel 12 per cent, Jordan 32 per cent, Lebanon 6 per cent, Syria 5 per cent, other Arab States 8 per cent, rest of the world 7 per cent. About 70 per cent of the total Palestinian population is living in diaspora.

The Syrians and Lebanese have a century old history of overseas migration. Their french connections have particularly facilitated their migration to francophone West Africa and Europe, Sizeable Syrian/Lebanese communities also live in Argentine, Brazil and the U.S.A. The total diasporic population of the Syrian and Labanese is estimated at over 4 million. The North African Arab Diaspora can be sub-divided into two categories; Egyptian and Maghrebi. There does not seem to be a distinct pattern of Egyptian migration and settlement abroad except for the fact that a large number of Egyptians have been working in the Gulf countries. More than 3 million are said to be living abroad. People from Algeria, Morocco and Tunisia are mainly settled in Europe and particularly in France.

The contemporary Turkish diaspora, estimated at about 3.5 million, is mainly concentrated in Germany. Small Turkish communities also live in Australia and in the European and North American countries. The Iranian diaspora, estimated at around 3 million, was mainly formed in the aftermath of the Islamic revolution in 1979, and is located in European and North American countries. The over 1 million strong Kurdish diaspora is centered in Western Europe, particularly Germany. All these WANA diasporic communities send considerable amounts of remittances to their respective homelands.

POPULATION CHANGE AND ECONOMIC DEVELOPMENT

Population and development are related through a complex network of linkages. The size and rate of growth of population determines the number of potential producers and consumers which in turn influences the economy. The sex and age composition of the population tells us not only about the potential working population and the proportion of dependents but also the rate of growth of the labour force, and consumption and saving patterns. Similarly, the spatial distribution and movements of population in terms of levels of urbanisation and internal migration also have important effects on economic development. Different regions, and particularly rural and urban areas, significantly differ in their quality of labour productivity and patterns of consumption and investment, and in the different economic and social opportunities they provide. 'Rural-to-urban migration, and the consequent transfer of labour from agricultural sectors may have particularly wide-ranging consequences for the growth and distribution of income, levels of consumption and investment as well as demand for social services.'[19] While considering the relationship between the population and economic development, it is also important to recognise that differentials in fertility and mortality by economic status or class, ethnic groups, and rural-ruban regions have significant repercussions for socio-economic, group and regional inequalities. The relationship between population and economic development is a two-way process and the latter also has important effects on the former. It is a well-established fact that accelerated socio-economic development leads to decline in fertility as well as mortality rates.

From the above discussion it can easily be understood that in the context of the WANA countries the effects of demographic factors on their economic development are far too numerous to be comprehensively discussed in the short space of this chapter. Therefore, only a few general observations would be made here. To begin with, excepting a few small oil-rich countries, most of the region usually suffers from problems of unemployment and under employment as the rapidly expanding labour force cannot be absorbed by their underdeveloped and dependent economies. In a situation of rapid population growth 'it is particularly difficult to create the entry-level jobs that the (very young) labour force requires, especially when skilled older workers are so scarce. Since for the non-oil (and increasingly for the oil-exporting) states, funds for investment are very scarce, rapid population growth slows the pace of growth and development.'[20]

The very young population of these countries also require increasing amounts of money to be spent on education which most of the WANA countries are trying very hard to do. Moreover, these countries have to invest in such social overheads as housing, sewage and water systems, public health facilities and city administration. An even more far - reaching consequence of rapid population growth has been the soaring demand for food in the WANA countries which are already deficient in the 'food security' system due to natural and social factors. Finally rapid population growth leads to increased supply of labour relative to capital and raises the ratio of unskilled labour to skilled labour resulting in economic and social inequalities.

POLITICAL IMPLICATIONS OF POPULATION CHANGE

Population in most countries seldom remains at or achieves an optimum level. It is either too large or too small, and both situations can have serious political implications. In countries with large populations such economic problems as unemployment, food shortage, industrial backwardness, etc., often bring about serious political problems. In the face of these problems, the rising expectations of the masses leave much to be done by the political elites. Such situations in a country usually lead to considerable emigration. In the WANA region Egypt, Turkey and Yemen have immensely benefited from the remittances sent by their countrymen abroad. Exactly the opposite situation exists in the case of small-sized oil-rich countries which are short of manpower and thereby have to depend on foreign workers. The GCC countries provide good examples of varying sizes of immigrant populations within their respective borders, ranging from 50 per cent to 75 per cent.[21] Such a large number of 'sojourners' are not only potential 'settlers', given the opportunity, their presence has also given rise to a sense of political insecurity among the native ruling elites.[22] Not surprisingly, the Gulf countries are extremely cautious and strict about their immigration and naturalization laws.[23] Perhaps an even more serious 'political' problem in the GCC countries that has emerged from their low population base is the problem of raising their own viable armies for defending their borders. The 1990-91 Kuwaiti crisis fully illustrates this point. Even a proposal to raise a combined GCC armed force failed not only due to the politics among the member states but also because of demographic and 'tribal'/ ethnic reasons.

Differential fertility among various ethnic/sectarian groups in a plural society can also lead to serious political problems. Aptly termed as 'the politics of differential fertility', this problem is acute in Labanon and Israel where political representation in the national parliaments are made on the basis of the numerical strength of various religious / sectarian/ ethnic groups.[24] What makes the situation more acute is the fact that the communal boundaries often correspond to their differential socio-economic status, and the disprivileged groups naturally demand more power commensurate to their population size.

One major political implication of the youthful profile of the WANA countries is that only half of the population is legally adult and is therefore entitled to vote and can stand for elections. Unfortunately, democracies are an exception in this region. Another serious implication is that a vast majority of the youth in these countries is susceptible to the influence of various political and religious ideological currents ranging from Islamic fundamentalism to Marxism, Zionism to Pan-Arabism and nationalism to internationalism. Evidently, the youth has played a significant role in the Islamic Revolution in Iran and other kinds of political developments in Algeria and the Sudan, not to mention the sacrifices they made in the Iran-Iraq War.

CONCLUSION

The demographic profile of the West Asian and North African countries is characterised by a persistently high population growth rate, youthful age structure and a moderate to high degree of urbanisation by the Third World standards. The persistence of high fertility levels in the WANA region is often attributed to either the Islamic culture or the low socio-economic status of women or both. These hypotheses, however, could not be supported by empirical evidence. It is argued here that although there is a great merit in the women's status hypothesis, it ought to be placed within the context of the political cultures of these societies which at present are less conducive to providing education and non-farm job opportunities for women and implementing family planning programmes.

Of the twenty countries considered here three countries, Iran, Turkey and Egypt, alone account for over 55 per cent of the total population of the region. Whereas these and some other countries with large populations face various socio-economic problems, the smaller and especially oil-rich Gulf countries suffer from an inadequate population-base and have to rely on heavy immigration in order to meet their manpower needs.

The youthful profile of populations coupled with a fairly high degree of urbanisation render the West Asian countries politically volatile and subjects them to various kinds of youth activism and urban violence, which in turn may well lead to increased state authoritarianism.

Notes

1. Palestinian territories West Bank and Gaza, and Western Sahara are not included here. Currently their respective population is 3.1 million and 260,000.
2. See World Bank, *World Development Report 1992,* New York: Oxford University Press, 1992, p. 30
3. Carla Makhlouf Obermeyer, 'Islam, Women and Politics: The Demography of Arab Countries', *Population and Development Review*, 1992, 18 (1), p. 35.
4. *The Cambridge Encyclopedia of the Middle East and North Africa,* Cambridge University Press, 1988, p. 114.
5. Carla M. Obermeyer, op, cit., pp. 42-43
6. M. Ghallab, 'Population Theory and Policies in the Islamic World', in J. Clarke (ed.), *Geography and Population*, Oxford: Pergamon Press, 1984, pp. 232-241.
7. J. Chamie, 'Polygyny among Arabs', *Populations Studies*, 1986. 40 (1), p. 56.
8. See, T. Burch, 'The Impact of Forms of Families and Sexual Unions and Dissolutions of Unions on Fertility', in R. Bulatao and R. Lee (eds.), *Determinants of Fertility in Developing Countries*, New York: Academic Press, 1983, Vol. 2, pp. 532-561 ; J. Weeks, 'The Demography of Islamic Nations', *Populations Bulletin*, 43 (4).
9. S. Farid, 'A Review of the Fertility Situation in the Arab countries of Western Asia and Northern Africa,' in United Nations, Department of International Economic and Social Affairs, *Fertility Behaviour in the Context of Development: Evidence from the World Fertility Survey*, New York, 1987, p. 347.
10. P. Fargues, 'The Decline of Arab Fertility', *Population*, 44 (1), pp. 147-175.
11. Carla M. Obermeyer, op. cit., p. 46
12. Alan Richards and John Waterbury, *A Political Economy of the Middle East: State, Class and Economic Development*, Boulder: Westview Press, 1990, p. 88
13. Carla M. Obermeyer, op. cit., p. 51
14. Alan Richards and J. Waterbury, op. cit., p. 89.
15. Julien Conde, 'Rapid Population Growth in Developing Countries', in Pradip K. Ghosh (ed.), *Population, Environment and Resource, and Third World Development*, Westport: Greenwood Press, 1984, pp, 102-125.
16. See, John I. Clarke, Contemporary Urban Growth in the Middle East', in John I. Clarke and Howard Bowen-Jones (eds.), *Change and Development in the Middle East*, London: Methuen, 1981, pp. 154-170.

17. For details, see Prakash C. Jain, *Population and Society in West Asia: Essays in Comparative Demography*, Jaipur and New Delhi: National Publishing House, 2001, chapter 4.
18. For details see Prakash C. Jain, op. cit., chapter 9.
19. UN Department of Technical Co-operation for Development, 'Population and Development Strategies', in Pradip K. Ghosh, op. cit., p. 250.
20. Alan Richards and J. Waterbury, op. cit., p. 93.
21. See J.S. Birks, 'The Demographic Challenge in the Arab Gulf', in B.R. Pridham (ed.), *The Arab Gulf and the Arab World*, London: Croom Helm, 1988, pp. 131-152.
22. See Georges Sabagh, 'Immigrants in the Arab Gulf Countries: "Sojourners" or, "Settlers"?' in Giacomo Luciani and Ghassam Salame (eds.), *The Politics of Arab Integration*, London: Croom Helm, 1988, pp. 159-182.
23. See Sharon Stanton Russell, 'Migration and Political Integration in the Arab World', in Giacomo Luciani and Ghassam Salame, op. cit., pp. 183-210.
24. For brief case studies of Lebanon and Israel, see Alan Richards and John Waterbury, op. cit., pp. 96-99.

Minorities in the Middle East
An Inquiry

P. R. KUMARASWAMY

It may be emotionally satisfying, but it is intellectually dishonest to compare one's theory with the other's practice. It is equally misleading to compare one's best with the other's worst.

Bernard Lewis[1]

Are there minorities in the Middle East?[2] If so, who are they? Unlike some of the other issues such as terrorism, defining minorities is least problematic. It is possible to draw easily recognisable parameters and identify minorities in various countries of the Middle East.[3] Despite inherent difficulties and conflicting claims, demography can be used to identify, define and delineate various minorities in the region. The real problem, however, lies in the unwillingness of most countries to recognise the existing realities. If there are no minorities, the argument goes, there is no need to discuss issues such as status, discrimination, etc.

The question of minorities has been singularly absent in the Middle East political discourse. Even the Islamists have been careful to avoid the issue or have taken refuge in the traditional interpretations of Islam's benevolent treatment of the *ahl al-Kitab* or the people of the book.[4] Often discussions on minorities are dismissed as external, mainly Israeli, conspiracies to undermine the Arab and Islamic world. Israel's policy towards the minorities has come under closer scrutiny and severe criticism. Reacting to Israeli policy of dividing the non-Jewish population, Lisa Hajjar observed:

> The Israeli state has always utilized divide-and-rule strategies to govern its non-Jewish citizens, the Palestinians who remained inside the 1948 borders. They were categorised into discrete 'nationalities': 'Arabs', 'Druze', 'Bedouin' and 'Circassians.' Construction of these

minority identities was intended both to fragment an Arab collectivity within Israel and differentiate citizens' rights according to communal affinities.[5]

The Arab citizens of Israel and their socio-political marginalization had drawn widespread attention in the Arab and Islamic world. But the fate of minorities in the rest of the Middle East has rarely received adequate attention or treatment.

However, the issue is not of definition or official acceptance but of the existence of minorities. What Ami Ayalon says about Copts of Egypt is true for other states vis-a-vis minorities: 'a curtain woven of intense sensitivity, perpetual denial, and a profound reluctance to discuss what is behind it.'[6]

Who is a Minority?

It is obvious that none of the countries in the region is homogenous. Despite the dominant Arab and Islamic character, the region has substantial non-Arab and non-Islamic minorities. Some of them pre-date the birth of Islam and the Arabization of the Middle East. Most minorities originate 'either from the region's ancient pre-Arab inhabitants or from the three monotheistic religions and their subsequent offshoots.'[7]

Writing at the end of the Second World War, Albert Hourani defined Middle East minorities as those communities that differ from the Sunni Arab majority in their religious affiliation and/or their ethno-cultural identity.[8] If one accepts this broad definition, one can identify the following types of minorities:

Religious communities that are non-Sunni Muslim, but are ethnically or culturally Arab: Christians: Greek Orthodox, Greek Catholic, Copts, Maronites, Latins and Protestants. Muslim heterodox sets: Shia, Alawis, Druze and Islamaili.

Ethnic or national groups that are non-Arab but Sunni Muslims, viz., Kurds, Turkomans and Circassians; or neither Arab nor Muslim, viz., Jews, Armenians, Assyrians and Christian tribes in southern Sudan.[9]

Problems of Minorities

The existence of the minorities and their deliberate non-acceptance as a distinct group by most of the countries raises a number of questions.

Table 1: **Demography (by Religion)**

	Sunni Muslim	Shia Muslim	Chris-tians	Druze	Jews	Kurds	Others
1. Algeria	99.0						1.0
2. Bahrain	75.0	25.0					
3. Djibouti	-						
4. Egypt	94.0		6.0				
5. Iran	10.0	89.0					1.0
6. Iraq	42.0	55.0					3.0
7. Israel	14.1[1]		2.8		81.4		1.7
8. Jordan	96.0		4.0[2]				
9. Kuwait	45.0	40.0					15.0
10. Lebanon	21.0	32.0	21.0[3]	6.0			10.0
11. Libya	97.0						3.0
12. Morocco	98.7		1.1		0.2		
13. Oman	18.8	6.2[4]					75.0[5]
14. Palestinian areas	90.0		10.0				
15. Qatar	70.3	24.3					5.4
16. Saudi Arabia	92.1	5.0					2.9
17. Sudan	NA						
18. Syria	74.0		10.0[6]	16.0[7]			
19. Tunisia	98.0		1.0				1.0
20. Turkey	79.8	20.0[8]					0.2
21. UAE	62.5	15.0					22.5
22. Yemen	62.0	36.0					2.0

Source: *The Middle East Military Balance*, *1999-2000*, Cambridge, MA: MIT Press, 2000,

1 'Muslims' no separate classification
2 Greek Orthodox and other Christians
3 Maronites
4 And Hindus
5 Ibadi Muslims
6 Greek Orthodox, Gregorian, Armenian, Catholics, Syrian Orthodox, Greek Catholic
7 Alawi, Druze and Shia Muslims
8 Alevis

Table 2: **Demography (by Ethnicity)**

	Arabs	Persians	Jews	Berbers	Kurds	Others	Others	Others	Others
1. Algeria	78.5	-	-	19.4	1.0	1.0	-	-	1.1
2. Bahrain	73.0	8.0				13.0[1]			6.0
3. Djibouti									
4. Egypt	98.4					1.6			
5. Iran	3.0	51.0			7.0	24.0[2]	8.0[3] 2.0[4]	2.0[5] 2.0[6]	1.0
6. Iraq	73.5	-	-	-	21.6	4.9		-	-
7. Israel	-	-	81.4	-	-	18.6			
8. Jordan	98.0	-	-	-	-	2.0			
9. Kuwait	35.0	4.0	-	-	-	45.0[7]	16.0[8]		
10. Lebanon	95.0	-	-	-	-	4.0[9]	-	-	• 1.0
11. Libya	97.0[10]					3.0[11]			
12. Morocco	59.6	-	-	39.5		0.9[12]			
13. Oman	90.6	-	-	-	-	9.4[13]			
14. Palestinian areas									

Arabs	Persians	Jews	Berbers	Kurds	Others	Others	Others	Others	
15. Qatar	40.0	10.0	-	-	-	18.0[14]	18.0[15]	14.0[16]	
16. Saudi	91.4	-	-	-	-	5.0[17]			3.6
17. Sudan	NA								
18. Syria	90.3	-	-	-	-	9.7[18]			
19. Tunisia	98.0[19]	-	-	-	-	1.0[20]	-	-	1.0
20. Turkey	-	-	-	-	20.0	80.0[21]			
21. UAE	50.0	-	-	-	-	43.8[22]	6.2[23]	-	-
22. Yemen	91.7	-		-	-	6.3[24]	-	-	2.0

Source: *The Middle East Military Balance, 1999-2000*, Cambridge, MA: MIT Press, 2000.

1. Southest Asians
2. Azeris
3. Gilaki and Mazandarani
4. Lurs
5. Balouchis
6. Turkmens
7. Kuwaitis
8. Southeast Asians
9. Armenians
10. Arabs and Berbers
11. Greeks, Maltese, Italians, Egyptians, Pakistanis, Indians, Tunisians and Turks
12. Europeans and others
13. Africans, Persians and Southeast Asians
14. Pakistanis
15. Indians
16. Mostly Southeast Asians
17. Afro-Arabs
18. Kurds, Armenians and others
19. Arabs and Berbers
20. Europenas
21. Turkish
22. Southeast Asians
23. Europeans and Persians
24. Afro-Arabs

One of the principal problems in discussing the question of minorities is the absence of reliable demographic data. When the census process itself is absent in countries such Saudi Arabia and Lebanon, identifying the strength of the minorities is almost impossible. As a result, more often than not the population statistics of the minorities are no more than educated guesses or projections based on earlier census. Opposed to the demands of the minorities, governments of the region tend to underestimate their numbers and for the same reason, the minorities tend to inflate their number. For example, in the mid-1980s the estimates of Kurdish population in Iran, Iraq and Turkey ranged from less than 7 million to nearly 17 million.[10] While the Coptic leaders put their strength at 18 per cent of the population or 11 millions,[11] the official version claims that only 5.6 per cent (or just under 3.3 million) Egyptians are Copts.[12]

Some of the brutal violence and conflicts in the Middle East are rooted in the inability of the states to recognise social diversity and their unwillingness to accommodate the demands of those who are different from the majority. Even the passage of time has not enabled some of these countries to come to terms with their past. The massacre of Christian Armenians under the reign of Ottoman Sultan Abdul Hamid II and subsequently by Young Turks is still contested by Turkey. If the Armenian massacre did not happen, the question of Turkey's culpability does not arise. The civil wars in Sudan and Lebanon as well as the Arab-Israeli conflict are basically ethno-religious disputes.

The end of the Ottoman Empire proved ominous for minorities in the areas under its erstwhile control. The emergence of the new entities and their pre-occupation with territorial nationalism circumvented the *millet* system, which granted and guaranteed communal autonomy. The *millet* system was a significant improvement for the minorities who despised the demeaning and shameful *dhimmi* status. Under the new arrangement, Christians and Jews enjoyed recognition and religious freedom. Despite insecurities, the system functioned well. Largely due to pressures from the European powers, the poll tax imposed upon the non-Muslims was gradually abolished. Likewise the status of *dhimmi* was abolished in the nineteenth century by the Ottomans and the Qajars.[13]

The emergence of new states in the post-Ottoman era should have improved the status of minorities further. On the contrary, the authoritarian nature of much of the Arab regimes presented 'a major obstacle to the expressions of minority identities and aspirations'.[14] Driven by the need to forge a new identity based on territorial nationalism, these states strived for homogeneity and viewed any other identity as divisive, counterproductive and externally sponsored. In their determination to forge a national identity based on territorial loyalties, the post-Ottoman polities viewed internal diversity as a divisive factor and a 'potential challenge' to the unity of the nation.[15] As a result, unlike other citizens, minorities have to suffer both as individuals and as communities.[16]

Moreover, one of the significant developments of decolonisation was that Maghreb was emptied of any sizeable non-Muslim minority and following the formation of Israel, Judaism almost vanished from the Arab world.[17]

Thus, the consolidation of the nation-building process has not facilitated a reappraisal of the minority question. For example, in 1971 a Turkish official maintained: 'We accept no other nation as living in Turkey, only the Turks. As we see it, there is only one nation in Turkey: the Turkish nation. All citizens living in different parts of the country are content to be Turkish'.[18] Similarly, discussions in Egypt on the Copts have scrupulously avoided the expression 'minority'.[19] If Golda Meir was unwilling to recognise the existence of Palestinian people, Turkey's attitude towards the Kurds is no better: 'They are not Kurds, but Mountain Turks!'

Leaders who otherwise are known for their socialism, secularism and modernising influences initiated some of the harshest anti-minority moves. It was Kemal Ataturk, who in his bid to consolidate the post-Ottoman ethnic Turkish identity proscribed the teaching of Kurdish language. The present rulers of Turkey are merely implementing his 1924 policies. In 1957, it was Gamal Abdul Nasser, the champion of secular Arab nationalism, who enforced teaching of Islam as a basic subject in the curricula, including in Christian schools.[20] Because of their exclusion from political participation, the

Copts became active in business and hence when Nasser nationalised private properties, they became his principal victims. In 1994 when Saad Eddin Ibrahim, director of Cairo-based Ibn Khaldoun Centre, sought to organise a conference on minorities, veteran journalist Muhammad Hassanein Heikal launched a fierce attack on the move. In Heikal's view, there are no minorities in Egypt because Copts are a 'part of Egypt's unbreakable fabric'.[21] The government eventually banned the conference and Saad Eddin Ibrahim shifted it to Cyprus.

The growth of religious extremism has also adversely affected the status of minorities. The 1971 Constitution of Egypt proclaimed Islam as state religion with Sharia as 'a principal source of legislation' and less than a decade later Sharia became 'the principal' source of law. Likewise, the secularist Ba'athist ideology was insufficient to withstand pressures from the Islamists and in 1973 Syria ruled that the head of state must be a Muslim. The same is true for Iraq where the Ba'ath party recognises Islam as an essential component of the Arab culture.[22] According to Article 13 of the Iranian constitution, minorities are denied the presidency, the prime ministership, the ambassorship, ministerial posts and top-level military positions.[23] As Hilal Khashan rhetorically asked: 'If Arab sheikhs and princes build mosques in Christian lands and brag about it, they should, on grounds of reciprocity, allow Christians to build churches to serve Christian migrant communities in the Gulf area.'[24]

In the absence of guaranteed and constitutional protections, minorities become vulnerable and susceptible to pressures and exploitation. More often the rulers found minorities useful for specific tasks. For example, the Ottoman Empire employed Maronites as police officials; Baha'is proved useful to the Pahlavis; and Berbers and Circassians have played a pivotal role in internal security for Morocco and Jordan respectively.[25]

In some cases minorities benefit from affirmative actions. For example, out of the 88 seats in the Palestinian Legislative Council six seats are reserved for Christians; two each for Jerusalem and Bethlehem and one each for Ramallah and Gaza Strip. In other words, they have 7 per cent representation in the Council or 'more than double their proportion in

Palestinian society'.[26] Likewise, Iran's affirmative action works in favour of the minority representation in the *Majlis*. Even though their combined population is less one million (out of 35 million) they have five seats in a 270-member parliament. However, these exceptional representations in parliament or the high profiled positions given to minorities by some states (Boutros Boutros-Ghali in Egypt, Tariq Aziz in Iraq or Hanan Ashrawi in the Palestinian Authority) do not alleviate the vulnerable position of the minority community.

There are noticeable exceptions. In Iraq, Syria and to a lesser extent in Jordan, the minorities are in control of the state and have successfully taken over the state and politically marginalized the majority community. Syria is a classic example: the Alawis constitute about 10 per cent of the population and by co-opting other minorities such as Christians, Druze and Isma'ilis they have successfully marginalized the majority Sunni Muslims. Likewise, Palestinians constitute the majority in Jordan even though the Jordanians of the Transjordan or East Bankers control the state. Both Bahrain and Iraq have a Shia majority but the power rests with the Sunni leadership.

A number of historical as well as social developments diminished the Christian population in the Middle East (see Table 3). Even those places where Christians constituted substantial portions of the population, if not the majority, have witnessed a noticeable shift. Traditional Christian towns such as Bethlehem and Nazareth ceased to have a Christian majority. At the more immediate level, 'under the Young Turks and then under the Kemalist Republic, nearly 3 million Christians were to pay the shock of nationalisms and the birth of modern Turkey with their lives or by their exile'.[27] Youssef Courbage attributes a number of reasons for this population shift: conversion of individuals, families and entire groups; immigration and emigration, by coercion or by free choice; inter-marriage between Muslim men and Christian women, which leads to a second generation of uniquely Muslim children; and birth and death rates of different magnitude.[28] These processes are valid for the demographic shifts that affect other minorities of the region.

Table 3: **Christians of the East (by Rite and Country) (in thousands, 1995)**

Church	Egypt	Lebanon	Syria	Iraq	Jordan	Israel	Palestinian areas	Turkey	All countries
Copts (all rites)	3238.9	1.9	0.0	1.8	1.2	0.8	2.8	0.0	3298.0
Greek orthodox	4.4	294.8	503.0	0.8	81.4	33.0	41.6	13.9	972.9
Maronite	2.5	490.9	28.0	0.0	0.0	7.3	0.3	0.0	529.0
Greek catholic	4.7	255.2	111.8	0.7	22.1	43.9	4.4	0.0	442.8
Armenian apostolic	7.6	196.4	111.8	25.0	3.5	1.3	2.9	68.3	416.8
Chaldean Catholic	0.5	4.9	6.7	390.3	0.0	0.0	0.0	6.8	409.2
Jacobite	0.2	14.7	89.4	37.2	2.2	0.1	2.5	39.9	186.2
Latin	3.8	2.9	11.1	5.2	34.9	13.2	15.2	5.7	92.0
Protestant	20.9	20.2	20.1	5.8	4.4	4.5	4.8	5.2	85.9
Syrian catholic	1.3	19.7	22.4	55.5	0.0	0.1	0.5	1.7	101.2
Nestorian	0.0	4.9	16.8	87.7	0.0	0.0	0.9	0.0	110.3
Armenian Catholic	0.6	19.7	24.6	5.5	0.4	0.1	0.3	5.1	56.3
Total Christians	3336.4	1326.2	945.7	615.5	150.1	104.3	76.2	146.6	6700.6
Percentage of total populations	5.7	43.8	6.4	2.9	4.2	2.1	3.8	0.2	4.0

Source: Youssef Courbage, 'Christianity and Islam: Demography in the Middle East,' ISIM Newsletter no.3/99, July 1999, p.26.

The dispersal of minorities across the region transcends the national boundaries which emerged after the Second World War. This transnational dispersal works against the interests of minorities. Despite territorial contiguity, the Kurds are scattered in Turkey, Iran and Iraq and 'their nationalist movements in each country have functioned very much independently of each other'.[29] As a result, countries, which in the past supported the Kurdish struggle, abandoned them when the political climate changed (for example, the Algiers Accord of 1975 between Iran and Iraq). Despite political differences with neighbouring countries, Iran has been wary of granting autonomy to the Kurds. If Kurds were to be granted autonomy, 'what about the Turkomans, Baluchis, Azeris and the Iranian Arabs?'[30]

Table 4: **Iranian Minorities**

Ethnic groups	Religion	Estimated strength
Arabs	Sunni and Shia	615,000-2 million
Azeri	Shia	8.8-10 million
Bakhtiari	Shia	300,000-1 million
Baluch	Sunni	500,000-1 million
Kurd	Sunni, Shia and Sufi	3-8 million
Lur	Shia	300,000-580,000
Qashqai	Shia	800,000-1 million
Shahsevan	Shia	310,000
Turkman	Sunni	1.1 million
Armenian	Mostly Apostolic	150-250,000
Assyrians & Chaldeans	Mostly Nestorian	16-18,000
Baha'is	Baha'i	150,000-300,000
Jews	Judaism	20-30,000
Zoroastrians	Zoroastrian	50,000

Source: Eliz Sanasarian, *Religious Minorities in Iran*, Cambridge: Cambridge University Press, 2000, pp.10-13 and 36-37.

In a number of cases the minorities share the same ethno-cultural background, language and social classes. They neither live in separate enclaves nor wear clothes that would distinguish them from the rest. During nationalist struggles, they joined hands with the rest of the population and fought against colonialism and imperial domination (for example,

Berbers in Algeria and Copts in Egypt). As with the Copts, only religious beliefs differentiate them from the majority. Likewise, with notable exceptions like the Kurds, Maronites and pre-1948 Yishuv in Palestine, secession and political independence is not an option for most minorities. Nor do they demand autonomous regions where they are a majority.[31]

At the same time, some of the minorities forged a close linkage with Western powers, enjoyed their protection and benefited from their patronage; for example, Maronites in Lebanon and pre-state Jews in Mandate Palestine. But not all minorities follow this practise; the Greek Orthodox Christians in Syria, never identified with Western Christianity.[32] The same is true for the Copts. Yet, Arab Christians are perceived, especially during political turmoil, as Western agents.[33]

People of the Book

The traditional frameworks such as *dhimmi* (non-Muslim subject of the Muslim state) and *ahl al-Kitab* are not adequate to address a number of problems facing minorities. First and foremost, this conservative interpretation adopts religion as the marker and classifies people into believer and non-believer; among the latter category, Christians and Jews, who have revealed sacred texts, are given the status of 'people of the book' and are treated differently from other non-Muslim minorities. However, much of the minorities in the Middle East are Muslims and this traditional approach is insufficient to address their position. Ethnic, national and linguistic minorities, who figure in most of the problems in the Middle East, are simply left out. For example, like the majority Muslims in the region, most of the Kurds are Sunnis. This religious affinity however, has been subservient to their Kurdish ethnic identity and the latter forms the basis for their longing for political autonomy and independence.

As the *majority determines the Dhimmi status*, it puts the minority, especially those sects which branched out of Islam, under great jeopardy. Even legitimate Islamic sects are not part of the majority ruling group; Shia minority under Sunni rule or vice-versa. The Baha'i, an offshoot of Shia Islam, suffers from this problem, as the Islamic Republic of Iran does not recognise them, neither as Muslims nor as people with revealed sacred texts. Hence the limited protection accorded to other religious minorities such as Jews, Armenian Christians or Zoroastrians is not available to the Baha'is and they remain the most persecuted minorities in Iran.[34] Even Christian converts are also excluded from the privileges bestowed upon recognised religious minorities in Iran. The Sunni-dominated states and religious leaders consider a number of heterodox Islamic sects such as Shia, Alawi, Druze and Ismaili as deviators from Islam and even as heretics.

The problems of the Alawites in Syria are somewhat different. Under pressure from the Islamists, in 1974 the Syrian Constitution declared that the head of state must be a Muslim. The Islamic credentials of the Alawites, the sect to which president Hafiz Al-Assad belonged, are questionable. Since Syria is under the control of the minority Alawites, the state managed to secure the endorsement of the *ulema* who recognised Alawites to be Muslims. The question therefore arises: should they lose control of the state, would the Alawites still be considered Muslims? Despite arguments supposedly based on religious considerations, when it comes to determining one's status as minority, the issue is fundamentally political. For example, Ahmadias are declared *kafirs* or non-Muslims in Pakistan, primarily due to political pressures than because of religious considerations.

Even the protected status is not automatic but is contingent upon the formal acceptance of Islamic rule by the non-Muslims. In short, the protected people are 'given "citizenship", protection of life, dignity, and property and freedom of worship, and in return they are obligated to pay special taxes, accept Islamic civil law, and respect the sensibilities and beliefs of their Muslim protectors.'[35]

This tolerance is no longer acceptable to the *other* and in the words of Palestinian sociologist Bernard Sabella:

> A majority-minority relations means either you don't have equal rights before law or that you are dependent on the goodwill of the majority for these rights. At the dawn of the 21st century, this status is simply no longer acceptable to Palestinian Christians. I exist in Palestine not because Muslims or the PA (Palestinian Authority) or

> Israel 'protects' me. I exist here by virtue of my birth, my ancestors and, above all, because I am a Palestinian. I don't owe this existence to anybody. The age of *Ahl al-Dhimma* is over.[36]

Islamists have paid only limited attention to the issue partly because its puts them on the defensive and 'they resort to apologetics to try to defend the good name of Islam'.[37] In short, the traditional 'people of the book' favoured by the Islamists 'does not stipulate a position in principle with regard to the status of non-Muslims who are neither Christians nor Jews, or on the significance of the quantitative "balance of power" among the various communities'.[38] In the words of Lewis:

> ... it is only very recently that some defenders of Islam have begun to assert that their society in the past accorded equal status to non-Muslims. No such claim is made by spokesman for resurgent Islam, and historically there is no doubt that they are right. Traditional Islamic societies neither accorded such equality nor pretended that they were so doing. Indeed, in the old order, this would have been regarded not as a merit but as a dereliction of duty. *How could one accord the same treatment to those who follow the true faith and those who wilfully reject it? This would be a theological as well as a logical absurdity.*[39]

It is therefore essential that the question of minorities need to be examined taking into account the shortcomings of the traditional approach of protected people.

Conclusions

None of the Middle Eastern states are homogenous and each state has a number of ethnic and religious minorities. Most of the states rarely recognise the existence of minorities within the national boundaries and often see the issue as a conspiracy to undermine national unity and integrity. Traditional discussions of minorities within the paradigm of 'People of the Book' are inadequate and outdated and hence not able to deal with the growing problems facing minorities. Religious groups, which do not come under the purview of 'People of the Book' such as the Baha'is, have faced institutionalised discrimination.

Affirmative action in favour of officially recognised minorities ensure significant representation in parliament and provide certain constitutional protection and safeguards but are inadequate to deal with the question of power sharing. In a few exceptions, ethnic or religious minority groups actually control the state apparatus; for example, Syria, Iraq, and Gulf Sheikhdoms. Though most of the Muslims in the Middle East are Sunnis, they form a substantial minority in Iran. A number of conflicts in this region can be traced to disputes over ethnic or religious minorities; for example, the Kurdish question, the Arab-Israeli conflict, civil wars in Iraq, Lebanon and Sudan.

Notes

1 Bernard Lewis, *The Jews of Islam*, Princeton, NJ: Princeton University Press, 1987 pb, p.7

2 Even though West Asia is the popular and official nomenclature in India, the countries of the region define and present themselves as part of the Middle East and hence the paper uses 'Middle East' rather than ' West Asia'.

3 The term Middle East is applied in a larger context and denotes all countries ranging from Morocco on the West to Iran in the East. Hence it includes Algeria, Bahrain, Egypt, Iran, Iraq, Israel, Jordan, Kuwait, Lebanon, Libya, Morocco, Oman, Qatar, Saudi Arabia, Syria, the Palestinian Authority, Tunisia, Turkey, UAE and Yemen.

4 For a recent assessment see, Uriah Furman, 'Minorities in Contemporary Islamist Discourse', *Middle Eastern Studies*, 36(4), October 2000, pp.1-20

5 Lisa Hajjar, 'Israel's Interventions among the Druze', *Middle East Report*, 26(3), July-September 1996, p. 2

6 Ami Ayalon, 'Egypt's Coptic Pandora's Box', in Ofra Bengio and Gabriel Ben-Dor (eds.), *Minorities and the State in the Arab World*, Boulder, CO: Lynne Reinner, 1999, p.53

7 Moshe Maoz, *Middle Eastern Minorities: Between Integration and Conflict,* Washington: WINEP, 1999, p.5

8 Quoted in ibid., p.2

9 Ibid.

10 Edwar Chaszar, 'International Protection of Minorities in the Middle East: A status report', *Middle East Review*, 18(3), Spring 1986, p.40. The same can be said about other minorities.

11 Quoted in Imad Boles, 'Egypt-Persecution', *Middle East Quarterly*, 8(1), Winter 2001, p.23
12 Quoted in Philippe Fargues, 'Demographic Islamization: Non-Muslims in Muslim Countries', *SAIS Review*, 21(2), Summer-Fall 2001, p.109
13 Ibid., p.104
14 Mordechai Nisan, 'The Minority Plight', *Middle East Quarterly*, 3(3), September 1996, p.29
15 Fargues, n.12, p.109
16 Nisan, n.14, p.29
17 Fargues, n.12, p.110.
18 Turkish official statement of May 1971 quoted in Chaszar, n.10, p.41
19 Karim al-Gawhary, 'Copts in the "Egyptian Fabric" ', *Middle East Report*, 26 (3), July-September 1996, p.21.
20 Fargues, n.12, p.112
21 For a discussion on this controversy see, Ayalon, n.6, pp.63-67; and al-Gawhary, n.19, p.21.
22 Ray J. Mouawad, 'Syria and Iraq-Repression', *Middle East Quarterly*, 8(1), Winter 2001, p.57
23 Eliz Sanasarian, *Religious Minorities in Iran*, Cambridge: Cambridge University Press, 2000, p.70
24 Hilal Khashan, 'Arab Christians as Symbols', *Middle East Quarterly*, 8(1), Winter 2001, p.12
25 Nisan, n.14, p.30
26 Daphne Tsimhoni, 'Israel and the Territories-Disappearance', *Middle East Quarterly*, 8(1), Winter 2001, p.41
27 Youssef Courbage, 'Christianity and Islam: Demography in the Middle East', *ISIM Newsletter*, no.3, July 1999, p.26
28 Ibid.
29 Chaszar, p.10, p.40
30 Ibid. The same can be said about other minorities.
31 For an interesting discussion on enclaves see, Walid Phares, 'Are Christian Enclaves the Solution?' *Middle East Quarterly*, 8(1), Winter 2001, pp. 61-70
32 Fargues, n.12, p.112
33 Khashan, n. 24, p.10
34 However, the persecution of Baha'is is rooted in Iranian history and can be traced as far back as 1845.
35 Furman, n.4, p. 4
36 Quoted in Graham Usher, 'Palestine's dwindling Christians', *Middle East International*, 28 January 2000, p.23
37 Furman, n.4, p.1
38 Ibid., p.2
39 Lewis, n.1, p.4

Globalisation and Literature

SADIK J. AL-AZM

The India International Centre provided us with an excellent concept paper. I would like to take off, in my observations, from the concept paper which broadly outlines the general themes of the seminar as well as some of the main terms of the debate in which we were engaged. I shall start with two remarks, the first critical of and the second complementary to two important points raised in the Centre's document.

The paper foregrounds the concept of 'West Asia' by emphasizing, first, that it restores what is more commonly known as 'The Middle East' to its Asian anchor and, second, that it transcends the Eurocentric classification of lands, cultures and peoples in terms of their distance from Europe itself in such names as the Near East, the Middle East and the Far East. Still, as an Arab from the so-called Middle East, I have certain reservations about the concept of 'West Asia' as an accurate and viable alternative to the currently prevalent concepts in the political, scholarly and daily-life discourses about the part of the world I come from.

From an Arab point of view and on first sight, this West Asia anchor seems to leave out Egypt and the whole of North Africa from our own perception of ourselves as the Arab World. Although the concept paper includes Egypt's Nile-Delta civilisation within the compass of the 'West Asia' concept, we have to remember that Egypt is after all in Africa and that Egypt's ancient Nile civilisation is African and not Asian.

Another troubling aspect of the West Asia anchor from the Arab point of view, is that it seems to completely neglect or submerge or even dismiss the Mediterranean dimension—historical, cultural, political, economic—of our own perception of ourselves and of our identity, of who we are, where we have come from, and so on. It is this Mediterranean dimension which organically links us as 'West Asia' to the other side of the Mediterranean Sea, i.e. to Greece, Alexander the Great,

Hellenism in general, the Roman Empire, Muslim Spain (Andalusia), the Christian Crusades, the shared experience of Ottoman rule with Eastern Europe, European modernity in general, and so on. Add to that the fact that one of the three prophetic religions that the concept paper says arose in West Asia not only crossed over to the European side of the Mediterranean but became supreme and dominant there for a long time indeed—I mean Christianity.

My second remark complements the dual concern of the concept paper about our local literary traditions, intellectual accomplishments, performing arts and local creativities in general on the one hand, and about today's *mantra* of universalism and transuniversalism on the other. As a result, I have chosen to write about globalisation and literature and this for two reasons: (a) It has become impossible these days to discuss the *mantra* of either universalism or transversalism save under the aspect of the globalisation process currently taking hold of mankind; and (b) it is a well-known fact that literature condenses in itself the artistic traditions, intellectual accomplishments and local creativities that form the concern of the concept paper.

CENTRE-PERIPHERY AND WORLD LITERATURE

The seventies of the last century ended with a major international debate sparked off by the publication of Edward Said's book *Orientalism*.[1] At the time, I contributed, both in Arabic and English, to the polemics, debates and discussions raging practically everywhere about the vexed questions and issues raised in and by Said's book.[2]

As the controversy unfolded, I was struck by a vague but persistent feeling that there is something special, unique and/or qualitatively new about the universality of the discussions over this whole Orientalism issue. They seemed international, world-encompassing and transcendent of habitual geographical locations, national borders and cultural differences in a most unprecedented way, especially for a work emerging out of the American academy. No book in recent memory, no matter how great, revolutionary, critical and/or offensive, had managed to simultaneously draw such complex and powerful reactions, both positive and negative, from Arabs, Indians, Africans,

Americans, Europeans, Latin Americans, Russians, Muslims, Christians, Jews, etc., as well as from Marxists, liberals, nationalists, islamists, rightists, leftists, neutralists, culturalists, universalists, nativists, postmodernists, and much of it through the medium of English.

Similarly, no book before Edward Said's *Orientalism* had succeeded in commanding the simultaneous and spontaneous attention of highly articulate sociologists, psychologists, political scientists, linguists, literary critics, historians, philosophers, humanists, orientalists, journalists, politicians, diplomats, public intellectuals, immigrants, and so on, in all four corners of the earth.

In the early eighties, I found myself explaining away novel features of the *Orientalism* debate by attributing them variously to: (a) a concatenation of some very special and exceptional circumstances such as had surrounded Boris Pasternak's novel *Dr. Zhivago*, leading to an unprecedented international crisis and debate over both the novel and the Nobel prize for literature awarded to the author in 1958. But, I, then, dismissed the Pasternak incident as no more than a highly unusual episode of the Cold War at one of its worst moments; (b) the random convergence of various lines of radical concerns, postcolonial interests, and critical intellectual approaches emanating from very many parts of the world and their seemingly accidental intersection at the time of the publication of Said's *Orientalism*; (c) the earlier stirrings within the field of Orientalism itself, indicating that perhaps the time is ripe for some critical stock-taking, soul-searching and consciousness-raising concerning what the discipline is all about, particularly these days.

But, then, the eighties of the twentieth century surprised us by ending with an even more protracted and massive transnational, transcultural and transcontinental controversy, row and struggle over Salman Rushdie's novel, *The Satanic Verses*. Again, I contributed, both in Arabic and English, to the polemics, debates and discussions raging literally everywhere on the surface of the earth about the vexed questions and issues raised both in and by the novel.[3]

As the Rushdie controversy unfolded, it dawned on me that the universalism of the earlier *Orientalism* debate was really neither an exceptional circumstance nor an accidental episode, but the beginning of a genuinely new worldwide movement and trend. This became confirmed, first, by the starkly global nature of the Rushdie affair and the singular sweep of the controversies over *The Satanic Verses* throughout the nineties; and second, by the equally universal and transcultural attention given practically everywhere around the world to the articles and books of Francis Fukuyama[4] and Sammuel P. Huntington[5] on 'the end of history' and 'the clash of civilizations' respectively. To be noted also is the fact that the latter two authors stake out overarching universalist claims themselves about the whole of humanity, its history, future and destiny. Like Said's *Orientalism* and Rushdie's *The Satanic Verses*, their work left no one untouched, and consequently the reactions came from everywhere on the surface of the globe. Actually, Huntington noted in the introduction to his book that according to the editors of *Foreign Affairs* his article 'stirred up more discussion in three years than any other article they had published since the 1940s... The responses and comments on it have come from every continent and scores of countries... Whatever else it did, the article struck a nerve in people of every civilization'. In brief, the universality that struck me as so exceptional at the beginning of the 1980s had become routine by the middle of the 1990s.

The consolation I drew from all this is that books still make a difference and on a scale never witnessed before, critical thought counts in the most unlikely quarters, fine literature remains capable of unsettling the whole world and authors continue to be alive, well and kicking. I say this in the face of such postmodern routine proclamations as the death of the author, the end of the novel and the demise of literature.

Eventually, I came to the conclusion that underlying this whole phenomenon stretching from the *Orientalism* debates to the Huntington controversies, is what we have come to call the process of globalisation. I came to this realisation by reflecting on what seemed to me, then, like certain urgent questions and considerations suddenly pressed on our consciousness by the Rushdie affair itself. For example:

(a) What does it mean in today's world and to today's world when a satirical 'English' novel that takes in

India, England, Islam, Khomeini's revolution, the East/West divide, immigrant communities and a lot of other hot issues, anomalies and paradoxes, generates unprecedented massive reactions in the West, no less than in the Indian subcontinent, no less than the Muslim World, no less than Africa?

(b) Is the world getting unified—or maybe over-unified—not only commercially, communicationally, scientifically and technically, but also culturally? Or, are we, perhaps, seeing the rise of a certain kind of super-culture or over-culture to be added to the well-known earlier cultural forms such as popular, middle-brow and high-brow cultures?

(c) Could we be seeing the formation of transnational, transcontinental and translinguistic cultural vanguards set on meeting the spiritual, intellectual and artistic needs of the emerging financial, technological, managerial and business elites that preside over and run the currently globalising world economy?

(d) Are we witnessing the rise of a world literature out of the myriads of local and national literary traditions and what is the role of the authors of the periphery in building and nourishing this new development? Furthermore, how is all this reacting on the Western core itself and affecting its own literary output and creative writers?

It seemed to me at the time that these important questions had never been posed so starkly, urgently and on such a global human scale as with the Rushdie affair and novel. Consequently, whatever one may think of the artistic merits of Rushdie's literary productions, whatever one may think of the religious status of *The Satanic Verses*—blasphemous or innocent—this highly challenging feature of his novel is sufficient to make the whole incident command our serious attention for a long time to come, both in the East and West. I say both East and West, because the uniqueness of the Rushdie affair lies precisely in the fact that a book has finally succeeded, and for the first time ever, in implicating at one and the same time, both the Muslim East and the secular West in the same religio-literary scandal and affair.

Now, I would like to return to my contention that the emerging universalism first noted in the *Orientalism* debate and which then come to fruition in the Rushdie controversies, would have been quite impossible without the globalisation process currently taking hold of humanity.

Globalisation is at bottom an economic process with the usual social, political, cultural, legal, etc., ramifications attendant on such major economic shifts and transformations. For my present purposes, it is enough to characterise globalisation as the most advanced phase of the capitalist transformation of mankind under the leadership and hegemony of the core countries. This massive process flows primarily from the centre to the periphery with a lot of feedbacks and refluxes impacting the centre itself.

I would like to couple this characterisation with George Lukacs' observation that 'artistic forms rise and decline with the rise and decline of the image of their epoch'. Lukacs' succinct formulation is, I think, inspired by Goethe's remark somewhere to the effect that 'literature deteriorates only as mankind deteriorates'.

What I am saying, then, is that: (a) globalisation is a new rising epoch encompassing the whole of humanity; (b) this epoch has its own image in-the-making at the present time; and (c) the artistic forms appropriate to and expressive of this image have started to rise and evolve as well (taking care here not to confuse artistic and/or literary forms with formal techniques).

In his *Testaments Betrayed*,[6] Milan Kundera described Europe as the society of the novel and called the modern Europeans the children of the novel. He, then, proceeded to castigate both Europe and the Europeans for failing so miserably in defending their mother, the novel, throughout the turmoil of the Rushdie affair. Kundera's rebuke illustrates very nicely, in my view, this idea of an intimate relationship—an elective affinity, if you wish—between the image of a rising European modernity on the one hand, and the concomitant rise of this new literary form that we call the novel on the other. One can as beneficially think, in this context, of Hegel's description of European modernity as the age of prose and the prosaic, as against the image of an earlier epoch of poetry, chivalry and heroism.

We know that Goethe was the first to formulate the pregnant idea and highly suggestive ideal of *Weltliteratur*, i.e. the idea of a universal world literature in-the-making and the ideal of a common world literature transcending national limits, cultural boundaries and provincial traditions. Now, consider the following extension of Goethe's suggestion: '... and as in material, so also in intellectual production. The intellectual creations of individual nations become common property. National one-sidedness and narrow-mindedness become more and more impossible, and from the various national and local literatures, there arises a world literature.'

This is Karl Marx echoing the great German poet while giving his own characterisation of the modern epoch and its image in the *Communist Manifesto*.

For Karl Marx, without the universalising drive of European capitalism, without its unquestionable world-historical commanding position and without the resulting *Weltmarkt* in all sorts of goods, products and exchanges, the idea of world literature would have been quite unthinkable. For Goethe as well, without the universalising drive of European literature (primarily the novel), its emerging world-historical commanding position and the resulting formation of a *Weltmarkt* in all sorts of cultural productions, the idea of *Weltliteratur*, would have also remained quite unthinkable. It is as if these two giants saw the present globalisation epoch, its image and its literary forms as somehow already immanent in the main universalising drift of their times.

This is not blind Eurocentrism on the part of either Goethe or Marx, but: (a) a recognition of the central place and privileged position occupied by European literature in the then rising *Weltmarkt* in everything; (b) an admission not only of that literature's role as the main vehicle of the cultural universalisation processes going on under their very eyes, but also of its status as paradigm and model; (c) a making of the best use possible of the extraordinarily privileged position that each of them found himself in as an observer capable of surveying the world's literary outputs from the commanding heights of the centre and with a fair amount of Olympian detachment; and (d) a heightened awareness of the historicity of literature and of the impossibility of severing literary practice from the pressures and tugs of a wider history.

As I reflect on this whole issue of globalisation and literature, I read both Goethe's proposal and Marx's characterisation as brilliant anticipations of the arrival of a new epoch which makes possible, for the first time, the rise of literary forms that appropriate the whole world under the image of a single entity. These forms have to seriously transcend the earlier understandings—be they noble or trivial—of world literature as not much more than:

(1) An act of bringing together, in some fashion or other, the great books of all times and places.

(2) An upholding of the ideal of a grand synthesis of all that is glorious and sublime in the world's high cultures.

(3) A collecting in one supreme formation of the greatest literary works produced anywhere around the world at any one time.

(4) The mere give and take that occurs (and has been occurring) among the world's various national and local literary traditions.

(5) The intense exchanges and interchanges that have been taking place among the world's national literatures through the preponderant medium of Euro-American literary productions.

(6) Those non-Western works that find great favour with and circulate widely among the readers of the core countries, particularly the works chosen in and by the West for prestigious prizes, high praise and critical acclaim.

(7) The idea of the rise of a cultural *Weltmarkt* as a neutral arena where all nations, cultures, authors, etc., offer their literary goods and services.

(8) The mere circulation and exchange of works of literature across national borders and cultural boundaries.

(9) The steady internationalization of reading publics and of writing elites, sort of a cosmopolitanism of reading and writing.

(10) The mere internationalization and/or commercial globalisation of the literary.

Thus, contrary to the currently shrill claims of the postmodernists, globalisation and the processes, images, forms and vocabularies attendant on it seem like the fulfillment of the very modernity that Goethe and Marx struggled with while trying to comprehend, express and explain. Or, to put the matter somewhat differently, the '*Weltliteratur*' attendant on globalisation and its forming image is precisely the product of this European modernity pushed to its logical consequences in the very act of its total universalisation. If I were to use the fashionable terminology of the poststructuralists, I would have, then, to say that this emerging *Weltliteratur* is really more of a variation and/or shift of emphasis within the same relentlessly universalising modernity-paradigm (or modernity-problematique), than a shift or leap from one paradigm (or problematique) to another.

The pains, fears and hesitations attendant on this shift of emphasis from an older, thoroughly Eurocentric understanding of the concept of *Weltliteratur* to its newer and more comprehensive meaning are already evident in the later work of the great German literary scholar, critic and theoretician Erik Auerbach. According to Edward Said's account in *Culture and Imperialism*:

> When Auerbach, in a justly famous essay entitled 'Philologie der *Weltliteratur*', written after world War Two, takes note of how many 'other' (i.e. non-European) literary languages and literatures seemed to have emerged... he expresses more anguish and fear than pleasure at the prospect of what he seems so reluctant to acknowledge.[7]

Rise of Global Art Forms

I find extremely interesting and instructive the fact that at the time when a new, more authentic and more accurate understanding of the concept of world literature seems to be emerging—at least as far as the novel is concerned—proclamations in the core countries about the end of the novel, the demise of literature and the death of the author seem to grow more emphatic, cynical and defensive. I find no less interesting and instructive the fact that a peripheral author like Salman Rushdie should come to the defense of the novel as *the global art form* in the face of these Western Cassandras.

In an article entitled 'In Defence of the Novel Yet Again', published in the special issue of *The New Yorker* magazine devoted to fiction,[8] Rushdie retorted by arguing that if the European novel is suffering from decline and exhaustion in the eyes of some of its practitioners and critics, it does not follow at all that the novel, as a universally established world art form, is either exhausted or in decline or anywhere near dead. For Rushdie, these Europeans have to be made to understand that 'it doesn't matter where the great novels come from as long as they keep coming', and now they are coming from India, Latin America, Asia, Africa, and so on. In other words, these Europeans have to finally reconcile themselves to the dual fact that the originally European art of the novel can and will certainly survive an exhausted Europe and that the decline of the European novel stopped a long time ago from being the same thing as the decline of the novel *per se*.

For, according to Rushdie, might not what seems to these European pundits and epigoni as the end of the novel, 'be simply that a new novel is emerging—a postcolonial novel, a decentered, transnational, interlingual, cross-cultural novel... If we include writers from beyond the frontiers of Europe, it becomes clear that the world has rarely seen so rich a crop of fine novelists living and working at the same time'.

In brief, what I am suggesting is that Goethe's and Marx's concept of *Weltliteratur* is an idea whose time has come.

In the light of all this, *The Satanic Verses* takes on the guise of the multicultural, multinational world-novel *par excellence*. Most probably it is the first such novel we know of. So many cross cultural themes, topics, activities, worldviews, characters, politics, and so on, are fused in it and interwoven into its fabric and texture that you can alternatively describe it as the supra-national novelistic synthesis of the *fin-de-siècle* (or *fin-de-millènium*), globalising condition that is currently taking hold of humanity, For example, in the novel India, England, Islam, Europe, Iran, the West, the Arabs—as a settled past, as a lived present and as an anticipated future—do not simply coexist and impact each other at the periphery (*à la* E.

M. Forster's *A Passage to India*), nor are they merely contemporaneous with and adjacent to each other, but mesh and interpenetrate at all conceivable levels: economic, commercial, scientific, colonial, anti-colonial, political, ideological, religious, cultural, artistic, personal, sexual, etc.

As a result, we find *The Satanic Verses* on the one hand ambivalently celebrating, in theme and form, the exhilarating dynamism of this world-historical globalising process sweeping away over-defined and over-ossified identities, breaking restrictive cultural, social, political boundaries of all sorts and expanding along the way the experiential possibilities of each self. On the other Rushdie's novel senses and laments the dark, diabolical, even Mephistophelian and destructive underside of this world historical dynamism as represented in its devastating effects on historical communities, ancient nations, sacred cultures, proud peoples, such that all that had been thought solid and taken to be permanent and abiding seems to melt into thin air in no time.

The Satanic Verses is also a tale of two cities: Bombay and that other London, the London of the immigrant minorities from India, Bangladesh, Pakistan and the Caribbean that the author calls, 'A City Visible but Unseen'. Rushdie does artistically to Bombay and the 'City Visible but Unseen' what we all know Balzac did to Paris, Dickens to London, Joyce to Dublin and Naguib Mahfouz to Cairo, but with a difference. Rushdie's two cities are novelistically taken in and represented totally under the aspect of the new global condition and its universalist regime, not excluding all its tragi-comic effects and details. Only under this new regime does it become possible for a novel like *The Satanic Verses* to present the inhabitants of the 'City Visible but Unseen' as people who left their settlement to settle nowhere and regard that as a normal condition to boot.

In addition, *The Satanic Verses* is a world novel in a new sense precisely because it cannot be construed exclusively as an English novel about India, or an Indian novel about Islam, or an immigrant novel about Britain or a Third World novel about Europe, for it is all these things and much more. It is this brilliantly crafted surplus which makes it not only the world novel of our times, but also a world-class novel in its own right. Its diverse cultural, linguistic, ethnic, national, religious, stylistic, etc., components are dispersed all over the globe, but the resulting synthesis is still far more than any sum of its originally mutually exclusive and often hostile parts. In other words, it is at present the unrivalled world novel on account of its organic composition whereby India, Britain, Europe, Islam, the immigrants and so on, not only stop coexisting alongside each other, touching at the peripheries only, but proceed to become, by force of global circumstance, seriously constitutive of each other in an unprecedented manner and in unheard of ways.

This is why we can safely say that *The Satanic Verses* remains the leading novel not written with an exclusively European and/or American and/or Arab and/or Indian and/or African readership in mind. It is certainly not a world novel just because bad luck, adverse political developments and certain international conjunctures forced it on the attention of the whole world in a previously unheared of fashion. We can safely say as well, it is a world novel because it depicts so well the transitional period in which the consciousness of a new phase of world capitalism is being formed and expressed.

Furthermore, it is inconceivable that such a world novel could have been produced in French, German, Urdu or Arabic, for only English would do, given its status as globalisation's world language *par excellence*. Hence, the intriguing question: Is *The Satanic Verses* English literature or is it simply literature written in English? Or, are we seeing the breakdown of such distinctions, categories and classifications in favour of a higher and more comprehensive synthesis still to come?

In any case, the decisive links between Rushdie's innovative artistic practices, the vocabularies he devises, the structures and figures of speech that he invents to express this unprecedented global condition and relentless process are all there to be noted, investigated and appreciated by those willing and able to take the time and make the effort, particularly the professional literary critics and the specialized scholars.

In all this, we have on display as well, an act of postcolonial poetic justice whereby this Indian Muslim immigrant appropriates to himself the *lingua franca* of globalisation, twists it to suit his purposes, bends it to conform to his experiences, distorts it to serve his particular ends, hybridizes it to satisfy his special needs, exotizes it to express his foreign world and then resplashes this whole new literary concoction all over the globe. Now the exalted temples of learning in the Anglo-Saxon core of the core find themselves tending and teaching an English literature shot through and through with the peculiarities, mannerisms, expressions, distortion and themes of what their old colonialist graduates once arrogantly dismissed as the 'babu' of the natives. This is poetic justice indeed.

The upshot of it all is not only a babu-English subversively and periodically produced by a superior mastery of the master's tongue, but also a new Indo-European language that Rushdie baptized as 'this Angrezi in which I am forced to write'. His Angrezi, is, (a) intentionally well attuned to the textures of the ordinary and everyday in defiance of the formality and artificiality of much contemporary peripheral literary culture; (b) directed at subverting both the standards of the imperial English to which a writer like him is supposed to conform as well as the norms of the nativistic tongues to which he and his peers are constantly being called to authentically adopt; and (c) meant to become the denationalised locus of the global and universal, by at the same time confirming, challenging and subverting the *lingua franca* of the centre. This is why Rushdie will neither assimilate into the centre *à la* Naipaul nor go back home to cultivate God's nativist little literary and linguistic acre, *à la* Nagugi wa Thiong'o of Kenya.

Literary Logic of Globalising Capitalism

The relationship of the Rushdie affair and novel to the globalisation process is complex and many-sided. For example, globalisation provided the necessary and sufficient conditions for a debate over an 'English' satirical novel to transcend its local origins, British context, immigrant themes, religious skepticism, etc., and turned it into a transnational, transcultural, transcontinental global controversy and international scandal. In other words, globalisation is what helped turn *The Satanic Verses* from what may have never gone beyond an internal Muslim scandal and quarrel into a world-wide explosion, from what may have done no more than precipitate an Iranian-British dispute into a universal crisis and from what may have remained no more than another revolutionary Muslim Shi'i 'fatwa' into an international impasse.

Critics have noted how *The Satanic Verses* documents, uses, mimics, satirizes, caricatures and parodies the process of globalisation. I would like to go further by claiming that the novel may prove to be to the globalisation epoch and its image, what Naguib Mahfouz's trilogy of novels[9] have always been to Cairo's *Lebens Welt* and its image between the First and Second World Wars on the one hand and the 1919 and 1952 Egyptian Revolutions, on the other.

Similarly, if Fredric Jameson, one of America's most prominent literary critics and theoreticians today, finds it appropriate to characterize postmodernism as the 'cultural logic of late capitalism',[10] I see nothing wrong in describing *The Satanic Verses* as the finest expression to date of the 'literary logic of globalizing capitalism'. Again, if the world-system economist and analyst, Samir Amin, could call the emerging world of globalizing capitalism 'the empire of chaos',[11] then nothing should prevent us from regarding *The Satanic Verses* as the novel of that empire.

Two more details are worth mentioning in this connection. Considering that the stage on which the more spectacular aspects of the globalisation drama are unfolding and its battles are being fought is the ex-Third World and the ex-Soviet Union, the fact that the author of this first world-novel happens to be neither an American nor a European, but a Muslim Indian immigrant to the most classical of the classical core countries, acquires additional symbolic significance. Of similar importance is the fact that *The Satanic Verses* should have appeared in 1989, the very year in which the last obstacle to the unbridled gushing of capitalist globalisation vanished, viz., the collapse of European communism and the consequent rapid demise of the Soviet Union itself. For all these reasons, I find it very impoverishing to deal with Rushdie's novel as a purely Anglo-Indian literary phenomenon.

Globalisation often appears in *The Satanic Verses* as the realm of necessity to which all have to adjust on pain of marginalization, if not historical extinction. It comes through—for ill or good or some combination of the two—as destiny, or as the newly emerging destiny. In characters like Mimy Mamoulian, Hal Valance and Whisky Sssizodia, we have a first depiction of what it means to be a thoroughly globalised man and/or woman, globalised in aspirations, values, beliefs, travels, outlook, chicaneries, foibles, love affairs, financial dealings, crookery, and so on. The resulting image is not pretty: highly elastic people, all surfaces but no interiors, plenty of roles without a role, piles of dreams without a dream, lots of sensing and sensation without either sense or sensibility, the cacophony of a thousand and one voices, where no one finds his voice. This is the result of a world experienced as nothing more substantial than an unending series of opportunities, risks, accidents, bets, chances, adventures, occasions, deals and affairs upon affairs of all possible sorts and impossible kinds.

True to form, *The Satanic Verses* never tires of self-referentially reminding the reader that it is directly implicated in the globalisation process gushing out from the centre to the periphery. In the process, globalisation's discourses are parodied, its tensions reflected, its paradoxes recalled, its contradictions mocked, its pretentions debunked, its heroes satirized and its mannerisms, banalities, vulgarities, farces and pseudo-tragedies exposed.

In the novel, even the Joycean-Faulknerian stream of consciousness (or semi-unconsciousness), falls prey to the logic of this new necessity. In other words, this supposedly last privileged sphere of human subjectivity, spontaneity and freedom simply succumbs to the requirements and exigencies of a surrounding world of globalised dead objects and fetishized commodities, i.e. a world 'thingified' to the bitter end. In this sense, globalisation is also the generalized commodification of everything, everywhere and everywhen. This turns the literary stream of consciousness from an ostensibly autonomous form of becoming propelled by its own creative energies into an operation that unfolds according to the necessities and needs of an overwhelming process rapidly imposing itself on humanity's outer world, inner processes and intimate experiences.

We all remember how in Jean Paul Sartre's most celebrated novel, *La Nausee*, a thingified world of inert objects, lifeless commodities and neutral things relentlessly besieges Antoine Roquentin and gives him his bouts of nausea. This is Sartre's nausea of the spirit from which Antoine finds temporary respites only in the world of art and its consolations. But, here nausea is still the sign of the human subject's immersion in the world and of his/her complicity with the very dead objects that bring about the nausea attacks in the first place. In *The Satanic Verses* globalised commodification simply absorbs the human subject, reconstitutes his subjectivity accordingly and puts a radical end to this kind of 'healthy' nausea. Now who needs a refuge in art and its consolations? Still better, why not announce the end of art *tout court*.

To be fair to Rushdie, I must add that he is no mere aesthetic scoffer at either the emerging globalised human condition nor at the philistinism of the human types it secretes and forms. He earnestly seeks, I think, to transcend both the cynicism of the ironist's scoffing stance and the philistinism of the objects of his ironies in a more meaningful, humane and promising direction. Thus, we find *The Satanic Verses* working hard at the literary level—and quite successfully in my view—to transcend the by now well rehearsed dichotomy in the high modernist European novel between the lifeless objectivism of the noveau roman—*à la* Alain Robbe-Grillet—on the one hand and the chaotic gushing of a monotonous stream of subjective states of consciousness, associations, impressions, ideas, anticipations, emotions, perceptions, illusions, desires, hallucinations, etc., on the other.

For example, the characters of Robbe-Grillet's novels of the fifties experience no nausea because the complicity of human subjects in the world of objects simply ceased to exist. What now exists are neutral objects abstractly and geometrically described in a narrative from which even the author has been refined out of existence in favour of static structure, lifeless form and the supremacy of technique. Or, as Robbe-Grillet once commented: 'Les choses son les choses, et I' homme n' est que I'homme.' Given this hard and fast separation of human agency from the objects out there, no wonder all of Robbe-Grillet's characters turn out to be schizoids.

His famous movie, *L' Année Derniere à Marienbad* (1961, directed by Alain Resnais), is the best visual illustration of what I am describing.

No wonder either, that in Samuel Beckett's play *Oh' Les Beau Jours*, the only meaningful activity that engages the ever-sinking Winnie is fiddling endlessly with a few lifeless objects in a silly bag, talking non-stop to no one in particular about her trivial collection of ordinary daily-life articles, tooth brushes and all. This is modern Euro-American *Chosisme* at its finest, starkest and most hollow.

But in Rushdie's art in general and *The Satanic Verses* in particular, the two sides of this antinomy are mediated in manifold ways in the hope of yielding happier, more authentic and revealing visions of reality even under the aspect of a mercilessly globalising and thingifying condition. This is especially evident in the hallucinations of a mentally deranged character like Jibreel Farishta, because 'fools never lie', as Naguib Mahfouz reminds us in one of his novels. The deeper truths are grasped by Farishta because in him the parallel lines of the objective and the subjective meet, touch, criss-cross and at decisive moments coincide to enrich each other by yielding a higher, more accurate multidimensionality of vision which combines and surpasses the tedious unidimensionality of each side of the original dichotomy.

George Lukacs once observed: 'With present-day techniques anything from the atom bomb to the interior monologue can be photographed, and it is ultimately the writer's approach to reality that determines whether he produces a painting or a photograph, an articulate statement or a mute babbling.' As far as *The Satanic Verses* is concerned, I think Rushdie's approach to the new globalised reality allowed him to produce—in theme and form—a real painting and not just a photograph, an articulate statement and not a mere babbling. I say a painting on purpose, for, first, painting is to Rushdie's later novel, *The Moor's Last Sigh*, what film and cinema were to *The Satanic Verses*; and second, because the multidimensionality of colour in painting acquires its analogue in Rushdie's art in the multidimensionality of word and phrase, for which he is justly famous.

Notes

1. Edward Said, *Orientalism*, New York: Pantheon Books, 1978.
2. 'Orientalism and Orientalism in Reverse', *Forbidden Agendas*, London: Al-Saqi Books, 1994. Also, Alexander Lyon MacFie (ed.), *Orientalism: A Reader*, New York : New York University Press, 2000, pp. 217-238. For the Arabic version, see my book *The Tabooing Mentality: Salman Rushdie and the Truth of Literature*, Damascus and Beirut: Al-Mada Publications, 3rd edition, 1997, pp. 13-92.
3. Sadik J. Al-Azm, 'The Importance of Being Earnest about Salman Rushdie', *Reading Rushdie: Perspectives on the Fiction of Salman Rushdie*, edited by D.M. Fletcher, Amsterdam: Rodopi Publications, 1994, pp. 255-292. For the much longer Arabic version, see *The Tabooing Mentality: Salman Rushdie and the Truth of Literature*, pp. 163-300.
4. Francis Fukuyama, 'The End of History', *The National Interest*, Summer, 1989, pp. 3-18. Also his *The End of History and the Last Man*, New York: The Free Press, 1992.
5. Sammuel P. Huntington, 'The Clash of Civilizations?, *Foreign Affairs*, Summer, 1993, pp. 22-49. Also his *The Clash of Civilizations and the Remaking of World Order*, New York: Simon and Schuster, 1996.
6. Milan Kundera, *Testaments Betrayed*, London: Faber and Faber, 1995.
7. Edward Said, *Culture and Imperialism*, New York: Alfred A. Knoff, 1995, p.45
8. Salman Rushdie, 'In Defense of the Novel Yet Again', *The New Yorker*, 24 June, 1996, pp. 48-55.
9. Naguib Mahfouz, *Palace Walk*, Cairo, 1956; *Palace of Desire*, Cairo, 1957; *Sugar Street*, Cairo, 1957.
10. Fredric Jameson, *Postmodernism or the Cultural Logic of Late Capitalism*, London: Verso Books, 1991.
11. Samir Amin, *Empire of Chaos*, New York: Monthly Review Press, 1992.

Exploring Composite Culture in India

NEERA CHANDHOKE

Historically significant moments arise in the biography of any polity, when that polity is forced to rethink, and perhaps renegotiate the basic categories that have served as its foundational concepts and norms till then. This re-negotiation may be prompted by a number of compelling factors. For instance, the normative concept may have been hijacked for a variety of purposes that prove antithetical to the norm itself, it may have been subjected to some abuse, or the validity of the norm itself may have come under challenge. Whatever be the specific cause for the challenge to the norm, what we need to recognise at this point is that the historical conditions within which certain concepts and norms first emerge on to the political horizon change, and they change dramatically. A different temporal experience may, therefore, call for either of two strategies; it may demand another set of conceptual categories altogether; alternatively the moment may call for the strengthening of a particular conceptual category simply because it is both politically desirable as well as politically relevant. This is not to say that there are no eternal answers for the eternal questions of the human condition. It is merely to suggest that answers to these eternal questions remain bound by temporality, even as the questions themselves continue to bedevil the human condition.

I will suggest in this essay that the idea that India possesses a rich composite culture has been threatened by two moments in the history of the country. The first moment arose when the strategies of the colonial power were to fragment the idea that Indian society had built upon various cultural resources to create a shared, a rich and a multi-textured composite culture. The second moment arose in the 1980s, when a series of historical events, most notably the consolidation of majoritarianism of *Hindutva*, challenged the notion that Indians across religious and cultural persuasions had much in common, and that this united them in projects of social co-existence. Both moments demanded and demand that the notion of a composite culture be strengthened, by the delineation of tangible political norms that guarantee the right to equality and freedom to all participants in shared ways of life that theorists call composite culture. To put it differently, I suggest that there are moments when cultural categories may need to be reinforced by liberal and democratic political norms that deliver justice to all.

I

Let me begin the argument by suggesting that the most troublesome question that hovers over the collective life of a multicultural, multireligious, and multilingual society like India is the following; what are the terms and conditions under which people who subscribe to different and perhaps incommensurable belief systems can live together in some kind of dignity and civility? What are the measures that allow for social co-existence and perhaps social co-operation? The answers to these questions acquire some urgency today, for we live in somewhat troubled times marked by incivility, intolerance, and communalisation; all of them being features of our contemporary moment. And the contemporary political moment in India has been forged by the politics of Hindutva, as well as by what has been generically called the global ethnic explosion.'

Provided that the question posed above is valid, that is, provided we accept that we need to think out the ways in which people in India who belong to different religious, linguistic and cultural persuasions can live together in some peace, we can proceed to choose any one of the following options. First, we can go back to the past, see how these questions have been historically negotiated, and transfer the discourses found there and then to the present. Second, we can renounce history and opt for the discourses of the present that may possibly offer a solution. Third, we can break with both our present as well as the past and start completely afresh to chalk out new ways of living. Fourth, we can begin to build on both our collective past and present in order to think out what political possibilities present themselves to our collective gaze.

The last option seems to me to be profitable, for we in India cannot renounce our past, simply because that past had brought together people across religion, caste, and language, in one of the most massive and magnificent movements for freedom from colonialism. Historians have told us that the extent to which the freedom movement in India mobilised the masses rivalled the most dramatic liberation movement the world has seen: that of China. This was not all, for the people of India were to throw up all the values that are indispensable for the modern democratic condition—freedom, equality, democracy, rights, and secularism in and through the process of struggle. And the gains of political struggle are of value because they signify the ways in which people make their histories together, the ways in which ordinary people insert themselves into history, which can be otherwise fairly elitist and exclusive. Further, any path that we wish to tread in order to arrive at a desired future cannot but be historically informed. After all in order to know where we are now and where we wish to go to from here, we first of all need to know where we have come from. Any sound political understanding has to be in other words sound historical understanding. There is no alternative to robust historically informed understanding.

Now one of the concepts that have been generated by and through the intricacies of Indian history is that of composite culture. The thesis of composite culture simply suggests that the inhabitants of Indian society during the course of working and living together, or through the *practices of everyday life*, had developed a common, transcendent culture that both merged as well as surpassed the best of component cultures. This development, that is, the merger or rather the transcendence of two or more cultures was of course purely unintentional. No one had deliberately set out to fabricate such a transcendental culture in art, in architecture, in music, in linguistics, or for that matter in the practices of everyday life. Indeed, if some one had attempted to do so, if someone had attempted to tamper with cultural practices to make them conform to the dictates of another culture they may have been faced with tremendous resistance and the closing in of minds and of cultural boundaries. This is at least what the recent history of our world tells us: whenever communities have been forced to set aside their own meaning systems and adopt those of others we have the makings of a politically explosive situation on our hands. But India's composite culture represented the outcome of an unintended but a creative process; inasmuch as when people who belong to diverse persuasions came together for the purposes of work or of recreation, when they drew upon their collective resources for facing natural calamities or when they celebrated their victories over these calamities together, they created a common culture.

Witness for example the evolution of the Hindustani classical music tradition, which represents perhaps the finest examples of India's composite culture. Recollect for instance the awesome devotional mood in which the maestro Ustad Bade Ghulam Ali Khan sings the Hindu *bhajan* 'Hari Om Tatsat'. To an outsider, the very idea that vocalist who had been born into a Muslim household can realise selfhood through and in the intricacies of a Hindu devotional raga, may seem inexplicable. What makes Khan Saheb's rendering of the *bhajan* seem such a sublime experience given that he professed a different religion altogether? This question may continue to perplex an outsider who is unfamiliar with the ways of the Indian people. But it will not perplex an Indian.

For the Hindustani classical tradition was to bring together both Hinduism and Islam to create a new genre of music that appeals both to Ram as well as Rahim, to Nizammudin Auliya as well as to the pranks of the child Krishna, to Salim Chisti as well as to Radha's yearning for fulfilment with her God. Now a cynic can suggest that this merger was dictated by patronage, by the fact of a Muslim vocalist composing and singing for a Hindu King or a Hindu patron, or a Hindu vocalist singing for a Muslim patron. This is true to some extent. After all, if the great Faiyyaz Khan composed music for the Hindu King of Baroda or for a Mohan Seth both of whom extended patronage to him, he could hardly sing of an idiom that was unfamiliar to them.

But this would be too mundane, too simplistic an answer, for the classical tradition draws its *raison d'etre* from another source altogether, the folk tradition. As any student of Hindustani music knows, up to the time of Kumar Gandharava (who it is said filled the pitcher of classical music with the water of the folk tradition), the classic tradition drew heavily upon folk music and the folk tradition. And since the Indian folk tradition is replete with, permeated by, dipped in, the stories of the immortal love of Radha and Krishna, the devotional mood of the Navratra's, the joyousness of a Holi, the happiness of the harvesting season, vocalists could not but be singing of experiences that may seem on the face of it to belong only to the Hindus. The important point is that this culture of everyday life belonged to all, it was the joint inheritance of all. A Hindu who writes in Persian of Arabic, or an M.F Hussain who sketches the figure of Saraswati with a few strokes of his artistic genius are both the beneficiaries of these shared cultural resources. Therefore, Bade Ghulam Ali Khan can sing 'Hari Om Tatsat' with as much ease as the poet Gulzar can compose lyrics in pristine Urdu. It is commendable that the classical musical, artistic, and literary tradition continues to retain this eclectic *espirit* despite attempts since the early twentieth century to purify and Sanskritise it in the service of Hinduism.

It was precisely this composite culture that was to find expression and codification in one of the most widely spoken languages of northern India: Urdu. It is interesting that whereas both Sanskrit and Persian remained confined to the intelligentsia in India's pre-colonial life, increasingly a third language was to eclipse other languages as the language of everyday life in the northern part of the country. This was Urdu. The term Urdu was founded by the poet Mir in 1752, who called it *Urdu-e-Mu'alla* or courtly language. But actually Urdu, which derives from the Turkish word *Ortu* (a military camp) was developed in the cantonments and in the bazaars. Evolving from *khari boli*, which is a branch of Hindi spoken in the region, and which owes its origins to one of the linguistic families of Sanskrit, Urdu is a *patois*, where a Persian-Arabic vocabulary has been grafted on to to a *prakrit* syntax and grammar. For these reaons a variety of people across religious and regional identities took to the language. Urdu acquired a still more communicable *avatar* in the form of Hindustani, which could be written in both the Persian-Arabic as well as in the Devanagari script, often along gender lines. In Punjab, for instance, the male section of the population essayed Hindustani in the Arabic script whereas women wrote the language in the Devanagari script. In effect, Urdu in its *avatar* as Hindustani became a link language in large parts of northern India. It is worthwhile to recollect that both Gandhiji as well as Pandit Nehru insisted that it was Hindustani rather than the Sanskritised Hindi that should become the national language of the country, for Hindustani could be written in two and possibly more scripts and thus serve to connect diverse populations.

Now if we view language as not only the spoken word but something that is connected deeply to the kind of human beings that we are, a shared language becomes the highest representation of a shared culture. For a language is after all connected to the collective understandings of a community, understandings that commonly go by the name of culture. To speak a language is simply to articulate presuppositions and assumptions that are culturally specific. Language, to put it differently, is *contextual* because it always refers to my being in a particular way of life. Urdu representing shared understandings and meaning systems, therefore, codified India's composite culture.

It was this composite culture that the historian Tara Chand spoke of when he suggested that the conquerors who arrived from Central Asia with a religion and a culture in many ways diverse and even contradictory, gradually evolved a number of common customs and common characteristics of culture with other people. For instance, people of a region began to speak the same language irrespective of their religion. Since language, Tara Chand goes on to suggest, is both the medium of expression and emotion as well as constitutive of expression and emotion, it is not surprising that literature produced by Hindus and Muslims in Indian languages shows remarkable closeness, mutual understandings, and similarity of attitude and feelings. This is because social interaction between members of different religious groups affected both the religious as well as the secular idiom, even as the two groups borrowed from each other their customs and manners. The same theme is echoed in the historical works of Ishwari Prasad, S. Abid Hussain, M. Mujeeb, Humayun Kabir and Asim Roy. M. Mujeeb, who told us that the Sufi Malik Muhammed who composed the *Padmavat* in the *avadhi* dialect greatly influenced the way in which Sant Tulsidas wrote the *Ramayana*, echoes Ishwari Prasad who wrote that the two communities shared their joys and their sorrows simply because they lived together.

Historians of composite culture such as Mushirul Hasan tell us that since Islam entered India through many paths and different entrances over large historical spans of time, and since Muslims settled in different regional settings, they acquired the hue and the complexion of their setting. There was no Muslim identity but only Punjabi Muslims, Keralite Muslims or the Muslims of Tamilnadu with little in common except a few common rituals. To put it differently, Hasan suggests that since Islam entered India not in a single time span but in succession, divided unevenly across different periods, its diffusion took place in a variety of forms. Ordinary Muslims were not, he insists, members of a monolithic community sitting sullenly apart, but active participants in regional cultures whose perspectives they shared. In fact, they saw Islam as a religion that was itself differentiated internally into a number of detailed commitments. And Asim Roy, in his evocative, *The Islamic Syncretistic Tradition in Bengal,* argues that precisely because an exogenous Islamic tradition based on Perso-Arabic literatures failed to interact with the world of the exclusively Bengali-speaking Muslims, it was set aside by them in favour of a local, a more familiar and meaningful syncretistic Islamic tradition.

The most eloquent articulation of the idea of India's composite culture was to come from two of India's most towering statesmen: Maulana Abdul Kalam Azad and Pandit Nehru. In Azad's well known words, since full eleven centuries had passed since Islam came to India, it now had as much a claim on the soil of India as the Hindu religion. 'Just as a Hindu can say with pride that he is an Indian and a Hindu so also we can say with equal pride that we are Indians and follow Islam.' And Pandit Nehru, India's tallest statesman, could say with equal pride that the strength of Hinduism was its 'cultural multiplicity', which had developed over thousands of years. He wrote:

> Hundreds of vivid pictures of this past filled my mind and they would stand out as soon as I visited a particular place associated with them. At Sarnath, near Benaras, I would almost see the Buddha preaching his first sermon, and some of his recorded words would come like a distant echo to me through two thousand five hundred years. Asoka's pillars of stone with their inscriptions would speak to me in their magnificent language and tell me of a man, who though an emperor was greater than any King or emperor. At Fatehpur Sikri, Akbar forgetful of his empire, was seated holding a converse and debate with the learned of all faiths, curious to learn something new and seeking an answer to the external problem of man.

Such was India to Pandit Nehru: a country in which an amalgam of all that is best in her constituent cultures created a shared symbolic world, a society where people could rise above the petty boundaries of narrow and chauvinistic faiths and glory in the many options of a composite culture. His *Discovery of India* unfolds with vivid clarity a series of snapshots that reveal common traits, habits, ways of living, artistic tastes in music, painting, architecture, food, clothing, common festivals, languages, and above all a common response to the problems of everyday life. This conviction was reflected in Pandit Nehru's politics. Because the culture of India was composed of a many and variegated strands, each of these strands had *place of pride* in the country's politics. *Each of the components of India's composite culture and of her multi-varied social fabric had rights by right, simply because they belonged integrally to the political and the cultural imaginary we call India.* Consequently, when he spoke at Aligarh Muslim University on 24 January 1948, Pandit Nehru was to make the following political commitment:

> For my part I wish to say that inspite of everything, I have a firm faith in India's future. Indeed, if I did not have it, it would not have been possible for me to work effectively. Although many of my old dreams have been shattered by recent events, yet the basic objective still

> holds and I see no reason to change it. That objective is to build up a free India of high ideals, and noble endeavours where there is equality of opportunity for all and where many variegated streams of thought and culture meet together to form a mighty river of progress and advancement for her people... You are Muslims and I am a Hindu. We may adhere to different religious faiths or even to none, but that does not take away from that cultural inheritance that is yours as well as mine. The past holds us together; why should the present or the future divide us in spirit?

Eloquent sentiments, conviction and passion permeated Nehru's commitment to the ideal of a composite culture simply because he realised that ordinary people had come together to both creatively build on their own traditions as well as create something new. This was to be the blueprint of his new polity. Therefore he was to suggest that whatever be the confusion that marks the present, 'in the future India will be a land, as in the past, of many faiths, equally honoured and respected, but of one national outlook, not I hope, a narrow nationalism living in its own shell, but rather the tolerant creative nationalism which believes in itself and in the genius of its people.'

Arguably Pandit Nehru's convictions presaged the currently fashionable themes of multiculturalism and minority protections that form a dominant part of contemporary political theory. But this was not born out of his personal conviction alone, or out of his adherence to the dictates of trendy political theorising. His understanding of India's past was historically constituted, forged as it was through the prism of a temporally specific experience. To put it differently, Pandit Nehru's commitment to the idea of India's composite culture was born out of two historical events. The first event related to the way the nationalists were to respond to the strategies of the colonial power to categorise and classify the people of India in the moulds of ascriptive identities. The second and a related event was equally nationalist: it drew upon the idea of a composite culture in order to create and construct a pan-Indian freedom struggle out of a diverse mass of people who had been split by the divisive strategies of the colonial power.

That the British set themselves out to deliberately fracture and fragment Indian society by the construction of categories whereby people came to be known by their religion or their caste is by now well known. The first ploy employed by the colonial power was to interpret major happenings in terms of religion. In the context of Ayodhya, for instance, the historian Sushil Srivastava tells us that Montgomery Martin, a British official charged with collecting information on Eastern India in 1838, observed that:

> ...the destruction [of the Hindu temples] is very generally attributed by the Hindus to the furious zeal of Aurangzeb, to whom is also imputed the overthrow of the temple at Benaras and Mathura. What may have been the case in the two latter, I shall not now take upon myself to say, but with respect to Ayodhya the tradition seems unfounded.

Matters were different twelve years thereon. By 1850 P. Carnegie, a British officer of the Bengal civil service, was to write thus: 'The Janamsthan was in Ramkot and marked the birthplace of Rama. It seems that in A.D. 1528, Babur visited Ayodhya and under his orders this ancient temple was destroyed and on its site was built what came to be known as Babur's mosque.' The British may have invented this myth, suggests Srivastava, in order to legitimise their annexation of the province of Avadh. Whatever be the reason for the invention of this particular colonial stereotype, we in India have had to pay heavy costs in terms of fractured communities and a divided people, simply because the stereotype plays neatly into the hands of communal elements. In this and other ways the politics of colonialism served to foster divisions among a people that had learnt to live together and work together.

The second ploy that the British adopted was equally divisive: that of the politics of enumeration or the census. Whereas on the one hand the way in which empirical data is accumulated for the census (what caste or religious group do you belong to?) *constructs* identites, the recognition that any given community has so many members *reinforces* identities. The first census in 1881, for instance, told Indians that Muslims constituted 19.7 per cent of the total population, the rest of the population was presumably constituted by the Hindu community. The politics of enumeration were naturally to influence the way in which people were to recognise themselves as well as others as those who belonged or who did not belong. They were in short to result in the politics of majoritarianism and minorityism. Consequently, even as identities were constructed along the axis of enumerated communities, whether of religion, caste, or language, the social fabric of Indian society was rent apart by the politics of exclusiveness.

Now identities, as any one knows, are multiple, conflictual, and overlapping. Our class, gender, caste, or religious identities are organised around different and often antagonistic sites and discourses. Therefore identities are neither fixed nor given, and which identity we privilege depends largely on the context of its articulation. But it is equally true that when one identity comes to bear the imprimatur of the state, it breeds spillover's in the way people conceptualise themselves in terms of who they are and what they stand for. This was more than manifest as we saw the freedom struggle degenerate into a host of competing identities in the early part of the twentieth century. We saw groups organising themselves along the axis of religion to make their demands, and we saw in the process the reinforcement of the very identities that the colonial power had given to us. Therefore, the idea that India has no shared culture and that therefore it could never aspire to nationhood came to command the imaginations of both the colonised as well as those who do the colonising. And these imaginations were to bear the same consequences: the dissolution of a shared composite culture.

Expectedly, the nationalists responded to both the divisive strategies of colonialism, as well as to the divisiveness of political identities in civil society by drawing upon the idea that Indians shared a composite culture. In other words, the notion that the country was not an *aggregation* of different communities but a *composite* that possessed a transcendental culture, was India's *nationalist* response to the colonial imaginary that India had no shared language, understanding, or tradition, and that it possessed but the history of conflicts and divisions. And as nationalist responses go, this particular response was to present the composite culture that had emerged out of the interaction of two cultures as non-conflictual. To put it differently, the idea represented *one* facet of Indian life, that people had, through the processes of working and living together, managed to carve out regions of shared meanings despite the fact that they professed different faiths. After all, a nationalist coalition had to represent shared visions, shared projects, and a shared culture. Therefore, the notion that India possessed a composite culture constituted the core of the nationalist imaginary. The idea was neither wholly fact nor wholly fiction but like all good ideas it worked, for some time at least, to bring together people in a wide ranging freedom struggle. But there were other dimensions of this phenomenon, which were perhaps *not* underscored for very good reasons, these reasons having to do with the exigencies of building a nationalist coalition.

In retrospect, it is difficult to escape the realisation that part of the reason why people in India in the period before the late nineteenth century could live together without clashing on every matter, little or small, had to do with the economic and the political context of the times. For communities, whether Hindu or Muslim, lived, as anthropologists put it, in a 'back to back' relationship with each other. They could speak the same language, sing the same songs, celebrate and mourn together, simply because they were *not* competing for either political or economic power in a society where competition happens to be the very logic of existence. The logic of pre-market economies, we need to understand, is very different to that of market economies; the former is characterised by what is known as the moral economy of the peasantry, the latter is marked by what is known as the instrumental economy of competition. And the logic of electoral competition as we know from our bitter experience in India, is not any less instrumental, constructing as it does exclusive identities in order to secure vote banks. People in pre-modern India, in other words, could show *tolerance* to each other and to other faiths because they were *not* caught up in the competitive populism of either the market or that of elctoral democracy.

Matters were undeniably different when the people of India began to organise themselves for the purposes of political representation in the 1880s in and through the Indian National

Congress, and when they began to organise themselves for the material benefits that power brings with it. The enervating logic of the market made its presence felt in the shape of competition for jobs, for economic benefits, and in the shape of contending projects of garnering wealth. And when people compete it is easy to organise projects around exclusive identities, which arguably may not be the main way in which they perceive themselves, but which may simply be convenient for purposes of garnering political and material support. In the process, divisions within religious and cultural blocs were flattened out and communities were homogenised for purposes of political representation and economic competition. It was difference more than commonality that began to command the political imagination of deeply divisive movements organised around Hinduism and Islam.

It was this development that the nationalists sought to counter by the thesis of India's composite culture. But somewhat expectedly, even as the freedom movement put forth the idea of India's composite culture as a *response* to the colonial manipulations, the common culture that had emerged unintendedly out of the myriad of social interactions and transactions between the Indian people began to fragment and fray at the edges. From the early twentieth century, therefore, we begin to witness what can be called the *paradox* of India's freedom struggle. On the one hand as the base of the national movement widened in the 1920s with the advent of Mahatma Gandhi, as he proceeded to finely hone the techniques of resistance he had developed in South Africa, as he proceeded to build up a mass struggle, and as previously marginalised groups were politicised and brought into the public arena of the anti-colonial struggle, Indian society was united as never before, under the overaching call for freedom and independence.

But somewhat contradictorily, deep social divisions were never quite as unequivocally discernible, as they were in that period. The hold of religion on the popular psyche was never quite as apparent, as when it began to be politicised and made the propellant of political movements, which were to finally divide India irremediably on the basis of religion. Groups organising themselves for and around Hinduism or

Islam played into every stereotype of the British who had declared religion to be the mainstay of identities in the country. This development understandably led to disastrous consequences.

Witness, for instance, the fate of Urdu in India. Once the language of the courts, of the judicial system, of the bureaucracy, and of literary transactions, today for a variety of political reasons Urdu has been excluded from the benefits that should naturally be attached to a creative language. If the language has survived it is because of its usage in the Bombay film industry, as the language of love, as the language of longing, or as the language of grief, but never a language of everyday life, which is connected to the street, the job, the bazaar, the coffee house, public meetings, and all the other institutions that constitute the public sphere of civil society.

Urdu, or its more communicable *avatar* Hindustani, as suggested above, had united people in northern India. But oddly it was Hindustani that was to become one of the main targets of the Hindi-Hindu *wallah's* when it came to notions of who belonged and who did not in the new nation. The issue was actually the reverse: who did the nation belong to? For projects of nation building inevitably embody within them projects of power. Therefore even as the movement for the hegemony of Hindi as the national language made its appearance in north India, we find a twist in the tale. For although the case for Hindi was primarily propelled by movements anxious to emancipate the country from the influence of an alien language like English, and though the idea of Hindi as the national language constituted an integral part of the national vision, increasingly it acquired a communal complexion. And the movement was simultaneously to position itself against Urdu and Hindustani as the spoken language of the people simply because Urdu was identified with Islam. Therefore, the movement for Hindi set itself out to purge the language of all Urdu words and symbols. Despite the efforts of Gandhiji who wanted Hindustani written in both the scripts as the link language of India, and who wanted scripts to resemble and reflect the spoken word, the spoken language of the people was once again subordinated to the language of power, precisely the way it had happened during the hegemonisation of Sanskrit, Persian, and English.

For instance, commonly used words like *padho* (study) were replaced by an archaic word like *adhyan*, and *trikon* or the triangle was replaced by *tribhuj*, even as Hindi was emptied out of its Urdu components. In the process, the spoken language of the people was stripped of its vitality and vibrancy. In sum, if one aspect of the movement for Hindi was connected to the politics of emancipation from colonial rule and colonized mentalities, the other aspect revealed a rankly communal face. In time the idea of Hindi-Hindu-Hindustan posited not only a close link between a language and nationhood, but also between language and religion.

We in India still bear the scars of this particular development. For even though the issue of linguistic states was settled in the 1960s, in a politically volatile country like India, language, like other indicators of group identity, can still prove combustible. Consider for instance that as recently as the 28th of September 1989, bitter riots erupted in Badaun in Uttar Pradesh (U.P.) around the decision of the state government to make Urdu the second language of the state. This of course has a history. On the 8th of October 1947, the state government of what was then the United Provinces had opted to make Hindi the state language even before the Constituent Assembly had taken a decision on official languages. The decision of the state-level Congress leadership, to make Hindi written in the Devenagari script an official language, violated the earlier preference of the Congress party for Hindustani written in both scripts as the official language. The reasons for this decision are not difficult to fathom. They had largely to do with the communalisation of Indian politics in the first half of the twentieth century when Urdu came to be identified with the Muslim minority, even though countless linguists and political commentators have argued that Urdu as spoken in north India has more to do with Hindustani than Persian. Arguably, the decision to allot Hindi written in the Devanagari script the status of the official language of U.P. made Urdu redundant in the very region where it was spoken.

Now decisions on official languages breed momentous consequences in terms of material advantages or disadvantages. On the one hand a group can feel that it is materially deprived because another language has been privileged as the language of material, social, cultural and political transactions. We have thus the makings of political alienation on our hands. For the speakers of the language that is widely used in these transactions have an unfair advantage over others who do not speak the language or those who are not bilingual. On the other hand, the speakers of the language that is termed official are empowered because their tongue has been included as the medium of the many transactions of a society, and because the survival of any language is connected with material benefits. Therefore, the decision to restore Urdu to its status as the second language in Uttar Pradesh in 1989 was to spark off communal riots in the name of language riots. The rioting remained confined to Badaun and did not spill over the borders, as most communal riots are prone to do in the country. But it testifies to the fact that the shared world of linguistic understanding had been fragmented by the pursuit of economic and political power.

In sum, the consequences of the paradoxical nature of the freedom struggle were significant. For leaders realised that the *notion of a composite culture could not by itself form the bedrock of the struggle*. If the movement had to mobilise vast masses of people in a struggle for freedom. It had to draw upon other more tangible resources. If it had to build coalitions among groups, many of which had been propelled politically to position themselves against each other, the movement had to convince all the participants that they were of equal importance and that they would not be discriminated agianst in the new state.

Now Gandhiji with his firm belief that religion established bonds among people could call upon the capacity of religious traditions, many of which were shared, to tolerate and respect other forms of worship. But for more pragmatic leaders like Nehru who were steeped in modernity, though India's composite culture was of value, one of its component that is religion could cut both ways. After all by the end of the 1920s separate electorates and rabidly communal organisations had erupted on the scene of Indian politics in the name of religion. For these reasons, at times Nehru showed profound discomfort with the evocation of religion in politics by Gandhiji:

> I [he wrote] used to be troubled sometimes at the growth of this religious element in our politics, both on the Hindu and the Muslim side. I did not like it at all... Even some of Gandhiji's phrases sometimes jarred upon me—thus his frequent references of Ram Raj as a golden age which was to return. But I was powerless to intervene, and I consoled myself with the thought that Gandhiji used tho words because they were well known and understood by the masses. He had an amazing knack of reaching the heart of the people.

Pandit Nehru was to express the same discomfort when Gandhiji undertook a fast in September 1932:

> I watched the emotional upheaval of the country during the fast, and I wondered more and more if this was the right method in politics. It seemed to be sheer revivalism and clear thinking had not a ghost of a chance against it. I felt I was drifting further and further away from him mentally in spite of my strong emotional attachment to him.

Experiencing deep apprehension as he watched this 'sheer revivalism', Nehru was convinced that though India possessed a vibrant composite culture to appeal to this fact alone *as the basis of civility and co-existence in the new and a rather fragile State, would be an appeal to too nebulous, too ambiguous a concept*. No society, which aspired towards the establishment of harmony between religious groups that had come to confront each other in such a murderous fashion, could build its foundations on such an unstable, on such a fragile principle alone. For if a shared culture forms the core of humanity, if it tell us how to be human, and if it binds us as Gandhiji said indissolubly to the truth, the most in human atrocities have also been carried out in the name of one of its components, that is, religion—crusades, jihad, holy wars, communal rioting and genocide. 'What a disgustingly savage people we are', wrote an anguished Nehru in his diary while in prison in 1935. 'Politics, progress, socialism, communism, science, where are they before this black religious savagery?'

In short, the idea of a composite culture was not just enough when it came to the construction of either the freedom movement or the postcolonial nation. Asture political leaderships realised that in order to forge alliances between groups, the movement had to appeal to principles that were strictly outside the internal ideology systems of the various groups themselves. It was in response to this that Nehru built on the Gandhian notions of *sarva dharma sambhava* to privilege the doctrine of secularism, citizenship rights, and minority protections, all the political norms which had been thrown up during the course of the freedom struggle. None of these neutralised the thesis of India's composite culture, but strengthened it immeasurably.

Consider that in the hands of Pandit Nehru *sarva dharma sambhava* which meant that each religion occupies an equal slot in India's composite culture, was to translate into secularism. Ironically in all these attacks on secularism, we often forget that secularism in India had been devised during the freedom struggle and reinforced during the deliberations of the Consituent Assembly, as a moral response to divisive strategies. Secularism had been devised precisely to negotiate inter-religious relationships; to grant the freedom of religious belief; to ensure equality of all the religious groups, and to assure the minorities that their identities would be safe. *It was meant to safeguard both shared understandings as well as grant people the right to their particular meaning systems.* It was in pursuance of these objectives, that Pandit Nehru was to declare, '[t]he government of a country like India, with many religions that have secured great and devoted following for generations, can never functions satisfactorily in the modern age except on a secular basis.'

On another occasions he was to reiterate this principle:

> It is perhaps not very easy even to find a good word in Hindi for 'secular'. Some people think that it means something opposed to religion. That obviously is not correct. What it means is that it is a state which honours all faiths equally and gives them equal opportunities; that, as a state, it does not allow itself to be attached to one faith or religion, which then becomes the state religion.

The norm of equality of all religions, and the distancing of the state from all religious groups, was specifically meant to assure the minorities that they had a legitimate place in the country, and that they would not be discriminated against. Correspondingly, secularism established that the majority group would not be privileged in any manner. The creed, therefore, discouraged any pretension that the majority religion had any right to stamp the body politic with its ethos.

In sum, the concept of secularism that emerged in India gave body and substance to the doctrine of composite culture inasmuch as it both recognised as well as revalued the *status specificity* of each component of the complex.

Correspondingly, the minorities were reassured that they would not be discriminated against in any way. 'Anything that creates such an apprehension in the minds of any group in India is to be deprecated. It tends to disturb and it is opposed to our secular ideal', wrote Nehru to the Pradesh Congress Committees in August 1954. Not to consider any of the religious minorities as much a part of India as any one else, 'immediately leads us away from both our secular and democratic ideals'.

But people could only transcend deeply divisive tendencies when they had tangible identities to draw on, firm solidarities and affiliations to sustain themselves with, political principles and norms to regulate their relationships with others and substantive loyalties that breed camaraderie and fraternity, all of which would support the idea of a composite culture. A further hope underpinned the leadership in the post independence period. It was hoped that people would in time transcend their religious affiliations and come to view themselves as citizens of the country just as they had historically transcended their religious affiliations and come to create a composite culture. The creation of an autonomous public sphere where people would act as citizens unencumbered by the political and the moral weight of their community affiliations was to reflect the best themes of this culture—unity in diversity. This would provide the key to a modern India. In a modern India, people would not spend their time in rituals that sapped and exhausted their energy because they filled their imaginations to the exclusion of other things. They would have access to other identities, other forms of solidarity, and other bondings in civil and political society.

Whatever their beliefs in their personal lives, in the public sphere they would be able to transcend religion and again reinstate the norm of a composite culture now translated as a shared political culture.

The three ideas of 'a composite culture, secularism and democracy', these were the gods of the newly independent countries of the 'third world'. Whenever, and wherever religion was invoked in the postcolonial world, it was as a component of, not as a substitute for, national identity. Despite the fact that the movement for Pakistan had been fought in the name of Islam, Jinnah ruled out the idea that a theocratic state would be established in the country. Inaugurating the Constituent Assembly of Pakishtan on the eve of the formation of the country on 11 August 1947, Jinnah promised equality to all citizens of Pakistan:

> Now I think we should keep that in front of us as our ideal, and you will find that in course of time Hindus will cease to be Hindus and Muslims will cease to be Muslims, not in the religious sense, because that is the personal faith of each individual, but in the political sense as citizens of the state.

On the other hand, Nehru insisted that whatever the shape of things may be in Pakistan, in India we must pursue with great vigour efforts to form a secular state, in which everybody could walk with his head held high. 'India', declared Pandit Nehru firmly, 'is a secular nation which guarantees equality of citizenship to people of all religions'.

At the same time, minorities were reassured that their identities were perfectly safe in India. Therefore, Article 29 (1) of the fundamental rights chapter lays down that 'Any section of the citizens residing in the territory of India or any part thereof having a distinct language script or culture of its own shall have the right to conserve the same'. This constitutional provision has two dimensions. One, it recognises that linguistic and religious cultures are valuable for their members; that members of minority cultures can face disadvantages in a majoritarian society, and that, therefore, these members need to be given explicit rights to their own culture. Two, the right to culture is an individual right. This article along with Article 30 which guarantees that all religious and linguistic minorities are given the right to establish and administer educational institutions of their choice, are grouped together under cultural and educational rights. These two articles have to be read along with Articles 25 to 28 that grant the freedom of religion in order to comprehend the range of protections afforded to religious groups.

In a manner of speaking, the grant of these minimal rights to religion and culture was historically overdetermined. Certainly the Constituent Assembly was itself historically constituted. In any case, constitutions are seldom written upon *tabula rasa*. The first democratic French constitution had as its referent point the revolution of 1789, the constitution of the United States of America was to codify the central tenets of the Declaration of Independence, and the first constitution of the Soviet Union aimed at the consolidation of what the Great Revolution of 1917 stood for. Equally, the referent point of the deliberations of our Constituent Assembly were historical events, such as the freedom movement, the political mobilisation of various communities on the basis of religion, and the political practices of the colonial government. Constitutional deliberations were simply burdened both by the promises as well as the pitfalls of history. And history, as well as historical understanding, is a hard taskmaster. No one has been able to escape the coils that histories fashion for us to date.

But equally, the proposed Constitution was a design for the future. Pandit Nehru was to acknowledge this in the following way, 'Many of our discussions here are inevitably derived from the past. We cannot get rid of them. None of us can, because we are part of the past. But we ought to try to get ourselves disconnected from the past if we are to mould the future gradually.' The Constituent Assembly, therefore, straddled the past and the future in an uneasy and contradictory present, a present that was constituted by partition, communal rioting, and bloodletting. The deliberations of the Constituent Assembly, carried on as they were in the shadow of the partition, were governed in a major way by the complete breakdown of life in northern India, and the fear of renewed civil war. This has left its stamp upon many sections of the Constitution, especially the federal provisions. Considering that the partition took place on religious grounds, when it came to the establishment of the right to religion, various problems reared their head. As K.M Munshi was to state, 'The most important task before the Constituent Assembly, was to secure political consolidation of the nation. Its basis had been destroyed by the British by statutorily fragmenting political idea into religious communities under the guise of protecting the minorities.'

Expectedly, the aspiration of building a strong nation-state sat uneasily with the idea of the rights of the minorities to their religion. Expectedly, the tussle between the legacy of the past, the perilous state of the present, and hopes for the future, was to govern debates on minority rights. Nevertheless, the Constituent Assembly showed profound sensitivity to the needs of the minorities. Pandit G.B. Pant, moving the resolution to set up an Advisory Committee on Fundamental Rights and the Rights of Minorities, explicitly stated that:

> [a] satisfactory solution of questions pertaining to minorities will ensure the health, vitality and strength of the free State of India... now it is necessary that a new chapter should start and we should all realise our responsibility. Unless the minorities are fully satisfied, we cannot make progress; we cannot even maintain peace in an undisturbed manner.

This, as I have already said, was historically overdetermined. The Congress had consistently maintained throughout the freedom movement, that it was committed to the protection of the religious, cultural and other rights of the minorities. In 1927 at Madras, the Congress declared that the basis of any constitution would be a Declaration of Rights. The Nehru Constitution of 1928 reiterated this and enshrined the full enjoyment of religious and community rights to all communities. And Jawaharlal Nehru, writing a note on minorities in *Young India* on 15 May 1930, was to state that:

> The history of India and of many of the countries of Europe has demonstrated that there can be no stable equilibrium in any country so long as an attempt is made to crush a minority or force it to conform to the ways of

> the majority. There is no surer method of rousing the resentment of the minority and keeping it apart from the rest of the nation than to make it feel that it has not got the freedom to stick to its own ways... It matters little whether logic is on its side or whether its own particular brand of culture is worthwhile or not. The mere fact of losing it makes it dear. Therefore we in India must make it clear to all that our policy is based on granting this freedom to the minorities and that under no circumstance will any coercion or repression of them be tolerated... we can also lay down as our deliberate policy that there shall be no unfair treatment of any minority. Indeed we should go further and state that it will be the business of the state to give favoured treatment to minority and backward communities.

The freedom movement was led by visionaries who were devoted to the idea that India has an equal place for everyone in its political imagination. It is time again to reiterate the idea that India possesses a shared culture, a common past, common languages, and common histories; it is also time that we strengthen these ideas by drawing upon the political reserves of rights and equality, democracy and freedom, dignity and human value. It is time that we reiterate the right of every individual to live a life of dignity as guaranteed by the Constitution, and his or her right to be respected not despite but because she belongs to different cultures, which accrues to human beings by virtue of being human. It is once again time to support the idea of a composite culture by the idea of a shared political space and values as Pandit Nehru had done during the freedom struggle.

Sanskrit's Legacy to the Arab Intellectual Heritage

ABDUL ALI

The Arabs had close commercial and cultural relations with the Indians in the pre-Islamic days. Their friendship dates back to very ancient times in history when Indian and Arab sailors plied their ships across the seas and established commercial links between India and the Arab world. As a result the Arabs built their permanent settlements on the western coast of India which played a laudable role in the interchange of Indo-Arab cultural and intellectual heritage.

It is worth mentioning in this context that in ancient times India was far ahead of the world in science, technology philosophy and wisdom literature. Chess, the game of mental gymnastics, was also invented in this country. It is a well-known fact that Indian exports were highly prized in foreign markets in those days both in the West and in the East. Indian *kapás,* called *qutn* in Arabic, became cotton in the English language, while the swords manufactured in India became as proverbial in Arab lands as the Arabian horses in the court of Harshvardhan (d. circa A.D. 647), whose reign marked a transition from the ancient to the medieval period. As a result of the age-old Indo-Arab relations, the Arabs had become acquainted with some facets of the rich intellectual heritage of India long before the advent of Islam as a political force in this country. They had a very high opinion of the Indians. They also found much affinity with this country as the cultural heritage of both peoples was characterised by the predominance of spiritual values. That was the main reason why books by Arab travellers right from merchant Sulayman of the ninth century to Ibn Battutah of the fourteenth century display the admiration of the Arabs for this country and its people. Their fascination for India was further reflected in the fact that one of the favourite names of their daughters used to be Hind. They also held the Indians to be a people of noble ideas and sound brains, who were credited with having made significant researches in mathematics, engineering, astronomy, medicine and philososphy.[1]

After the rise of Islam when the Arabs developed a keen sense of intellectual curiosity and a voracious appetite for learning, they were but naturally attracted to the intellectual legacy of India which served as a fount of knowledge to them, especially in the fields of astronomy, mathematics, medicine, philosophy and wisdom literature.[2] It is said that Yahyā Bin Khālid al-Barmakī[3] (d. A.D. 805), the powerful vizier of Caliph Harun al-Rashid, was the first Muslim administrator who took keen interest in the intellectual heritage of India, and invited its physicians and scientists to Baghdad. The main benefits which the Arabs drew from Sanskrit literature in different sciences are briefly expounded below.

Astronomy and Mathematics

Astronomy was practised in India in the Vedic times too. The Arabs were interested in this science for practical purposes. The need for determining the direction for travellers crossing the desert as well as for knowing the exact hours of prayer, the azimuth of Mecca and the first appearance of the moon of Ramadān gave religious impetus to the Arab-Muslim study of astronomy and geography. They first studied and translated into Arabic *Brahma-Sphuta Siddhanta*[4] (Ar. Sindhind), a treatise on astronomy in Sanskrit, in which the Indian astronomical system is set forth in verse form by Brahama Gupta (d. circa A.D. 665), the most accomplished of the ancient Indian astronomers. It was written in A.D. 628 for king Vyaghramukha.[5] This book was brought to Baghdad in A.D. 771 by a deputation of Indian scholars, as a result of which a systematic study of the stars was undertaken by Arab astronomers. The translation was done by Muhammad Ibn Ibrāhīm al-Fazārī, who subsequently became the first astronomer in Islam, and prepared an astronomical table which became popular among the Arabs.[6]

Ya'qūb Bin Tāriq (d. A.D. 796) was another distinguished Arab scholar and author who made a thorough study of *Sindhind*, and became aquainted with Indian astronomy, astrology and mathematics.[7] The main books written by him are *Kitāb Taqtī 'Kardajāt al-Jayb* (Division of the Kardajat of the Sine)[8]; *Kitāb Ma Irtafa'a Min Qaws Nisf al-Nahār* (What Rises in the Arc of Half a Day); *Kitāb al-Zīj Mahlūl Min Sindhind Darajatan Darajatan* (The Astronomical Tables Solved in the Sindhind Degree by Degree).[9]

Another recently discovered major Arabic work on Indian astronomy by al-Biruni, titled *Ghurrat al-Zījāt*,[10] was also based on the Sanskrit manuscript of *Karana Tilaka* which the author reportedly obtained at Multan from its local astronomer Durlabha, whose name he has mentioned in his *Kitab al-Hind* also. This Arabic book containing fourteen chapters discusses a wide range of matters of astronomical interest including various calendars and their inter-relations. Its main importance lies in the fact that it is a vital missing link between *Karana Khandakhadyake* (Ar. *al-Arkand*) of Brahmagupta and *Karana Kutuhala* (Calculation of Astronomical Wonders) of Bhaskaracharya,[11] (d. circa A.D.) the leading Indian mathematician and astronomer of the twelfth century, who served as head of the famous astronomical observatory at Ujjain. Other important Sanskrit works on the subject translated into Arabic were *al-Arkand* or Brahmagupta; *Kitāb Asrār al-Mawālīd* of Kanaka; *Kitāb Asrār al-Masālil* of Sanjhal; and *Kitab 'Ilm al-Nujūm* of Shānāq (Chanakya).

The most significant contribution of India in mathematics was its numeral system which the Arabs learned and adopted. The invention of this system in India is placed around the second century B.C. It is rightly reckoned as one of the greatest inventions of all time. The first Arab exponent of the Indian numerals including the zero was Muhammad Ibn Mūsā al-Khwārizmī (d. after A.D. 843), who wrote the *al-Jam' wa al-Tafrīq bi Hisāb al-Hind*, in which he used the zero and the decimal notation for the first time. He is celebrated as one of the greatest scientific minds of Islam, who influenced mathematical thought to a greater extent than any other medieval scholar could do.[12] He also composed the oldest work on algebra under the title *Hisāb al-Jabr w-al-Mugābalah* (The Calculation of Integration and Equation), the Latin version of which by Gerard of Cremona was used until the sixteenth century as the main mathematical text book at European universities. It was mainly through al-Khwarizmi's works that the Indian numeral system was introduced into the West where these numerals became known as Arabic numerals despite the fact that the Arabs always referred to them in their writings as Indian numerals. As is well-known, when introduced in Europe, they marked the beginning of modern European mathematics and brought about a revolution in the science of calculation.[13]

Another major Sanskrit book on mathematics and astronomy translated into Arabic was *Aryabhatiya* (Ar. *Arjband*) of Aryabhatta, the renowned Indian astronomer and mathematician of the fifth century A.D.[14] Contrary to orthodox views, he maintained that the earth rotated round its axis. He also explained the cause of the eclipses of the sun and the moon. In addition, he laid the foundations of algebra and made several new observations in geometry[15] including the use of the ratios, sine and tangent which were first introduced to the Arab world by Muhammad Ibn Jābir al-Battāni.[16]

It is of utmost importance to note in this connection that Indian astronomy continued to influence Arab astronomers both in the Arab East and in Muslim Spain even after the diffusion and popularity of Greek astronomy in the time of Caliph Mamun and later periods. Of the several later such Arab astronomers mention may be made of the above-mentioned al-Khwarizmi, Habash al-Hasib, and Maslamah Bin Ahmad al-Majriti. Al-Khwarizmi composed his *Astronomical Tables*, popularly known as *al-Sindhind al-Saghīr* (The Little Sindhind), on the Siddhanta system of astronomy by converting the Indian calendar to the Persian calendar. Habash al-Hāsib (d. between 867 and 874) was director of the observatory at Damascus, and author of three astronomical tables, the first of which was based on the Sindhind system of calculation. Maslamah Bin Ahmad al-Majrītī (950-1007), the most eminent Arab astronomer of Muslim Spain, enlarged, amended and adapted the *Astronomical Tables* of al-Khwarizmi to the Cordova meridian and to the Arab Hijri calendar.[17]

Thus the Arabs were greatly influenced by the astronomical and mathematical researches of Indian scholars and drew large benefits from them while making their own contributions in these fields. As such it can be appropriately claimed for the Indians that they became the teachers of the Arabs in astronomy, arithmetic and algebra, and through them of the nations of the West during the medieval periods.[18]

Medicine

In the pre-Islamic days medicine among the Arabs was practised on primitive and superstitious lines. Magical charms and talismans also had a role to play alongside dispensation of proper medicines, but when the Prophet Muhammad came, he gave so much importance to the maintenance of health as to give it primacy over religion itself. He not only laid down fundamental principles of preventive medicine but also exhorted his followers to undertake extensive research in the field of medicine. In this connection he himself used a number of Indian drugs and recommended their use to his followers. Of them *Qusṭ Indica* (a kind of Indian incense), *Zanjabil* and *Zarirah* are well-known. He described the medicinal properties of *Qusṭ*, saying: 'Treat with this Indian incense, for it has cure for seven diseases. It is to be sniffed by one having throat-trouble, and to be put into one side of the mouth of one suffering from pleurisy (inflammation of the lungs.'[19]

Indian Physicians in Baghdad

After the expansion of Islam, especially in the Abbasid period (A.D. 750-1258), the Arabs paid serious attention to the rich medical literature contained in the Sanskrit language, the golden period of which, extending from 800 B.C. to about A.D. 1000, was marked by the production of two important medical treatises known as the *Charaka-Samhita* and the *Susruta-Samhita*, written respectively by Acharya Charaka, a physician, and Acharya Susruta, a surgeon.[20] It was of particular interest to the Arabs that the Indian physicians practising *Ayurveda* laid emphasis on dietetic treatment in preference to medicinal treatment. The Arab physicians also became further enlightened on the ethical, moral and spiritual dimensions of health as incorporated by the Indian system of medicine. Some Indian medical men were experts in veterinary medicine also, and knew how to treat the diseases of different animals including elephants.[21] It is noteworthy that knowledge about the Indian system of medicine had already percolated to far-off areas in West Asia even in pre-Islamic times under the Sasanids through the famous Persian Academy of Jundi-Shapur where Indian physicians met their counterparts and imparted instruction in their system of medicine.[22]

Several eminent Indian physicians were invited to Baghdad, the capital of the Abbasid empire, and employed in state hospitals or in translation of works. Some among these were Manaka (Manikya), Ibn Dahan (Dhanapati), Ṣālih Ibn Bahlah, Kanaka, Sanjhal, etc., whose names have been frequently mentioned by Arab historians of science and civilisation.

Manaka is mentioned as a distinguished Indian physician by Ibn Abi Usaybi'ah in his famous book *Uyūn al-Anbā fi Tabaqāt al-Atibbā* (Sources of Information on the Classes of Physicians). It is related that once when Caliph Hārūn al-Rashīd (A.D. 786-809) fell seriously ill and his court physicians failed to cure him, Manaka was invited from India to treat him. When he cured the Caliph, he was given a high rank and position. He was also an expert in the Persian language, and translated a number of Sanskrit books into Persian which were later rendered into Arabic.[23]

While moving about in a market in Baghdad, Manaka is said to have come across a juggler who was displaying his drugs and explaining their medicinal properties. He described a certain medicine prepared by him as the panacea for all the diseases of man. Hearing this, the critical Manaka smiled and said that if that was the case why had the Caliph taken the trouble of inviting him from India. He further said that if the juggler was an imposter, the Caliph should kill him as the law permits the massacre of such persons. For if he was not killed, he would kill several persons daily. This shows how bold, confident and conscientious he was as a physician.[24]

Ibn Dahan was also invited from India for the treatment of the same Caliph. He was appointed as chief medical officer at the prestigious Barmakid Hospital in Baghdad in recognition of his merit. He also assisted in the translation of several Sanskrit works into Arabic.[25]

Sālih Bin Bahlah was another eminent Indian physician who visited Baghdad during the reign of the above Caliph. Ibn Abī Usaybi 'ah has related an interesting incident about this physician which shows how perfect he was in diagnosis and treatment. On a certain day Ibrāhīm Bin Ṣālih, cousin of Caliph Hārūn al-Rashīd, fell unconscious and remained in a state of coma for a long time. He was examined and treated by no less a physician than Bakhtishu, the Caliph's personal physician, who was well-grounded in the Greek system of medicine. But he lost all hope of Ibrāhīm Bin Ṣāliḥ's recovery and declared that the patient could not be saved. Then it was suggested to the Caliph that Ṣāliḥ Bin Bahlah, an expert in Indian medicine, should be consulted to save Ibrāhīm's life. Ṣāliḥ examined Ibrahim, felt his pulse and reported to the Caliph that there was no cause for him to worry, and that his cousin would be saved. In the meantime news reached the Caliph that Ibrāhīm had expired. The Caliph became very angry and started cursing Ṣāliḥ and the Indian system of medicine. And as preparations for the last funeral rites were in progress, Ṣāliḥ appeared on the scene and sought the Caliph's permission to examine Ibrāhīm once more. No sooner did the physician cast a look at the patient than he requested the Caliph not to bury his cousin alive. He took a needle and pierced it into the thumb of his left hand between the nail and the flesh, whereupon the latter withdrew his hand (feeling the pain). This established that Ibrāhīm was still alive.. Then Ṣāliḥ called for frankincense and bellows from the store, and blew the smoke of the incense into Ibrāhīm's nose. And within ten minutes the body of Ibrāhīm started agitating, following which he sneezed and awoke to the surprise of all, with cries of *Allāhu Akbar* (Allah is the Greatest) echoing all around to the credit of this physician. Ibrahim lived for a long time after that incident and enjoyed a good career.[26] This case clearly proves that the ancient Indian physicians could distinguish between external death and real death, and that they applied artificial breathing to treat some fatal cases, whereas Greek physicians were not aware of this technique.[27]

Translation of Sanskrit Books on Medicine

Several major and minor Sanskrit works on medicine were translated into Arabic in Baghdad with the assistance of the Indian physicians. The *Caraka-Samhita* and the *Susruta-Samhita* were two such major Sanskrit books. As mentioned by Ibn al-Nadīm[28] in his *Al-Fihrist* (The Bibliogrpahic Compendium), the *Susruta-Samhita* (Ar. *Susrud*), containing ten chapters written in the form of a compendium of medicine, was translated by Manaka at the instance of the above-mentioned Yaḥyā Bin Khālid al-Barmakī, while the *Caraka Samhita* (Ar. *Sirak*) was translated by 'Abdullāh Bin 'Alī al-Dandānī from Persian into Arabic, as it had been first translated from Sanskrit into Persian. Other important Sanskrit books on medicine translated into Arabic were *Ashtangahridaya* (Ar. *Istankar*) of Vaghbhata, translated by Ibn Dahan; the *Nidāna* of Madhavakar, a celebrated work on pathology; *Kitāb Sundastaq*[29] (The Book of Success) which was translated by Ibn Dahan; a short treatise on drugs derived from Indian medicinal herbs; *Kitāb 'Ilājāt al-Hubālā* (Book on the Treatment of Pregnant Ladies); *Kitāb Tuqashtal* (a treatise on a hundred diseases and their treatment); *Kitāb Rawse* by an Indian lady physician on female diseases; *Kitāb Asma 'Aqāqīr al-Hind* (Book on Indian Drugs) which was translated by Manaka for Isḥāq Bin Sulayman; *Kitāb Ra'y al-Hind fī Ajnās al-Hayyāt wa Sumūmihā* (Book on the Knowledge of India about Different Categories of Snakes and their Poisons) by Pali; *Kitāb al-Tawahhum fī al-Amrād* (Book on the Suspicion of Diseases and Their Effects) by Yuqastak and Siddhyayoga, etc.[30]

'Ali Ibn Sahl Rabbān al-Ṭabari (d. circa A.D. 861), was the first Arab physician and writer who gave a comprehensive and systematic account of the Indian system of medicine in his *Firdaws al-Hikmah* (The Paradise of Wisdom), one of the earliest Arabic compendiums of medicine, which is chiefly based on Indian and Greek sources. Of other Arab physicians who wrote on the Ayurveda, mention may be made of Muhammad Bin Zakariyā al-Rāzī (d. A.D. 930), author of *al-Hāwī*, and of Ibn Sīnā, author of *al-Qānūn fī al-Tibb*, both of whom included chapters on Indian medicine in their respective books and quoted major Ayurvedic works as authorities on different subjects of medicine. As a result, the Arab physicians became acquainted with the Indian knowledge of anatomy, physiology, embryology, pathology and therapeutics.

In addition to the above, the Arabic language also bears witness to the fact that the Arabs drew large benefits from the rich Indian medical literature. A number of Sanskrit words relating to Indian medicinal and aromatic herbs have found their place in the Arabic language. Some Arabic words of Indian origin along with their Sanskrit equivalents are listed below in support of this point:

Sandal (chandan)
nilufar (nuluphal),
qaranfal (kanakphal),
philphil (pipli pipla),
jaiphal (jaiphal),
itrifal (triphal),
shakhirah (shakhar)
balilaj (bahera),
halilaj (harh),
al-baladur (bhalatakah),
misk (moshka),
kafur (karpur)
zanjabil (zunjabera).

Besides, as described by Sayyid Sulayman Nadvi, a distinguished Indian Arabic scholar, there are at least three words of Sanskrit origin which have the honour of being used in the Holy Qur'an. They are used in the description of Paradise in the following verses:

1. Lo! the righteous shall drink of a cup whereof the mixture is of water of Kafur (Karpur).[31]
2. They are watered there with a cup whereof the mixture is of Zanjabil (zunjabera). [32]
3. They are given to drink of a pure wine, sealed, whose seal is musk (moshka)...[33]

Conclusion

From the foregoing it is quite clear that the Arabs drew large benefits from the rich Indian legacy in different branches of knowledge and learning. Simultaneously, it must be acknowledged that, like a civilised nation inspired by the teachings of Islam, they enthusiastically searched, preserved, translated and studied the ancient intellectual heritage of the world including that contained in the Sanskrit language, enriching it with fresh contributions of their own as well as diffusing its knowledge among all sections of humanity at large without any distinction of caste, creed or religion. It is also noteworthy in this context that it was transmission of the knowledge acquired and developed by them to the West which facilitated the emergence of the European Renaissance, and that they never presented the contributions of other nations as their own findings. That way they not only became the harbingers of the modern scientific era, but also set examples of intellectual honesty and diffusion of scientific knowledge on secular lines for the betterment of the lot of the entire human race. Although some aspects of the Indo-Arab intellectual interaction have been investigated by different scholars, a vast field still lies unexplored, and is a fertile area for further research which may be done more fruitfully through the coordinated efforts of both Indologists and Arabists.

Notes

1. Mahmud Hasan al-Tonki, *Mu 'jam al-Musannifīn*, Vol. I, Beirut, 1344 A.H., pp. 59-60.
2. For details about the contribution made by Sanskrit books to Arabic wisdom literature, see *Presidential Addresses on Arab-Islamic Studies* by Abdul Ali, New Delhi : Kitab Bhavan, 2002, pp. 117-128.
3. The distinguished family of Barmakids who served as *viziers* to the Abbasid Caliphs of Baghdad were originally *pramukhs*, a Sanskrit word meaning head or chief, which became Barmak in Arabic. They had earlier served as priests of Buddhist monasteries in the region of Balkh in Central Asia. They also had been closely connected with India long before the advent of Islam. Later, when they got the upper hand in Arab administration, they strengthened Indo-Arab cultural and intellectual relations.
4. The first two chapters of the book *Brahma-Sphuta-Siddhanta* (Opening of the Universe) are devoted to the discussion of mathematics and various geometrical theorems, while the remaining twenty-three chapters deal with the Indian astronomical system relating to lunar eclipses, solar eclipses, planetary conjunctions, the lunar phases, and the determination of the position of the planets, etc. (See *The Fihrist of al-Nadim*, ed. & tr. by Bayard Dodge, London, Vol. II, p. 710).
5. C.A. Nallino, *'Iim al-Falak*, Rome, Italy, 1911, p. 174.
6. P.K. Hitti, *History of the Arabs*, London, 1958, p. 307.
7. C.A. Nallino, *'Iim al-Falak*, op. cit., p. 164

8. The *kardajah* (pl. *kardajāt*), probably a corruption of the Sanskrit *cramajia*, was the arc or sine of each of the 96 parts in which the circle was divided in the ancient Indian tradition. (*The Fihrist of al-Nadim*, op. cit., Vol. II, p. 659).
9. *The Fihrist of al-Nadim*, op. cit., Vol. II, p. 659.
10. The only available original manuscript of this book consisting of 68 pages is kept in the library of the Dargah of Pir Muhammad Shāh at Ahmedabad (India).
11. S.Samad Hussain Rizvi, 'A Newly Discovered Book of Al-Biruni *Ghurrat-uz-Zijat*) and Al-Biruni's Measurements of Earth's Dimensions' in *Al-Biruni Commemorative Volume*, Pakistan, 1979, pp. 605-606.
12. P.K. Hitti, *History of the Arabs*, op. cit., p. 379.
13. Abdul Hamīd, *Āfāq Islāmīyah*, Cairo, p. 176; Will Durant, *The Story of Civilization*, Vol. IV, p. 241.
14. Mahesh Prasad, 'Bayn al-Lughatayn-al-'Arabīyah wa al-Sanskritīyah' in *Thaqāfat al-Hind*, New Delhi, March, 1950, p. 93.
15. A.A. Macdonell, *A History of Sanskrit Literature*, 5th ed., New Delhi, 1984, p. 402.
16. Tara Chand, 'India's Contribution to Arabic Culture' in the *Al-Arab*, New Delhi, October 1962, p. 22.
17. C.A. Nallino, *Ilm al-Falak*, op. cit., p. 164.
18. In view of the facts discussed above, it is historically incorrect to keep the Indian influence on the Arabs in mathematical sciences confined to the eighth and ninths centuries, as done by A.A. Macdonell. During the eighth and ninth centuries, the Indians became the teachers in arithmetic and algebra of the Arabs, and through them of the nations of the West; see A.A. Macdonell, op. cit., p. 435.
19. *Sahīh al-Bukhārī*, tr. by M.Muhsin Khan, Vol. VII, 5th edition, New Delhi, 1984, p. 402.
20. *Encyclopaedia Britannica*, Vol. XXIII, USA, 1994, p. 776.
21. Shawkat Muwaffaq al-Shatti, *Tārīkh al-Tibb*, Vol. I, Damascus, 1956, p. 15.
22. P.N. Chopra, 'Cultural Contribution of India to the Arab World', in *Al-Arab*, Delhi, Vol. I, No. 24 (15 September, 1962), p.3.
23. Ibn Abi Usaybi'ah, *'Uyūn al-Anbā fi Tabaqāt al-Atibbā*, Vol. II, Wahbiyah Press, 1882, p. 33.
24. Ibid., pp. 33-34.
25. *The Fihrist of al-Nadim*, op. cit, p. 710.
26. *'Uyūn al-Anbā fī Tabaqāt al-Atibbā*, Vol. II, op. cit. pp. 34-35.
27. Shawkat Muwaffaq al-Shatti, *Tarikh al-Tibb*, Vol. I, op. cit. p. 25.

28. Ibn al-Nadim was an eminent book merchant and encyclopaedist.
29. *The Fihrist of al-Nadim*, op. cit., p. 710.
30. Ibid., p. 710.
31. The Qur'ān, 76:5, tr. by M.M. Pickthall.
32. The Qur'ān, 76:17, ibid.
33. The Qur'ān, 83:25-26, ibid.

Indo-Arab Cultural Relations
Glimpses of Medieval Arabic Texts

Abdul Bari

Indo-Arab cultural relations are very old. After the spread of Islam in the West Asian region the bonds of friendship and cultural cooperation were further strengthened. They are still continuing and are in good shape.

The image of India and the Indian people among the Arabs and Arab scholars has always been good. Arabic historical and literary works depict appreciation and impartial viewpoints regarding India.

Al-Beruni, in his book '*Kitab-al Hind,* says with an open heart, that the Indians during the ancient days were good people in the sense that they were men of learning and religious tolerance. Another great Egyptian scholar and historian of the fifteenth century A.D. called Al-Qalqashandi appreciates India with these words, 'India is a big and wide country having enormous wealth. The king lives with pomp and glory. Its ocean is full of pearls, its earth with gold and its mountains with rubies and emeralds. Its valleys have fragrance of Sandal wood and camphor. The people are bestowed with wisdom. Peace and justice can be seen in the entire country.'[1]

Another modern Egyptian scholar, Abu Zohra, in his book *Mohaderat Fi Muqarinat al-Adyan* opines about ancient Indian religions and says, 'Indians have a glorious history. They were possessed of civilization and culture in the olden days. The history of their civilization is so old that one remains unable to trace its origin.'

So far as socio-cultural relation between India and West Asian regions are concerned, we should also keep in mind the fact that, after the invasion by the Mongolian hordes and the ruin of Baghdad, India had also become a great centre for Arab scholars and Islamic learning. It was but natural that exchange of ideas and scholars, as well as, cultural cooperation between the two regions should acquire momentum.

Indian scholars of Arabic learning like al-Saghani, al-Zabidi and Azad Bilgrami and some others were given equal status, side by side with Arab scholars.

We are fully aware that for better understanding and cultural cooperation between two countries, details about the temperament of the people concerned, their past history and cultural heritage, prove helpful and beneficial. In the case of West Asia and India, Arabic texts are no doubt very useful. These Arabic sources will provide insights into the real picture of cultural activities, as well as fresh information about our Indian cultural heritage, of which even we Indians are not fully aware.

Moreover, our source of information is generally provided by European historians and Orientalists but some times the facts are wrongly interpreted. The lacuna is found due to the translated version of the facts. But the original sources remain more authentic and unbiased. Moreover, some very important Arabic sources, specially related to the cultural side, are still untouched.

In this paper I have tried to bring to the reader some such sources whose details are not found in Arabic historical works. First of all, I would like to present some glimpses of Indian life and culture provided by al-Qalqashandi. He writes about India (in about 35 pages) in the fifth volume of his book *Subh al-Asha*. He elaborates the different aspects of Indian life in ten chapters, mentioning the fruits and vegetables, coins, market rates, routes and the King's life.

He informs that there are four types of *durham* and each *durham* is equal to 34 *aflus*. A man can have one full meal in only four *aflus*. Good cotton cloth is better in quality than that prepared in Baghdad. The salary of a chief justice is equal to the produce of ten villages.[2] While giving details about Delhi he points out that there are 70 hospitals in the city.

There is a branch of Arabic history, called 'Hadaya literature' which deals with the articles of gifts exchanged between monarchs of different countries. This valuable Arabic source is still untouched although as it throws ample light on the cultural history of India and the West Asian regions.

In this category, there are two types of works. The first one deals exclusively with articles of gifts. The second category gives general historical accounts along with some details of gifts.

Under the first category, I have been able to trace out the following eight books:

1. *Kitab al-Hadaya* by Ibrahim al Harbi
2. *Kitab al-Hadaya* by al-Jahiz
3. *Kitab al-Hadaya* by Abu Tahir Taifur
4. *Kitab al-Hadaya* by Abu Abdullah al-Marzabani
5. *Kitab al-Hadaya* by Judisaburi
6. *Kitab al-Hadaya* byAbu Abdullah al-Khurasani
7. *Kitab al-Zakhairwa al-Tuhaf* by al-Qazi al-Rashid
8. *Kitab al-Tuhafwa al-Hadaya* by al-Khaliddiyan.

Under the second category I have to point out the following two books:

1. *Al-Nibras* by Ibn Dihya al-Kalbi
2. *Mutali al-Budur Fi Manazil al-Surur*, by Ala al-Din al-Ghazawli

Two books, one by al-Qazi and another by al-Khaliddiyan are very important. Leaving aside all other details, I am giving a glimpse of articles of gifts exchanged between Indian monarchs and Arab Caliphs on the basis of information provided by the two books referred to. During the reign of Hisham, an Indian King sent a typical presentation of an automatic toy to one of the Umayyad governors. It was a she-camel entirely made of gems and jewels. Its udder was full of pearls. It was placed in a silver cart. The cart had some automatic moving system. The moment it was placed on earth, it started moving in such a way, as if the she-camel was walking. The wonderful working of the toy was demonstrated in the Caliph's court by a special Indian messenger. The man first touched the udder. Suddenly pearls came down, in a sequence, as if milk was coming out of the udder. The pearls were collected in a golden bowl. Then, the neck of the she-camel was pressed slightly and in no time, rubies gushed out in a liquid form, as if it was blood. It was a matter of great astonishment for the entire gathering at the Court.

The gift signifies on the one hand the friendly gestures of the Indian kings towards developing mutual understanding, friendship and cooperation and on the other India's scientific and technological capabilities in those times.

During the reign of Mamun al-Rashid, an Indian king called Duhmi or Ruhmi sent him some remarkable gifts which are listed below:

1. A cup made of ruby and filled with 100 precious pearls.
2. A mattress made of a very big python's skin. It was decorated with pearls. It was said that one who sits on the mattress for seven days need not have fear of contracting diseases like tuberculosis.
3. Three carpets along with pillows made of soft feathers of a bird called Samandal. It was presumed that the feathers were fireproof.
4. A soft and rare variety of Ud (a fragrant wood).
5. Thirteen mounds of camphor in the shape of tablets.
6. A translated version of the book entitled *Safwat al-Adhihan* (The Choicest Wisdoms.)

Al-Mamun reciprocated the friendly gesture of the Indian king with the following gifts:

1. A statue of a warrior along with his horse and weapons made of red chalcedony.
2. A dining table of a rare wooden log, having golden legs.
3. Finest varieties of cloth each consisting of 100 pieces of cotton fabrics from Egypt, brocade from Sus, silk from Yemen and Iskandria and woollen fabrics from Khurasan.
4. Carpets of Oirmz, Tabaristan and Susangazd.
5. Hundred pieces of mattresses of Hira with pillows, all made of fine silk.
6. An Egyptian cup with typical paintings.
7. A book entitled *Diwan al-Albab wa Bustan Nawader al-Uqul* (Collection of Wisdoms and Garden of Novelties of Intellect).

In short, we can very well say that such details of gifts throw ample light on the cultural and scientific development of the Arab world and the Indian subcontinent alike. We can trace through the Hadaya literature much new information about the cultural history of medieval India. Arrangements should be made for translating from important Arabic texts into English, just as al-Beruni's works are being translated. Moreover, incentives should be provided for the meaningful development of the Arabic language and literature giving emphasis to Indo-Arab literature in India. The language will serve as a link between India and the West Asian countries from the point of view of cultural relations.

Notes

1. Al Qalqashandi, *Subh al-Asha*, Vol. 5, p. 11.
2. *Subh al-Asha*, Vol. 5, p. 94.

South India and the Gulf

Trade and Diplomacy During the Late Eighteenth Century

A.K. Pasha

In the second half of the eighteenth century despite the decline in power the Mughal Emperor was still regarded as the sovereign with the large number of independent rulers in different parts of India constituting authorized representatives. As per accepted contemporary legal ideas, every Indian ruler had to acknowledge the supremacy of the House of Timur. In south India, thc Nizam of Hyderabad was the Viceroy of the Deccan appointed by the Mughals. Other centres were the Nawab of Arcot (Carnatic), the Marathas and the Kingdom of Travancore. Despite nominal Mughal control, *de facto* power and influence was exercised by the English and all the above south Indian rulers were dependent on the British.

Like other rulers in south India, the Mysore royal family were the tributaries of the Mughal Empire. But in 1768 the Nizam of Hyderabad had ceded the *diwani* of Mysore to the English. Haider Ali, an employee of the Mysore ruler, due to his military skills had extended the territorial jurisdiction (at the cost of the Nizam and the Nawab of Arcot) and become the *de facto* ruler of Mysore between 1761-1782. In fact, he had become the most formidable political and military power in south India. Despite his new status, Haider Ali technically remained an employee of the Mysore Maharajah (ruler) and he never claimed to be a ruler of Mysore himself. Nevertheless, the Nizam, the Marathas, the Nawab of Carnatic along with the Mysore Maharajah had been working to undermine Haider Ali. The Nizam viewed Haider Ali as a usurper with no legal right to his conquered lands. The British perceived Haider Ali as a mortal enemy and the greatest obstacle in the achievement of their ambition in India and the neighbouring Gulf region. Tipu Sultan, who had succeeded his father, 'forced by circumstances and the need to defend his position and patrimony decided to dethrone' the Mysore Maharajah and proclaimed himself as an independent ruler.[1] Unfortunately, Tipu Sultan failed to get legal recognition either from the Nizam or the Mughal government in Delhi mainly due to British opposition and influence.

This paper, after briefly examining the British challenge to Tipu Sultan, will study in some detail the diplomatic and economic initiatives which Tipu Sultan took in the Gulf region in order to neutralize the British challenge.

I

As is well known the British, through ingenious means, had extended their influence over large parts of India, subjugating numerous Indian rulers and making them vassals of the British Empire. In south India, Haider Ali and Tipu Sultan were the only major rulers who defied the British and refused to become tributary to the East India Company, not due to any intentional hostility towards the English but because the Mysore rulers could see the British imperial ambitions based on domination and territorial expansion. Nevertheless, both Haider Ali and Tipu Sultan expressed their keen desire on numerous occasions to live in peace with the British, but the latter remained hostile to both the rulers and worked hard for their overthrow. This is confirmed by the fact that Sir Eyre Coote, on hearing the news of Haider Ali's death, could not help writing, 'On the many beneficial effects, which may be expected to arise to our general interests in India by the important news of Haider Ally's death—it opens to us the fairest prospect of securing to the Mother Country the permanent and undisturbed possession of this Eastern dominions.'[2]

Haider Ali was fully conscious of British intentions and also their methods of acquiring territory. In his view 'the English first try to secure a footing in other territories by outward professions of friendship and then gradually they bring them under their full sway.' He saw the British as his 'inveterate enemy'.[3] This animosity continued when Tipu Sultan succeeded his father and built up a strong military machine, contrary to the expectations that after Haider's death his newly built power would cease to be a dominant factor in south Indian politics. The British regarded Tipu Sultan as a hurdle to their imperial ambitions because he was 'unquestionably the most powerful of all the native Princes of Hindustan,' and they feared that 'his steadiness in establishing that system of government and discipline in his army, which have raised him above the other Princes in India cannot fail to make him everyday, more formidable.' No wonder, Lord Cornwallis attacked Mysore and divested Tipu Sultan of half of his kingdom in 1784. Cornwallis was convinced that Tipu Sultan was a 'prince of very uncommon abilities and of boundless ambition, who had acquired a degree of power in extent of territory and wealth, and in forces that threatened the Company's possessions in the Carnatic and those of all his other neighbours with imminent danger.'[4] The British were keen to take over the Malabar areas (western Coast), which were rich in spices (pepper), sandalwood and pine trees, as also such ports like Calicut and Cannanore in order to increase the revenues of the Company. The possession of these very lucrative areas by the Company would have partially compensated for the loss of British colonies in North America.

The British with the help of the Nizam and the Marathas as also by launching direct attacks on Tipu's territories, demonstrated their hostility towards Mysore. Because of his attempts to work for an alliance with the French, the Ottoman Sultan, the Shah of Persia, the King of Afghanistan, the Sultan of Oman and other Gulf rulers, Tipu Sultan was seen as dangerous to British interests. The British saw Tipu Sultan's search for allies abroad and pursuit of an active diplomacy coupled with the possession of a strong military as a threat to their imperial interests. From the outset, Tipu Sultan appears to have had a clear perception of the political, economic and military advantages of having closer relations with the Gulf area. Even though, Europe and North America had become the centre for global trade, the Gulf region still remained a significant centre of political and economic activity in the late eighteenth century and no wonder Tipu Sultan paid special attention to building ties with rulers in this area (Arab Sheikhs).

In order to understand Tipu Sultan's diplomacy in the Gulf region one should note the imperial struggle throughout the eighteenth century which gave ample scope to the Gulf's tribal elites to initiate strong local resistance to contain European imperialism and economic hegemony, after it had been regarded initially as a mere annoyance which would disappear as time passed. The Sultan of Oman took the lead in eliminating the Portuguese influence from his country in the Gulf. Its impact was that many of the small Gulf rulers became, or made bids to become, independent.

The following are some of the significant developments in the Gulf region during this period:

(i) the emergence of Muscat as a regional commercial power from 1719;

(ii) the seperation of Lahej, Aden and Hadramaut from Zaidi Yemen as of 1728;

(iii) the efforts of Nadir Shah to unify Persia against foreign influence around 1747;

(iv) the founding of Kuwait as a commercial centre under the Al-Sabahs around 1752;

(v) the emergence of the Al-Qasimis as a local resistance power dating from 1777;

(vi) the founding of Bahrain as a commercial centre under the leadership of Al-Khalifah of the Utub about 1783;

(vii) the appearance of the Wahhabi movement on a regional basis under the leadership of Al Saud dating from 1792;

(viii) the emergence and economic role played by Kuwait as a mercantile port-of-call, instead of Basra, around 1792 as a result of the sectarian wars between the Persians and the Ottomans in Iraq. During 1791-92 the Gulf region saw the emergence in a big way of the Al-Qasimis in the area now known as Sharjah of the United Arab Emirates (UAE).[5]

The British easily defeated the Dutch and French in the Gulf area and after they had firmly established their control over India from 1690 onwards, proceeded to control the lucrative trade in the Gulf region. The subsequent treaties with the subjugated Gulf Arab rulers completed the domination of key strategic areas so very essential to retain their dominant influence in the region. These were the links in their grand imperial design. Interestingly, the British began the establishment of their control all over the Gulf region by weakening the Arab commercial and economic capacities (by destroying ships, boats, forts, and so on) and by subjecting them ultimately to the colonial administration of which they made India (Bombay) their base. In this scheme, Tipu Sultan was seen as a major stumbling block who could have undermined their grand imperial strategy. In order to achieve her goals, Britain resorted to various tactics and excuses (with which to hide her true aims) of which three were crucial; she accused thc Gulf Arabs (especially tribal leaders) of (1) piracy, (2) slave trade and (3) arms trade. Under the pretext of trying to put an end to piracy, slave trade and a stop to arms trade in the Indian Ocean and the Gulf region, the British had subjugated all the coastal Sheikhs in the Gulf area. Britain started the systematic sinking of the trading vessels of the Gulf Arabs merely on suspicion, instead of taking them to the nearest port, as the agreements had stipulated. Muscat was identified as the major target. Thus, Bruce, quoted by Arnold Wilson, asserts: 'the shipping capability of the Arabs of Muscat and their tremendous human potential was such that it aroused fear to their seizing control of the entire Gulf...' At another place he says: 'However, the Arab pirates of Muscat were the worst offenders. They had become so strong that they were able to drive the Portuguese from Mombassa' (near Zanzibar, Tanzania).

Even though British domination of the region started in 1688 but the real era of 'Pax Britannica' in the Gulf region started with the fall of Tipu Sultan in 1799. British ascendancy in the Gulf was thus total; it was not only military but also economic. In this, their control and domination of India undoubtedly played a decisive role in their success in the Gulf region. From all this, it is clear that the opportunity to maneuver for Tipu Sultan was extremely limited given British naval supremacy among other factors, which enabled them to have global reach and paramountacy.[6]

II

The British challenge to Tipu Sultan was formidable, prompting him to respond with equally forcible measures to tackle it. Most significant was his attempt to seek friendship with the Ottoman Sultan, with Oman, Persia, and with other Gulf rulers, who were also simultaneously under intense (British) pressure and vulnerable to British military (mainly naval) power. It must be stressed here that since most of the well known Indian rulers were too deeply committed to the British in securing short-term benefits, Tipu Sultan had no hopes of being fully recognised as an independent ruler by them. Under the circumstances he decided to approach foreign rulers to get his independent status acknowledged. In this connection he decided to send missions to the Ottoman Sultan, Persia, Oman, Afghanistan, France, Mauritius, Egypt and other places.

At this stage one may legitimately ask whether Tipu Sultan actually needed outside recognition for his position or was he merely using it as a cover to embark on a covert mission to seek outside military, political and diplomatic support in order to confront the British and his other enemies from a position of strength. What is clear is that he was at this stage pursuing an ambitious and bold policy to strengthen and consolidate his position *vis-à-vis* the British who had now become his mortal enemies.

Tipu Sultan, in a bold and extraordinary move, decided to approach the Ottoman Sultan to get his independent status acknowledged, since the Caliph at Istanbul was still regarded by Muslims worldwide as their political and religious head. The Ottoman Sultan received Tipu's emissaries in 1787 and accorded permission to Tipu Sultan to assume the title of an independent monarch with the right to strike coins and to have the Friday prayer, *Khutba,* read in his name. This proved to be a major gain for Tipu in his confrontation with the British who were simply furious at this breakthrough despite their best efforts to prevent it.

Despite involvement in wars and the huge burden of war reparations, whenever his economic and military position improved, Tipu Sultan sent embassies abroad as he believed in close cooperation with the Gulf countries in order to contain the British as also for trade purposes. Tipu Sultan's intense diplomatic activity with Oman, Persia and others, which had essentially political, economic and military considerations, not only showed his desire to keep up contacts with influential rulers but also to seek allies against the British. Thus, the guiding principles of Tipu's diplomacy were to neutralize his enemies, maintain the integrity of his kingdom and also maintain his strong opposition to British imperialism and expansionism.

The British were extremely suspicious of Tipu Sultan's relations with Oman and other Muslim rulers in the Gulf region because of their implications not only on their position in India but also on ties with the Mughal Emperor (as the English were after all still the servants of the then Mughal Emperor) and other Indian Muslim rulers as well. According to one writer, if Tipu Sultan had succeeded in rousing the Muslims, the British would have had to face much greater difficulties in controlling India.[7] Moreover, Tipu Sultan's letters were making an impact on the Muslim rulers in India.

More dangerous were Tipu's schemes of cooperation in political and economic spheres. Tipu Sultan urged the Muslim Gulf rulers to have trade relations, establishment of factories, development of new weapons and enhance naval power. An independent live centre of Islamic renaissance in India could not have suited British interests. The British were simply furious over Tipu Sultan's contacts with the French as well. Napoleon's triumphant arrival in Egypt and his letters from Cairo to Tipu Sultan via the Sultan of Oman strengthened the British determination to defeat the French in Egypt, as it had grave implications for their position in India, the entire Gulf, the Indian Ocean and the Arabian Sea region. In order to watch French-Tipu activities in Oman, the British used the company's Indian broker in Muscat, Narottam Ram Chander Raoji, widely known as Josey, to act as an informer on payment. Not only were the British concerned over preferential treatment of Tipu Sultan and the French by Oman but they also sought to curb their influence in Muscat. The Imam's acquisition of a lease for Bandar Abbas on the Persian coast at the very time of the French mission to Shiraz could not have been a mere coincidence. The superior diplomacy and naval power of the British frustrated and undermined Tipu Sultan's strategy of enlisting assistance from the Gulf region (abroad). Thus, the British decided to contain Tipu Sultan first and directed all their energies towards bringing about his downfall.[8]

III

Tipu Sultan was fully aware of how the British rose to become dominant in India and elsewhere (through trade) and also how they became prosperous and subsequently acquired territories. Tipu Sultan also had in mind the achievements of the Raja of Travancore, who made huge profits from oceanic trade. No wonder Tipu Sultan attached great importance to foreign trade and commerce as he viewed it as the basis of state power and prosperity. Towards this end, he decided to build a strong commercial fleet at Calicut and Mangalore, capable of moving in the Arabian Sea/Gulf with large quantities of goods. He also gave special importance to the building of naval ships and to establish factories in the Gulf region in which the state was the monopoly-trading agent. Tipu Sultan, aware of the rich potential of his kingdom, especially in the field of agricultural and other products that were in great demand, sought to establish state-to-state trade ties.

The lucrative trade, especially in spices/rice, had made Mysore the richest and most prosperous region in the country, which the British and the French sought to dominate and control. Tipu Sultan correctly analysed the reasons for the political decline of the Muslims, the most important being their indifference to trade, commerce and industry. The Europeans, through extensive monopoly of trade, had elbowed the Muslims out of this field and were controlling and dominating the Muslim states. During his rule, Haider Ali had established close trade ties with Oman's ruler, Ahmad bin Said, with a factory at Muscat while a *wakil* had been appointed at Mangalore to represent Omani interests. Realising the immense significance of the Gulf region, which still remained the hub of global economic activity linking the Red Sea, the Arabian Sea and the Indian Ocean, Tipu Sultan maintained factories at Muscat, Hormuz, Basra, Bushire, Bahrain and Jeddah, At Muscat Tipu Sultan maintained a large staff to look after Mysore's extensive trade interests there and in the region. In the first two years of Tipu Sultan's rule, he had a *wakil* [or *darogha*] at Muscat and the ruler of Oman maintained an agent at Mangalore. Their names were respectively Mir Qasim and Ghouse Mohammed Khan. Tipu's chief broker *(dallal)* at Muscat and Bushire was Maoji Seth and at Basra a Jew called Abdullah.[9] Tipu maintained extremely cordial ties with the ruler of Oman who gave special privileges like lower customs duty to Mysore merchants. This was reciprocated by Tipu Sultan. In fact, by 1785-86, Tipu Sultan and the ruler of Oman were negotiating a mutually beneficial trade arrangement. In response to Oman's favour to Mysore merchants, Tipu Sultan promised to remit half of all duties on Oman's vessels trading at Mysore ports. He had also advanced plans either to set up new factories at Aden, Bushire, Basra and other important places in the Gulf region or to extend their operations to new areas.

One of the objectives of Tipu Sultan's embassy to the Ottoman Empire was to seek exclusive trading rights in the ports of Basra, Muscat and offer similar facilities at Mangalore or in other parts in his kingdom. He urged the members of the delegation to break journey at Muscat and Bushire to strengthen trade ties with Oman and Persia and to secure further trade privileges. It might be recalled that trade and commerce between Mysore and Oman had greately increased as shipping facilities were provided at the ports and reciprocal trade pacts had been concluded. As a result of these agreements Oman reduced customs duties on products from Mysore to 6 per cent from a high of 10 per cent. The duties imposed on Omani traders to Mysore ports were reduced by half. Keeping in view the crucial role played by the Gulf region in the trade from this area, Tipu Sultan also wanted his delegation to make a detailed study of the Gulf region from all dimensions which would enable him to better understand the prevailing conditions there because of their direct bearing on his kingdom.

According to one writer, Tipu Sultan kept himself up-to-date with regard to market trends in the Gulf region. This was possible for him as his ships and French ships, as well as the ships of Oman, plied frequently between Mangalore and Muscat. Tipu Sultan also maintained a brisk correspondence with his agents in Oman.[10] Undoubtedly, all of Tipu's diplomatic missions had commercial objectives. Since products from Mysore like spices, sandalwood, ivory, silk, rice, cardamoms, timber and cotton cloth were in great demand, he appointed Commercial Attaches and Consul Generals abroad. He maintained a large staff at Muscat to look after Mysore's extensive trade interests there and in the entire Gulf region. Imports from Oman to Mysore were dates, horses, and mules and from the Gulf (via Muscat) silk worms, sulphur, pearls, saffron seeds, pistachio nuts, copper, china wares, rock salt and raisins.

Tipu Sultan encouraged Armenian and Arab merchants from the Gulf to come and settle in Mysore and gave them special privileges as they were seen as successful businessmen. The goods brought by them to Mysore ports were exempt from duty. They were also free to buy and sell merchandise in the Kingdom of Mysore and enjoyed full freedom of movement. One of the crucial reasons why Mysore was prosperous during Tipu Sultan's reign was due to the state monopoly of trade. Tipu Sultan placed severe restrictions on European trading companies, especially the English. The British, in order to circumvent Tipu's restrictions, used to send other merchants disguised as Omani traders to make cheaper purchases from Mysore in different products, especially spices, rice and teak wood for the Chinese market. Tipu Sultan's example of state monopoly of trade was being followed all along the western coast of India. The Prince of Cherikal, and Bibi of Connanore were some instances. His huge military machine, very efficiently supervised by him and his trusted associates enabled Tipu to enforce his monopoly over trade, especially pepper and rice, which the British intensely resented. More and more south Indian rulers followed Tipu Sultan's example of trade monopoly to keep the Europeans out of India's lucrative markets.

According to Tipu Sultan's thinking once the barriers became costly and unprofitable for the British, they would leave the country peacefully. This in the final analysis was what prompted the British to put an end to Tipu Sultan's experiment least other rulers might follow.[11] Tipu Sultan urged the Gulf rulers to send him skilled people and technicians who would assist his government in the setting up of modern industries. This was possible due to his knowledge of the advanced countries, extensive foreign trading contacts and familiarity with foreign goods. Thus, he undertook the role of an international trader, manufacturer, banker and moneychanger.

It was due to Tipu Sultan's efforts that Mysore, now called Karnataka, has become India's leading silk producing state. His foreign economic diplomacy, which primarily aimed at increasing Mysore's exports, was largely successful in trade with the Gulf States due to his pragmatic plans. The British viewed him as a dangerous trade competitor and they were determined to put an end to all his trading activities and imaginative enterprises. His efforts to have extensive trade ties with the Gulf countries received a setback when the English, due to their much larger ships and strong navy, virtually cut him off from the Arabian Sea. After Tipu Sultan's defeat, the first thing the British did was to close down Tipu's factories and Agency at Muscat.[12]

Tipu Sultan's relations with the Gulf countries charted a new and unprecedented course. His embassies in the Gulf states not only gave legitimacy to his rule but also promoted flourishing trade with them. These were undoubtedly bold and courageous initiatives taken by a shrewd and ambitious ruler who had a clear global vision.

Tipu Sultan's skillful diplomacy pushed the British to redouble their efforts to neutralize his diplomatic initiatives, friendship and achievements. The British, due to their world wide contacts, modern means of transport and communications networks were able to reach out to places where Tipu Sultan intended to send his envoys and take effective and tangible steps to neutralize his initiatives in advance. Since the English had already elbowed out the other Europeans, including the French, effectively from the region, it was far easier for them to frustrate Tipu's energetic diplomatic moves. The room to maneuver for Tipu Sultan was extremely limited as the British concentrated all their power, skill and resources to bring about his downfall. It must be mentioned that Tipu Sultan was ready for a compromise or reconciliation with the British but all his overtures were spurned by them and he was repeatedly rebuffed because they considered him an adversary and his ideas too dangerous and hence they decided to overthrow him.

To sum up, Tipu Sultan's historical stature is guaranteed by two great qualities he showed through his statecraft; his ability to take innumerable diplomatic initiatives that transcended the force of circumstances and his ability to take risks even in the face of setbacks. That Tipu Sultan could survive several wars and rule for so long was mainly due to his many shrewd diplomatic and astute military moves. From the very outset, it was clear that a war between Tipu Sultan and the British-led coalition would have been an unequal contest. But what is significant is Tipu Sultan's courage to dare the British and all his other enemies. The success of Tipu Sultan's diplomacy, that brought name and fame from abroad especially from the Gulf region, ended his isolation throwing his enemies in confusion. The British correctly analysed Tipu Sultan's comfortable and secure position at home, which propelled him to seek outside recognition and success; hence they did everything to pull him down from within using his enemies and their manipulative skills. But he offered such stubborn resistance as even the British could never contemplate. He died a hero's death in May 1799 at Sriranganpatna near Mysore. In the ultimate analysis all of Tipu's intricate and complex maneuverings were primarily aimed at upliftment, and improving the life of the people of Mysore and in providing them security.

Notes and References

1. Ishtiaq Hussain Qureshi, 'Tipu Sultan's Embassy to Contantinople, 1787', in Irfan Habib, ed., *Resistance & Modernization under Haider Ali & Tipu Sultan,* Delhi: Tulika, 2001, p. 75.
2. Ibid., p. 70; see also B. Sheik Ali, *English Revolution with Haider Ali*: Mysore, 1963); and Hiden Furber, *Rival Empires of Trade in the Orient 1600-1800,* London: OUP, 1976.
3. Qureshi, n. 1, p. 70; see also A.K. Pasha, ed., *India & Oman: History, State & Foreign Policy,* Delhi: Gyan Sagar, 1999, pp. 1-21; Birendra Varma, 'Tipu Sultan's Embassies to Constantinople & Kabul', *Journal of Historical Research*, 16 (1), August 15, 1973, pp. 51-56.
4. Mohibbul Hassan, *History of Tipu Sultan*, Calcutta: The World Press, Pvt. Ltd. 1971, p. 148; see also K.M. Pannikar, *Asia and Western Domination*, London: Allen & Unwin, 1953, and *Malabar & the Dutch* Bombay: 1931.
5. Khaldoun Hassan al Naqeeb, *Society & State in the Gulf & Arabian Peninsula: A Different Perspective*, London: 1990,

pp. 38-43; see also I.H. Qureshi, 'The Purpose of Tipu Sultan's Embassy to Constantinople', *Journal of Indian History* (Travancore), Vol. 24, 1945, pp. 77-85.

6. Arnold Talbot Wilson, *The Persian Gulf*, Oxford: Clarendon Press, 1928, p. 322; see also Sultan Bin Muhammad al-Qasimi, *The Myth of Arab Piracy in the Gulf*, London: Routledge, 1988, pp. 26-28; Edward Ingram, *Britain's Persian Connection, 1798-1828*, and *Prelude to the Great Game in Asia*, Oxford: Clarendon Press, 1992.
7. Qureishi, n. 1, p. 76; see also K.N. Chaudhri, *Trade & Civilization in the Indian Ocean; An Economic History from the Rise of Islam to 1950*, Cambridge, 1985; A.K. Pasha, *India & West Asia: Continuity & Change*, Delhi: Gyan Sagar, 1999, pp. 1-15.
8. M. Redha Bhacker, *Trade & Empire in Muscat & Zanzibar: Roots of British Domination*, London, 1992, p. 34-35; see also Muhammad Abdullah al Azzawi, *France's Political Activity in the Arabian Gulf & British Counter Measures, 1793-1798*, Al Khalij al Arabi (Basra University) 18 (3-4) 1986, pp. 29-43 (in Arabic); A.K. Pasha, 'Tipu & the Ottoman Empire', in B. Sheik Ali, ed. *Tipu Sultan: A Great Martyr,* Prasaranga: Bangalore, 1993, pp. 219-232; Sultan Bin Muhammad al Qasimi, *Omani-French Relations, 1715-1900*, London: Forest Row, 1996.
9. See Sultan Bin Muhammad al Qasimi, n. 8, and als0 *Power Struggles & Trade in The Gulf, 1620-1820*, London: 1999. p. 178-182; A.K. Pasha, *Perspectives on India & the Gulf States*, New Delhi: Detente Publications, 1999, p. 1-23; Calvin H. Allen, 'Sayyids, Shets, & Sultan's Politics & Trade in Masqat under the Al Bu Said, 1785-1914.' Ph. D. Thesis, University of Washington, 1978.
10. Translation by Iqbal Husain, 'The Diplomatic Vision of Tipu Sultan; Briefs for Embassies to Turkey & France, 1785-86', in Irfan Habib, ed. *State & Diplomacy under Tipu Sultan; Documents & Essays*, New Delhi: Tulika, 2001, pp. 19-65; Mohibbul Hassan, *Waqai Manazil I Rum,* Aligarh: 1980; Charles Rathbone Low, *History of the Indian Navy (1613-1863)* 2 vols. London: Richard Bentley, 1877.
11. Translation by I.G. Khan, 'State Intervention in the Economy: Tipu's Order's to Revenue Collectors 1792-97, A Calendar,' in Charles Rathbone Low, n. 10, pp. 66-81 (p. 80); see also C. Northcote Parkinson, *Trade in the Eastern Seas, 1793-1813* Cambridge, 1937.
12. Ashin Das Gupta and M.N. Pearson eds. *India & the Indian Ocean, 1500-1800*, New Delhi: Oxford, 1999, p., 142; see also A.D. Gupta, *Malabar in Asian Trade 1740-1800,* London, 1967.

Medieval West Asian Critical Appreciation of India

M.A. SALEEM KHAN

There is something mysterious that our existence does not vanish though for centuries the cycle of time has been our enemy.

This couplet from the famous *Tarana Hindi* of Iqbal contains a profound truth whose historical, cultural and philosophical dimensions have not drawn much attention from scholars. India is a country of continental size, its religious and philosophical depth is unfathomable and ever new. While the Vedas of divine songs are among the oldest books of the world, the Puranas, the *Ramayana* and *Mahabharata* are treasures of cultural and anthropological lore, and the Upanishads are the deep oceans of thought. Its philosophies, its classical literature and its popular stories and legends are an unending flood of wisdom and entertainment. This should be as it is because India has been an ancient and large country with its lofty mountains, its large rivers, its vast plains, its luxuriant forests, and not the least, its patient, wise and vast humanity. The larger civilisation and ideational framework has been established from ancient times, leaving scope for cultural changes. Another couplet of the same poem reminds us that Greece, Egypt and the Roman Empire though the first two exist as countries their civilisations have vanished but India exists both as a country and a civilisation. This resilience of India can hardly be explained.

India's head is crowned by the lofty Himalaya and its feet are washed by the Indian Ocean. The Indian continent itself is a Pacific Ocean—*shant*, *prashant*, profound though at times it is a tempestuous ocean. It is not strange that India did not look outside except for a short while at Southeast Asia. While many conquerors and several peoples came to India, from Alexander to Abdali, from the Dravadians to the English, India remained engrossed in its philosophies, its religions, its internal wars and its caste restrictions. This isolation was not beneficial. It did not know what changes were taking place in the outside world. Even Ibrahim Lodhi, who should have known best, did not perceive that Babar was coming with an artillery. The conquerors have come and gone and peoples have come and got absorbed and now India is settled, stabilized and left to itself to recreate itself. However, the most marvellous feature is its large heart, large mind and large compass. While the Vedic-Brahmanic period was passing, the Jaina and Buddhist religions emerged, the Trimurthy age came, the Sad-darsana evolved, the Bhakti and Sufi movements humanised society, the Guptas and the Mughals put their stamp of grandeur and the British ruled and left, India emerged peaceful, profound and democratic.

In West Asia Turkey is the only country which has assiduously developed democracy and secularism, though the military has to intervene from time to time to maintain these features. Independent India from day one has been democratic and secular though sometimes, when disturbances occur in the stratosphere, fog covers the atmosphere and visibility and vision get blurred. However, the basic enduring nature of India is the product of our freedom struggle against the British. This in turn is the reflection of our profound philosophy, humanism and tolerant temper. This has made India a unique country and not for humanism alone.

This is the reason that from classical antiquity countless fanciful tales and amusing fables circulated throughout Europe concerning India's people, its animals and plants, its sun and rains, its mountains and rivers, and these continued to be retold until the Middle Ages. But all was not fancy and fable. Even though Alexander had invaded India he was impressed by the wisdom of India's holy men. He is said to have conversed with some of the 'gymnosophists' (naked philosophers). He was impressed by the brusque and incisive manner of these men. Eventually he asked one of them to succeed his preceptor Aristotle as his consistent companion and counsellor. This naked philosopher seems to have been a Jain Muni of the Digambra sect.[1]

Source of Knowledge and Wisdom

While a few Chinese travellers came and left their accounts and Megasthenese wrote *Indica* the people of West Asia showed the greatest interest in India. They came and wrote travelogues, they marvelled at and studied its religions and philosophies, and they admired its people's wisdom. Despite being strict monotheists they never criticised India's polytheism. As a matter of fact they described India's gods and goddesses objectively and explained religious practices with no adverse comment. There was an unending fascination and absorbing interest in the people of India. India was not the land of fancy and fables alone, it was also the source of knowledge and wisdom for the Arabs of West Asia. They knew about India much before the advent of Islam through their trade in the Indian Ocean and along the coast of India. But their knowledge of Indian culture was desultory and patchy.

With the conquests of the Fertile Crescent, Persia and North Africa, within a few decades of the Prophet's death Muslim Arabs came into contact with the peoples of older religions and older civilisations which were more complex than the simple religion of Islam and the primitive culture of the Arabian Peninsula. This impact produced many perplexing questions and different schools of thought and sects. Arabs had risen from the sands of the desert, but they became alive and receptive. They absorbed, produced and contributed to the cultures and civilisations of the world and attracted people from outside. In the early Abbasid period they established the *Bait al-Hikmah* (The House of Wisdom) in Baghdad and began to translate books from Greek, Syriac Persian and Sanskrit, a unique event in the culture and education of the world. The town became a centre of international learning and a hub of thought and philosophies. The impact of this translation activity was so great that within a few decades Baghdad's scholars began to develop various sciences and produce philosophy, and this exercise continued for many centuries even after the decline and disintegration of the Abbasid empire. For three and half centuries (750-1100) Muslim scholars became the leaders of science throughout the world.[2] While the Greek, Syriac and Persian contributions are of great interest various manifestations of Arab interest in India are relevant here. These will be briefly discussed.

Mathematics and Astronomy

Sarton has given a broad perspective with reference to mathematics in the world. In the second half of the eighth century, with the sole exception of Alcum in Europe, who composed some very elementary texts for teaching purposes, all the mathematical and astronomical work was done by the Muslims. In the previous period mathematical work had been done almost exclusively by the Chinese. Both in Islam and China some amount of stimulation had come from India. In the previous century Indian influence had reached China. Now it reached the Islamic world.[3] During the reign of Abbasid Caliph Mansur (754-775), an Indian delegation of scientists reached Baghdad in 770 with books of astronomy and mathematics. These books were translated into Arabic. They were *Brahmasphuta Siddhanta* (translated as *Sindhind*), *Aryabhatiya* (translated as *Arjabahad*) and *Khandya Khadyaka* (translated as *Arkand*).[4] In the fourteenth and twenty-seventh chapters of the *Siddhanta*, mathematics was discussed. Indian numerals derived from here brought about a revolution in mathematics.[5]

The story of how the Indian numerals were transmitted from the Islamic world to Europe is interesting. In the first half of the ninth century Greek mathematics, in the form of Euclid's *Elements,* was translated by Hajjaj b. Yusuf b. Matar. He also translated *Almagest* of Ptoleny. Then came al-Khwarizmi, from whose name the words 'Algorithm' and 'Angrim' were derived. He synthesized Greek and Indian mathematics. His arithmetic was transmitted to Europe. His astronomical and trigonometric tables as revised by Maslama b. Majriti were translated into Latin in 1126.[6] The earliest Muslim documents containing Indian numerals date to 874 and 888. The earliest example of zero is found in an inscription of 876 at Gwalior.[7]

Medicine

In addition to mathematics and astronomy the Arabs acquired the science of medicine from India. Some Greek and Syriac books of medicine had been translated during the Umayyad Caliphate. During the Abbasid Caliphate a *vaid* called Manka or Manik was called from India to treat Caliph

Harun al-Rashid. He cured him and paved the way for the admission of Indian medicine to the Arab world. In the promotion of medicine as in other fields the Baramika (Barmicides), the ministerial family of the early Abbasids, played a vital role. They appointed an Indian *vaid* as the director of their own public hospital. Yahya b. Khalid al-Barmiki sent an emissary to India to fetch Indian medicinal herbs and appointed an Indian physician in the government translation bureau to translate the medical books into Arabic.[8] Among the books of Indian medicine which were translated into Arabic two are famous: *Susrata Samhita* and the *Caraka Samhita*. Many other books were also translated.[9] These books were translated in the eighth century and influenced European medicine during the Middle Ages. *Caraka Samhita* was last printed in Arabic in 1550.[10] Many other books on Indian medicine were translated into Arabic in the Abbasid period. In the same way books on serpents, poisons, veterinary medicine, astrology, palmistry, gynaecology, music, politics, art of war and strategy, chemistry, prosody, magic, etc., were translated.[11]

Shortcomings in Transmission

The shortcomings in the transmission of knowledge were galore. There was a dearth of translators of Sanskrit while there was an army of translators of Greek and Syriac. No scholar was sent from the Arab world to India to collect Sanskrit books while many scholars had been sent to Constantinople and other Roman cities to collect books in Greek and Syriac. In philosophy while many important books of Greek philosophy were translated no book in the field (from India) was touched, as Indian philosophy was inalienably mixed up with religion which was not the case with Greek philosophy. It is also not surprising that neither Greek nor Indian mythology was translated. Unfortunately, the history and literature of the Greeks were also not translated, although these could have given the Arabs and other Muslims a new vision. There was a yawning gap in the Arab understanding of the Greeks. Mere philosophy and science isolated from history and society gives an incomplete picture. It is not surprising that Muslim philosophers could not go beyond the commentaries on Greek philosophy in most of the cases, and the Muslim flowering of knowledge and wisdom, as against the European Renaissance later, wilted within a few centuries.[12] In the same way no book of literature was translated from Sanskrit. While the science of history itself had not developed in India, very imperfect and simple-minded accounts of Indian history were given by Yaqubi and Masudi. Even Al-Biruni, who came later and settled down and worked for years, could not deal with Indian history except in terms of legends. So far as Indian philosophy is concerned no book appears to have been translated into Arabic. Even Al-Biruni dealt only with two systems. Indian philosophy could not be understood without the knowledge of Indian religions which were too complex for the West Asian monotheists.

Wisdom from Stories

In popular sciences the wisdom of India has no parallel. While India developed serious philosophy and theology of a high order its wise men did not ignore the common man, busy rulers and women. They were taught through stories on popular levels of wisdom. These books of stories became so popular that they were translated into many languages of the world. Among the books that were translated into Arabic are : (1) *Triya Charitr* (Deceit of Women); and (2) *Panchatantra* (translated into Arabic under the name *Kalila wa Dimma* by a famous early Arab writer, Ibn Muqaffa). Later on it was translated and retranslated even in verse. (3) *Budhasafa Wa Blohar* (Boddi Sattva and Prohitar).[13]

Two famous games, i.e. *chausar* or *narad* (backgammon) and *shatranj* (chess) travelled from India to West Asia. Yaqubi (d. 897) gave great details about these games which were supposed to represent two different philosophies.[14]

Arabs had been visiting the Indian coast much before the advent of Islam and knew something about India. But after some of them travelled to India or read about the Indians they were impressed by the Indian character and wisdom. Al-Jahiz (d. 869), famous writer, wrote about the superiority of Indians. He wrote that Indians were advanced in many sciences, in the useful and fine arts including dance, music, poetry and elocution. They had a high standard of philosophy and literature.[15]

Finding a Spiritual Anchor in India

It was not surprising that the West Asian Muslims found a spiritual anchor in India, particularly in the legend of Adam's descent into India when he was sent down from Paradise after he committed the sin of tasting the forbidden fruit. There are many Traditions (*Ahadith,* plural of *Hadith*) of Prophet Muhammad, stories cited in the commentaries of the Quran and in popular legends, which testify to the spiritual interest of Muslims in India. A Tradition says that Adam descended on a mountain in Sarandip (Sri Lanka), and this island in the eyes of Muslims was a part of India.

There were writers such as Ibn Jarir, Ibn Abi Hatim and Hakim who claimed that Adam descended in the Indian region called Dajna (Dakna or Deccan). It was believed that Adam brought to India many perfumes, spices and fruits from Paradise. Therefore India became famous for them. Another story directly connects Prophet Muhammad with India. It was believed that Adam in India received the first *wahi* (divine revelation) from God. The Light of Muhammad had been preserved in his forehead. There is a Tradition in which the Prophet says, 'I feel the divine perfume coming from India'.[16]

Syed Ghulam Ali Azad Bilgrami (1707-1786) of India wrote a booklet in Arabic which he later included as a chapter in his book *Sabhat al Marjan*,[17] on the spiritual importance of India in the eyes of Muslims. In support of his contention he cited famous scholars such as Jalaluddin al-Suyuti, Ibn Saad, Ali al-Rumi, al-Ghazali, Al-Zamkhshari, Al-Masudi, Sharfuddin b. Yunus, Mullah Ali al-Qari.[18] Bilgrami concluded his book with three Arabic couplets of his own whose translation is given below:

The Creator deposited His Light in Adam shining like the radiant star.

India is the land of descent and living place of our grand father (Adam).

This is a true assertion supported by the best of authority.

The inner part of India began to shine from the beginning.

With the Light of Ahmed (Muhammad), the possessor of glories.[19]

It is to be noted that the concept of Light of Muhammad had developed in early Islam and it was believed to be invested in Adam. However, most of the stories cited in the book are not given much credit. Then the question arises as to why an eighteenth century Arabic scholar of repute laboured so hard to collect them and write the book so enthusiastically. The editor of the book is of the opinion that this was because of the patriotic zeal of Bilgrami and the sacredness of India. It is however a fact, as the editor asserts,[20] that, 'In the early Arab writings India was almost always a place of superiority. This attitude sometimes exaggerated and fantastic, derived its inspiration from the progress which India had achieved in different spheres of life, spiritual as well as material.'

Natural and Unrevealed Religions

While Islam, like Judaism and Christianity, is a revealed religion some Muslim thinkers developed the concept of natural and unrevealed religions. Among them was Al-Masudi (896-956). While the Quran states that God sent to every people (*umma*) a prophet (X, 47, for example), Masudi held that some nations derived their laws not from the divine revelations of prophets but through the reason and wisdom of their kings and sages. These were 'natural religions' and India and China developed such religions. He calls India the land of 'virtue and wisdom'.[21] Such views had already been expressed by unorthodox Muslim philosophers of the ninth century. The famous Arab philosopher Al-Kindi's student, Ahmad b. al-Tayyab al-Sarakhsi (d. 899), was one of them. Other free thinkers such as Ibn al-Rawandi and Abu Bakr Muhammad al Zakaiyya al-Razi (d. 925 or 932) also did not believe in the necessity of prophets.[22]

Muslim Travellers and Geographers on India

There are a large number of Arab and Persian travellers who wrote on India. For the sake of brevity only the names of important ones are given here:

1. Ibn Khurdadbeh (d. 912).
2. Sulaiman, the Merchant (9th century)
3. Abu Zaid al-Sirafi (early 10th century)
4. Yaqubi (d. 897).

5. Al Masudi (d. 956)
6. Al Istakhri (flourished c. 950)
7. Ibn Hauqal (flourished 977)
8. Buzug b. Shahriyar (d. 1009)
9. Abu Dulaf Misar b. Muhalhil (d. 942)
10. Bishara al-Maqdisi or Muqaddasi (d. 1000).[23]

The writers on Indian religions were:[24]

1. Maqdisi (d. 985)
2. Ibn al-Nadim (d. 998)
3. Gardizi (d. 1060)
4. Marvazi (d. 1125)
5. Shahrastani (d. 1153).

It is interesting to note that the famous Abbasid Wazir Yahya b. Khalid al-Barmaki had sent an emissary in A.D. 800 to India to collect medicinal herbs and to write a book on the religions of India. The *baramika* (plural of *Barmaki* which is the Arabicised form of *paramukh*) were the descendants of the hereditary *paramukhs* (chiefs) of the famous Buddhist *vihara* of Balkh, now in Afghanistan. The Barmaki Wazir was naturally curious to know the religious situation in India, the land of Buddhism, the religion of his ancestors. The emissary was able to report on both the Buddhist and the Hindu sects. The name of the emissary's report has been given in Ibn al-Nadim's book *Al-Fihrist* (completed in 987) as *Kitab fihi Milal al-Hind wa Adyanuha* (A Book containing Sects of India and Its Religions). It attracted so much attention among Arab scholars that the famous philosopher Al-Kindi (d. 873) copied it in his own hand. Its contents, amplified with other information, were presented in *Al-Fihrist*.[25]

However, an unfortunate fact is that almost all the writers on Indian religions whose names were given above copied from the emissary's book written in A.D. 800 with some additions. They did not visit India as others had done. Even Shahrastani, who came after Al-Biruni, and whose book *Kitab al-Milal wa al-Nihal* (Treatise on Religions Sects and Philosophical Groups) and whose treatment of the West Asian religions is believed to be a standard one, committed blunders when he wrote on Indian religions.[26] This indicates that Shahrastani did not read Al-Biruni's book nor was otherwise inspired by him. This shows the decline of Islamic scholarship. As a matter of fact a steep Muslim intellectual decline had started from the twelfth century, a phenomenon which awaits detailed study.

While the early West Asian travellers, geographers and writers on Indian religions were brief in their treatment of Indian culture and history, Al-Biruni (Abu Raihan Muhammad b. Ahmad, 973-1050) was not only exhaustive but serious, imaginative and critical. He was well equipped to understand India, trained as an objective scholar and sympathetic to the soul of India. He had written an important book, *Chronology*, on the culture and history of western Central Asian peoples. Al-Biruni was also a scientist writing about Indian sciences. Born in Khwarizm in the region of Oxus (Amu-Darya) delta on the southern shore of the Aral Sea, he had been captured and brought from his native state of Khwarizm (where he was also an important courtier) by Mahmud Ghaznavi to India in 1017. He lived in India (mainly in Ghazni, in Afghanistan now but at that time a town of India) till his death. He wrote several books and papers. E.S. Kennedy has given an account of Al-Biruni's 146 works of which the major ones number 14, those that are extant are 22 and thirteen have been published. His three lost astronomical works run to 360,550 and 600 folios. The largest of all his books is *India*[27] which runs in 700 folios. His total output is in the order of 13,000 folios (pages). Roughly four-fifths of his works have been lost beyond the hope of recovery.[28] Fortunately his book on India is extant.

Al-Biruni lived in the first half of the eleventh century, an era when Islamic sciences and philosophy were on the decline. *Bait-al-Hikma* (The House of Wisdom), established by the Abbasid Caliph Al-Mamun (813-33) had passed into history, the Abbasid empire had been disintegrating and small states were patronizing the sciences but they were unstable. Ibn Sina, a physician and philosopher and a junior contemporary of Al-Biruni was wandering from court to court in search of security and patronage. Al-Biruni, who had learnt no profession depended only on patronage. In his early life he had also gone into wilderness when his native state was conquered and occupied by another king. However, he had returned and settled down to work before Mahmud Ghaznavi attacked and annexed it. It was his good fortune and that of India that he had been brought to India by Mahmud, though his relations with the king were strained.

Only a few aspects of Al-Biruni's contribution to the understanding of India will be dealt with here.

Hindu Religion: Al-Biruni makes a basic difference between the popular religion of idol-worship and the elite's religion of one God. He does not quote from Hindu books of religion but from books of philosophy such as from Patanjali. So far as Al-Biruni's 'book' of Patanjali is concerned Sachau remarks that it is totally different from the Yoga Aphorisms of Patanjali.[29] He describes Hindu belief in God in the following words:[30]

> The Hindus believe with regard to God that he is one, eternal, without beginning and end, acting by free will, almighty, all-wise, living, giving life, ruling, preserving, one, who in his sovereignty is unique, beyond all likeness and unlikeness, and that he does not resemble anything, nor does anything resembles him.

He never discusses the gods and goddesses of the Vedic period nor of later Hinduism of the Trimurthy (three gods, viz. Brahma, Vishnu [and his *avatars*] and Siva). Thus, he presents the God of the Hindus in absolute terms, resembling Islamic God. Was there any purpose behind this treatment? He quotes from the *Gita* also, but the quotations given by him are not found in the present *Bhagvadgita*. Sachau examines the passage given by Al-Biruni with the extant *Gita* and comes to the conclusion that it does not exist in the latter.[31] Another passage from the *Gita* which Al-Biruni quotes resembles the famous chapter of the Quran called *Ikhlas*.[32] One is struck by the apparent neglect in Biruni of the fact that what he was quoting from the *Gita* in the name of God was actually a conversation between two human beings, i.e. Krishna and Arjuna. It is strange that this did not strike Al-Biruni, a Muslim monotheist as in Islam there is no concept of man-god and even the Prophet did not claim to partake of divinity.

Hindu Religious Literature: Al-Biruni's treatment of Hindu religious literature is peculiar. Much before his time Muslims had studied their own religious literature particularly the

Quran and the *Hadith* on the one hand, and the derived literature as *'Fiqh'* (religious law), life of the Prophet, and the exegesis of the Quran meticulously on the other. They had of course not studied other religions until very late. When Al-Biruni got an opportunity to study Hindu religious literature and he evinced great interest in it; he could have studied at least some important books like the Vedas. But he did not. He wrote something about the Vedas on the basis of the Puranas which are a different and later category of literature. Of course, the Vedas were out of bounds for him but he did not mention this fact. He wrote about who could read and teach the Vedas but did not say much about what they contained. One can see from the following quote how vague, partial and irrelevant a characterisation of the Vedas he gives: 'The Veda contains commandments, and prohibitions, detailed statements about reward and punishment intended to encourage and to deter, but most of it contains hymns of praise and treats of various kinds of sacrifices to the fire, which are so numerous and difficult that you can hardly count them.'

He patterned the first part of his description of the contents of the Vedas in terms of the Quran and the *Hadith*. He of course mentions 'hymns of praise' but does not say whose praise they sing. He avoids the mention of gods and goddesses. He does not give the name of even the goddess of fire. Did he purposely avoid mentioning them? He gives stories which are not very relevant. One does not of course expect Al-Biruni to make a detailed and precise study as the modern writers do. It appears that the Pundits he engaged not only did not allow him to touch the Vedas but they also took him for a ride. He did not also mention the *Brahmanas*, the *Aranyakas* and the *Upanisads*, which are believed to be the parts of the Vedas.

Al-Biruni's treatment of the Puranas is also inadequate. He does not discuss the nature of the Puranas. This fact appears strange for a person who had a rational and logical mind because the Puranas unlike many other books of Hindu religion are loaded with strange myths and legends. He gives two lists of the Puranas,[33] and informs us that he saw some portions of *Matsya*, *Aditya* and *Vayu* Puranas. He also gives the names of twenty *Dharmasastras* (law books)[34] and calls the *Smrithi* a book. He notes that Hindus have written books an jurisprudence, theosophy, asceticism, on the processes of becoming god, and seeking liberation from the world. It has to be remembered that Al-Biruni's attempts to cover the whole conspectus of Hindu literature in the eleventh century is remarkable at a time when systematization was not known.

He mentions the *Mahabharata* which the Hindus[35] hold in such veneration that they assert that everything that occurs in other books is found in this book, but not all that occurs in this book is found in other books. He calls it *Bharata,* composed by Vyasa at the time of the great war between the children of Pandu and those of Kuru. The book has 100,000 slokas in 18 parts, each of which is called Parvan.[36]

Al-Biruni almost ignores the *Ramayana*. He mentions it briefly in a chapter on Puranic geography where a mention of Lanka is made. He briefly narrates the story of how Rama killed Ravana and his brother killed Ravana's brother.[37]

Hindu Caste System: Of the Muslim travellers and writers who came to India Al-Biruni was the only person who studied the caste system meticulously and in great detail and was generally correct in his observations. He wrote connected chapters on: a) The Hindu caste system; b) Life and duties of the Brahmanas and other castes; and c) Four stages (*Asrama*) in the life of Brahmanas,

It is surprising that the peculiar caste system of India did not strike him as strange as it should have, since he was a Muslim, who believes in the concept of equality. Among Hindus the human hierarchy had been sanctified by religion, even by the Vedas (e.g. by *Purusa Sukta*) and *Manava Dharma* Sastra and there was a widespread practice to such an extent that it had become pernicious and oppressive, though at the beginning it was innocuous. Al-Biruni, on the contrary, enthusiastically supports it in chapter IX because he was of Persian in origin though born in Khwarimz, a Turkish-influenced region. How enthusiastically he supports hierarchy in Hindu society will be evident from the following:[38]

> If a new order of things in political and social life is created by a man naturally ambitious of ruling, who by his character and capacity really deserves to be a ruler, a man from conviction and unshaken determination, who even in times of reverses is supported by good luck, in so

far as people then side with him in recognition of former merits of his, such an order is likely to become consolidated among those for whom it was created and to continue as firm as the deeply rooted mountains.

Then he draws the picture of antiquity saying that the kings 'who industriously devoted to the duties of their office' gave most of their attention to the division of their subjects into different classes and orders, which 'they tried to preserve from intermixture and disorder'. He illustrates this by the history of ancient Iranian kings who had created great institutions of this kind which could not be broken through the special merits of any individual nor by bribery. He gives the Iranian classes and castes as: (a) Knights and princes (b) Monks, fire-priests and religious lawyers, (c) Physicians, astronomers and other men of science, and (d) Husbandmen and artisans

Within these classes there were sub-divisions 'like species within a genus'. One finds that Al-Biruni uses his knowledge of biology and applies it to human society as if human society is an organism. However, later as an afterthought and only as a formality he adds. 'We Muslims, of course, stand entirely on the other side of the question, considering all men as equal, except in piety, and this is the greatest obstacle which prevents any approach and understanding between Hindus and Muslims.'

This interpretation is partially wrong because pious people in Islam are not superior in the eyes of law though they are respectable in the eyes of God, and if they commit any sin they are equally liable to punishment.

Al-Biruni gives a description of the four castes and even of those below the Sudras.[39] He also describes the life of the four castes, though that of the Brahmans[40] is given in greater detail.

Idol-Worship among Hindus: Here Al-Biruni does not justify idol worship among the Hindus, but denies its existence, except among the common people, the vulgar lot. The distinction between the educated and uneducated people is explained in great detail. This is a sociological problem which is common in every religion. However, so far as the Hindus are concerned he says[41] : 'For those who march on the path of liberation, and those who study philosophy and theology, and who desire abstract truth which they call *sara*, are entirely free from worshipping anything but God alone, and would never dream of worshipping an image manufactured to represent him.'

Thus the Brahmanas who belong to the highest caste and are educated theologians, if not philosophers, should not have been idol-worshippers. But they were the greatest idol worshippers and custodians of temples and religion. They are not an uneducated vulgar lot. In this way the thesis of Al-Biruni is rendered hollow. Then why does he offer this thesis?

In order to prove his contention he relates a story which Saunaka told King Pariksha.[42] There was a king, he relates, called Ambarisha who had obtained an empire as large as he had wished for. He retired from the world and devoted himself to worshipping God. Finally God appeared to him in the shape of Indra and spoke to the king, 'Demand whatever you like and I will grant.' The king thanked him and said he would not ask for anything from him but only from he who created him. Indra was angry and threatened to kill him if he did not yield. But the king did not budge. He insisted that he would ask the real God. Then the Lord appeared in the shape of a man of gray lotus colour, riding on a bird called Garuda, holding in one of his four hands the *sankha,* in the second the *chakra*, in the third an a emulet, and in the fourth a *padma*. When the king saw him he prostrated before him. The Lord promised to give him what he wanted. Then the king told him that his only wish was to be liberated from the world. The Lord ordered him to occupy himself with his empire in the best possible way and turn his thought to him (the Lord). He told him to make an image of him and worship it so that he may not forget him.

One wonders whether Al-Biruni duped himself or wanted to dupe his readers. The god who had appeared earlier whom the king did not accept was Indra, the Chief god of the Vedic period who had been dethroned in the later period. The god who appeared later and whom the king accepted as his lord was Vishnu, one of the three gods of a later period. He was not a real god as Al-Biruni could conceive. However, the answer to the question as to who is the real god is elusive. Believers in each of the three gods consider themselves to be worshipping the real god. The surprising thing is the Lord asking the king to make a figure of him and worship it. This goes directly against Al-Biruni's contention that only the vulgar indulge in idol worship. Al-Biruni, who worked on Hinduism, should have known this. The question is why Al-Biruni engaged himself in such delusion.[43]

Ghaznavi's Attempt to Reconcile with the Hindus: It is a well known fact that Mahmud Ghaznavi was a great conqueror and for the sake of maintaining his machinery of war did not hesitate to plunder Hindu temples, an act of sacrilege which early Muslim conquerors, particularly during the Pious Caliphate, had never resorted to. Al-Biruni condemned it in his *India* and showed sympathy with Hindus. He also admired Hindu progress in science and philosophy and distinguished them from the pre-Islamic Arab pagans who had no science and philosophy. Al-Biruni was not a theologian who would take a compulsively narrow view but a historian and sociologist and thus had a breadth of vision and understanding. Suniti Kumar Chatterji, one of the great Sanskritists of modern India, had great admiration for him.[44]

After discussing Mahmud's temple looting Al-Biruni states a paradoxical fact. He relates that after the conquest and annexation of the Punjab, Mahmud issued special kinds of coins for his Hindu subjects. On these coins something was written. This has never been done before or after in the annals of Islamic numismatics. On all the coins from the Umayyad Caliphate the Islamic *kalima* (creed), *'Lailaha Illallah Muhammad Rasulullah'* (There is no god except Allah and Muhammad is His Prophet) was inscribed only in Arabic. But the coins of Mahmud were bilingual. On one side there was the *kalima* in Arabic, inscribed as usual but on the other side there was its translation in Sanskrit, which was an innovation and a concession to the Hindus, according to Chatterji. However, the more surprising thing was the translation which read *avayaktum ekum, Muhammada avatara*. This was not a literal or exact translation as accepted by Chatterji. This was the one as cast in the mould of Hindu concepts and was far from the original one both for Allah and the *Rasul* (Messenger). The literal translation of the Sanskrit sentence as given by

Chatterji himself is, 'The Unmanifest is one, and Muhammad is his incarnation'. One may say this was nothing but 'a Hinduisation of Islamic creed'. Chatterji insists that Al-Biruni was associated with his translation. This is improbable. However, seeing the attitude of Al-Biruni in other matters, as discussed above, one may not be surprised if he did approve this translation.[45]

Al-Biruni may be called an exception in the field of study of medieval India. No author before him nor after him till modern times has studied India in such depth and with such sympathy. Further, he wanted to study India on a larger scale and would have revived the Indian sciences which had declined and at the same time would have resurrected Islamic sciences which were on their last leg in the eleventh century. But he could not do so because of Mahmud's lack of patronage and unsympathetic attitude. If he had been able to do so, it may be presumed the Renaissance might have taken place in India and West Asia rather than in Europe. Another important aspect of his contribution, as discussed above, appears to be that he wanted to establish an atmosphere of reconciliation and amity between the Muslim rulers and the Hindu subjects. For this purpose he presented the latter in the best possible light.[46] His academic service was a diplomatic exercise also but unfortunately it did not fructify. No dialogue was started between the two sides. Mahmud died and his kingdom was shattered after his death. Al-Biruni's book disappeared from the scene as the age of Persian had dawned and readers of Arabic, in which the book was written, became rare. There may have been other reasons.[47]

Notes

1. Klaus K. Klostermaier, *A Survey of Hinduism* New York, 1989, pp. 18-19.
2. See George Sarton, *Introduction to the History of Science*, Vol. I, New York, 1975 reprint, p. 62.
3. Ibid.
4. Syed Sulaiman Nadwi, *Arab Wa Hind Ke Taaluqat,* Azamgarh, 1984, new edition, p. 137.

5. For details see M.A. Saleem Khan, *Early Muslim Perception of India and Hinduism,* New Delhi, 1997, p. 173.
6. Sarton, n 2, pp. 562-63.
7. Ibid., p. 601. For further transmission of Indian numerals to Europe see a summary in Khan, n. 5, p. 169.
8. For details see Nadwi n. 4, p. 146.
9. For details see ibid., pp. 146-52.
10. See *The Gazetteer of India: Indian Union*, Vol. I *History and Culture* ed. P.N. Chopra Ministry of Education and Social Welfare: New Delhi, 1990, p. 208.
11. For details see Nadwi n. 4 pp. 152-72. See also Ibn al-Nadim, *Al-Fihrist* (Cairo, n.d.) pp. 435-501.
12. See Khan n. 5, pp. 175-7.
13. For details regarding this book see Khan n. 5, pp. 176-7.
14. For details see chapter 'Yaqubi and Indian Wisdom' in Khan n. 5 pp. 197-207.
15. For details see Khan n. 5, pp. 180-81.
16. See Nadwi, n. 4, pp. 1-3.
17. Syed Ghulam Ali Azad Bilgrami, *Sabahat al Marjan fi Athar Hindustan* edited by Muhammad Fazlur Rahman al Nadwi, Aligarh, 1976.
18. For a summary see Khan n. 5, pp. 146.
19. Bilgrami n. 17, p. 152.
20. Muhammad Fazlur Rahman Nadwi al-Sivani, Introduction in Bilgrami, n. 17.
21. Masudi devoted a whole chapter of his famous book, *Muruj al-Dahab wa Maadin al Jawahir*, Vol. I, to India in which the wisdom of India constitutes the dominant part.
22. See Khan n. 5, pp. 213-14.
23. For details on the above see ibid., pp. 184-235.
24. For details see ibid., pp. 238-303.
25. For details see ibid., p. 238-39.
26. See ibid., pp. 276-303.
27. Full name of Al-Biruni's Arabic book on India is *Kitab al-Biruni fi Tahqiq ma lil Hind min Maqalatin Maqbula fil Aql aw Marzula* (Dairatul Maarif al-Usmania, Hyderabad Deccan, Al-Hind) New Series No. 11, which forms the oldest extant MS in the *Bibliotheque Nationale*, Paris, Schefer 6080). Edward Sachau translated it under the name *Alberuni's India* Vol. I & II, bound in one volume (London, 1910, reprint 1983, New Delhi).
28. E.S. Kennedy, 'Al-Biruni' *Dictionary of Scientific Biography* (New York, 1980), p. 151.
29. See Sachau's Annotations in *Alberuni's India* pp. 263-64.
30. As cited Sachau, Vol. I p. 27.

31. See Sachau p. 264-66. See also Klaustermair n.1, p. 94, for the contention that since Shankarchariya's Commentary on *Bhagvadgita*, which is prior to Al-Biruni, there has been no change in the text.
32. See Sachan. 130-31.
33. Sachau, pp. 130-131.
34. Ibid., p. 131
35. Ibid., p. 132.
36. Ibid.
37. Ibid., pp. 306-307.
38. Ibid. p. 99.
39. For details see M.A. Saleem Khan *Al-Biruni's Discovery of India: An Interpretative Study,* New Delhi, 2001, pp. 128-34.
40. See ibid., p. 137-39.
41. Sachau p. 133.
42. Ibid., pp. 113-115.
43. For further discussion see Khan n. 39, pp. 141-44.
44. See Sumiti Kumar Chatterji, 'Al-Biruni and Sanskrit' in *Al-Biruni's Commemoration Volume,* Iran Society: Calcutta, 1951, pp. 83-100.
45. For discussion see Khan n. 39, pp. 60-63.
46. For greater discussion see ibid., pp. 256-272.
47. See ibid., pp. 267-271.

India-West Asia Interaction

AKHTARUL WASEY

Interaction between India and West Asia goes back to the pre-historic or legendary period and has been an uninterrrupted process till today. The two regions have been the cradle of some of the great cultures and have influenced each other in numerous ways. The agents of this interaction have been traders, adventurers, conquerors, men of religion and, in recent times anti-colonial freedom fighters.

The West Asian region stretching from Afghanistan to Egypt has a variety of geographical features from the mountainous land of the Afghans to the fertile plains of Persia (lran), and further on to the Arab lands that include the arid desert vastnesses of Arabia and the green valleys of the rivers Euphrates, Jordan and Nile. The geographical features of these areas determined the mode of interaction of each region. India was a land of plenty in ancient times, the legendary golden bird; its inhabitants felt no need to look beyond its shores. In contrast, people of West Asia were inclined to benefit from other lands through trade and conquest; several of them found India to be a better habitat than the lands of their origin and made it their home, over the centuries producing a rich, colourful cultural melange.

The Arabs of the region were seafaring people, their economy depending mainly on trade. They carried the produce, especially spices, of not only India but of the entire Southeast Asian region to Europe. There are hardly any authentic Indian accounts of the early period because, for some reason, Indians were as disinclined to recording history as they were to leaving their shores. The reason, it may not be wrong to surmise, could be that they felt overwhelmed by the transitoriness of earthly life and their mind remained preoccupied with the contemplation of timeless eternity; history, being recognition of the boundaries of time, was not worthy of intellectual labour. The result is that our knowledge is confined to extant legend literature and accounts of Arab travellers. India was the best staging post for these traders and travellers; the former set up colonies in the coastal regions of India while the latter explored the region to provide information to them.

The affluent trading Muslim communities of Gujarat and of the Deccan peninsula are relics of that period. They brought Islam to India and from here carried it further to Malaysia, Indonesia as well as China. The near-total absence of hostile feeling for their non-Muslim neighbours indicates that they had been treated as honoured visitors to be welcomed; they had, after all, contributed to the economic prosperity of this land through their trading activities. The message of Islam that they brought after its revelation in Arabia was welcome as a new way of contemplating man, society and God that appealed to the catholic spirit of the hosts. The impact was felt not only in terms of winning more adherents to Islam but also as a catalyst to Vedantic thought.

Indo-Arab relations were marked by mutual appreciation and respect. Though accounts of this relationship are better known from the period after the emergence of Islam in Arabia, there is evidence of this relationship persisting in pre-Islamic times as well. K.A. Nizami refers to British historian Elphinston as evidence that:

> There were large numbers of Arab colonies on the western coast of India and many Indian settlements in the Arab countries. Ubulla, for instance, was known as *arz-ul-Hind* on account of the large number of Indians who inhabited that region. When Islam spread and the Arabs got converted to Islam, these colonies continued to flourish as before. The Indian rajas appointed Muslim judges, known as *hunarman*, to decide their cases and provided all facilities to them to organize their community life (Foreword to *Arab Accounts of India*, ed., M. Zaki).

Nizami further writes:

> Commercial contacts led to clutural relations and while a large number of Arab navigational and other terms were adopted by the Indians, Indian customs, institutions and practices found their way to Arabia. Philologists have traced three Sanskrit words—*mishk* (musk), *zanjbil*

(ginger) and *kafur* (camphor)—in the Quran. An Indian raja is reported to have sent Indian pickle to the Prophet. The Prophet's remark that 'he received sweet fragrance from India' has been quoted by many later writers (ibid.).

Maulana S. Suleiman Nadvi, in his scholarly work *Arab-o-Hind ke Ta'luqat*, points, for the origin of early Indian scripts, to Arabic as they are written from right to left in contrast to the practice in Sanskrit and the languages derived from it. In support of the contention that Indians knew Arabic, he has discovered evidence in Swami Dayanand's *Satyarth Prakash*. He quotes him: 'In *Mahabharat*, when *Kauravas* planned to burn *Pandavas* in a lac-house, Vidurji informed Yudhishthir in Arabic and Yudhishthirji replied in the same Arabic language.' If Swamiji is right, it proves Indo-Arab intimacy to be as old as the *Mahabharat*.

On the high regard for India in the post-Islam Arabia ample evidence is available in the extant writings of the Arab traders and travellers. Jahiz, a resident of Basra, wrote a whole book, *Kitab-ul-Asnam*, describing the religions of India. Though that book is no longer available, his extant works contain rich compliments to the eloquence of Indians and their religious practices and intellectual achievements. In his journal *Fakhr-us Saudan'Alal Baizan*, he writes:

> The inhabitants of India are highly meritorious in astrology and medicine. They have a peculiar script. In medicine too they have a supreme insight. They have in their possession some strange secrets of the art of Aesculapius. They have medicines for some very fell diseases. In making busts and statues, in making pictures out of colours, and in architecture they are superb. They are the inventors of chess which is a game of mental gymnastics. They make fine swords and know how to wield them. They know incantations to annihilate the effects of poisoning and cure aches. Their music is also enchanting. One of their musical instruments is known as *kanka* (?) which is played on by striking a chord strung in a gourd. It sounds like the guitar and the conch-shell... there is every variety of dance, and they have got different kinds of script. There is an uncommon fund of poetical wealth

> and oratorical affluence in their possession. They know the arts of medicine, philosophy and ethics. The book *Kalah wa Dimnah* has come to us from them. They have plenty of courage and commonsense and many qualities that are wanting even in the Chinese. Cleanliness is a noted feature. They have good looks, tall stature, and a taste for perfumes. It is from their land that the peerless ambergris comes for the use of kings.

Jahiz goes on with the panegyric:

> Streams of high thinking flowed down from India to Arabia. They know incantations which, when chanted, annihilate the effects of poisoning. They are the inventors of astronomical calculations. Their women are expert singers and their men are expert cooks. Dealers in monetary transactions do not entrust their purses to any except them. The treasurer of every such dealer in Iraq must be a Sindhi or a son of a Sindhi. Their natural bias is towards figuring, monetary transactions and things like these. They make very honest and faithful servants.

Another Arab intellectual, Idrisi, at the instance of his royal patron, the king of Sicily, collected information about various countries of the world and compiled it into a book called *kitab al Rujari*. About India he reports:

> The Indians are naturally inclined to justice, and never depart from it in their actions. Their good faith, honesty and fidelity to their engagements are well known, and they are so famous for these qualities that people flock to their country from every side; hence the country is flourishing and their condition prosperous. Among other characteristic marks of their love of truth and horror of vice, the following is related: When a man has a right to demand anything from another, and he happens to meet him, (he) has only to draw a circular line upon the ground and to make his debtor enter it, which the latter never fails to do, and the debtor cannot leave this circle without satisfying his creditor, or obtaining the remission of debt.

If this appreciation of India was uni-dimensional, if no dark spots were seen, these accounts could as a whole perhaps be described as the diplomatic efforts of Arab rulers and tradesmen to curry favour and secure their political and commercial interests. But that is not the case. Of the seamy side of life also due note has been taken, For instance, kidnapping for ransom has been mentioned with horror and concrete examples have been narrated. These thugs are reported to be moving in gangs in search of their victims and kidnapped merchants, whether Indian or foreigner, and demanding ransom money on pain of death. In this connection one of the writers, Buzurg bin Shaharyar, relates an interesting story on the authority of one Muhammad bin Muslim who had spent twenty years in Thane (near Mumbai). A gang of a dozen such thugs kidnapped the only son of a rich merchant and demanded ten thousand *ashrafis* as ransom. The merchant offered one thousand instead and the kidnappers rejected the offer. The merchant then sought help of the raja and prayed for justice. The raja expressed helplessness and explained that if he took action to punish the robbers it might result in the death of his son whose rescue is sought. At that the merchant entreated the raja not to let the devils go scot free even if it meant the death of his son. The raja ordered that the abode of the kidnappers be set on fire and that resulted in the death of the merchant's son along with the gang of thugs.

Such opinions were held at a time when Islam was at the pinnacle of glory and Muslims had conquered large parts of Africa and Europe. Intellectual interest in India got a boost with the shift of the Caliphate from Damascus to Baghdad and Caliph Mamun set up *bait-u'l-hikma* and intiated a programme of translations from Sanskrit to Arabic. That touched off a movement to study Indian culture and social life. Shahristani, Masudi, Ibn Khurdazbih, Sulaiman Tajir, and a whole line of scholars collected information and wrote about Indian society, religion and politics.

What we have quoted above indicates answers to the queries of trading interests but commercial interests are hardly ever completely divorced from interest in political conditions. Not only those who were keen on territorial expansion of their rule but also those engaged in commerce and trade wanted to acquire information about the rulers and the political system prevalent in the countries in which they sought to operate.

Naturally therefore, there are numerous accounts of history and politics of India.

Masudi, an eminent historian, geographer and traveller attempted to reconstruct the ancient history of India on the basis of traditions and legends in currency in those days. Regarding the origin of man he quotes the tradition current among the people around him that Adam had descended in Ceylon (then included in India) with the leaves of a paradise tree on his body. Those leaves when dried were scattered by the wind throughout India which is why there are so many perfumes in this country. This is not a part of *hadith* (authentic traditions and sayings of the Prophet) but the Islamic scholars of *hadith* like Suleiman Nadvi and Husain Ahmad Madni have recognised the belief as evidence of Muslim claim to India as their ancestral homeland and the land where first of all the light of Islam appeared.

Masudi interpreted the Indian story of Creation as the early process of integration of India that is mentioned by M. Zaki in the introduction to his book *Arab-Accounts of India* thus: In the remote past when all other nations were divided into various tribes (i.e. when others were at the tribal stage) certain people of India adorned with the qualities of nobility, rectitude, wisdom and learning were trying to bring together people under a central government. They first established a central authority and claimed to rule over others. They appointed the great Brahman, the Supreme Leader, their ruler. It was the age of ascendancy of the learned. The people made progress in all fields of life. They explored iron mines, made swords and other weapons, built palaces, studied the Heavens and stars and the movement of the sun. They wrote books on various sciences, the details of which Masudi claims to have given in his other book, *Kitab-ul-Ausat*.

During the first hundred years of Islam, Arabs showed more interest in Africa and Europe where the Omayyids, with their capital at Damascus, extended their empire. As the Caliphate shifted from Damascus to Baghdad with the ascendance of the Abbaside, the focus of their attention shifted from Europe to Asia and India. Jawaharlal Nehru was greatly attracted by this development particularly because of the prominence of Arab interest in science and learning. In one of the letters in *Glimpses of World History* he pays fulsome compliments to the scientific spirit of the Arabs: 'Among the ancients we do not find the scientific method in Egpyt or China or India. We find just a bit of it in old Greece. In Rome again it was absent. But the Arabs had this scientific spirit of inquiry, and so they may be considered the fathers of modern science.'

They showed an insatiable hunger for knowledge, reminding one of the Prohet's advice to go up to China in pursuit of knowledge. According to Nehru Arabs were more interested in cultural interaction with India than in conquest, hence they did not extend their domain beyond Sind which he does not find of much consequence. Cultural contact he finds of greater interest. He however bemoans that the Arabs profited from this contact more than India:

> 'Arab students came in large numbers to the northern university of Takshashila or Taxila, which was especially famous for medicine. It is said that in the days of Harunal-Rashid Indian scholarship had a high place in Baghdad and physicians from India went there to organize hospitals and medical schools. Many Sanskrit books on mathematics and astronomy were translated into Arabic.

India, on the other hand, only 'got to know something of the new religion, Islam'.

The introduction of religion, even conversion, did not create any trouble or friction because it was not then seen as a part of conquest as happened later, especially in the case of Afghan invaders like Mahmood Ghaznavi, though his interest was more in plundering wealth than in spreading religion.

The Arab interest in India during the Abbasid period is exemplified by the comment of Yaqubi, an officer in Baghdad's department of Correspondence, who wrote in his *Tarikh*: 'The Indians are men of wisdom and vision, and in wisdom are superior to all other nations. Their views on astronomy are most authentic. Their dictums in medicine are preferable.'

The political interest of the Arabs was more in understanding the system of administration than territorial conquest. That is why even the introduction of Islam and building of mosques and *madrassas* created no friction or ill will. Indeed, they had very friendly relations with the rulers of the Deccan, the region where they had established their colonies. Their appreciation of the rajas is testified by M. Zaki, on the basis of the writings of Maqdisi, Yaqut and Istakhari, in the following words:

'These rulers, we are told, were very tolerant and had special regard for the Arabs. It was generally believed that they enjoyed long reigns (40 to 50 years) due to their love and affection for the Arabs. The Muslim Arabs enjoyed full religious freedom in their kingdom and regularly offered their prayers in the mosques. This is why all the Arab writers regarded them as the greatest pro-Arab rulers in India.

'Similarly they give a vivid description of the Muslim principality of Sind which, according to them, denoted the area lying between Hindustan on the one hand and Kirman and Sijistan on the other, comprising several provinces including Multan' (Introduction to the *Arab Accounts of India*, p.33).

Multan, under Muslim rule, is also described in glowing terms as *Bait uz Zahab* (House of Gold), its people praised as 'happy, prosperous, hospitable, honest and well-behaved'. References also are found to other kingdoms of India like Kashmir, Gujarat and Qannauj. In these accounts there are significant observations about the administration. For instance, it is mentioned that kingship is generally recognised as a hereditary institution, and so are the posts of *vizier* and all other important officials of the king. How closely they observed the political scene is reflected in the following description of the ceremony held on the raja's ascendance:

> Some of the kings of India, when they ascend the throne, have a quantity of rice cooked and served on banana leaves. Attached to the King's person are three or four hundred companions, who have joined him of their own free will without compulsion. When the King has eaten some of the rice, he gives it to his companions. Each in his turn approaches and takes a small quantity and eats it. All those who eat the rice are obliged, when the King dies or is slain, to burn themselves to the last man on the very day of King's decease. This is a duty which

> admits of no delay and not a vestige of these men ought to be left (Abu Zaid, supplement to Sulayman's *Silsilat-ul-Tawarikh*, p.116).

So far as religion is concerned the Arab-Indian relationship was marked by perfect understanding and a spirit of free inquiry. Elaborate details of various schools of religious thought in India are found in the writings of the Abbaside period. Quoting Abdul Karim Shahristani, a twelth century scholar of comparative religions, Zaki writes that according to him, 'Indians are a great nation and a great (religious) community (*Ummat-e-kabirah wa Millat-e-Azimah*) but they have divergent views and ideologies.' He cites another scholar, Mutahhr bin Tahir Muqaddasi, as saying that:

> ...according to some people there are nine hundred sects in India, only ninety-nine are known which are based on forty two sects, the latter are the off shoots of four main religions, and these four fall under two main categories i.e; Brahmanism and Samanism or Buddhism. Broadly speaking the Samanis do not believe in God or have faith in a powerless God. The Brahmans are divided into three main groups. The one believes in monotheism (*Tauhid*) and retribution and punishment (*jaza wa saza*), but does not believe in prophethood; the second one believes neither in monotheism nor prophethood but accepts retribution in the form of metempsychosis.

Another significant observation is by Qazi Said who, in his book, *Tabaqat-ul-Umam*, says that 'Hindus generally believed in one Supreme God, having no partner, but differed further regarding the nature of the universe. A section of the Brahmans believe it as accidental while others regarded it as eternal, but none of them had faith in prophethood. All of them were against animal slaughter.'

Buzurg Shahryar, captain of a Persian merchant ship, has recorded his personal experiences in a book *Ajaib-ul-Hind*. In it he records a tradition surviving till his time, the tenth century:

> When the people of Sarandeep and places roundabout learnt of the Prophet of Islam, they sent an intelligent

person from among themselves to Arabia for inquiry. When at last he reached Madinah the Prophet was already dead. The period of Abu Bakr's caliphate was also over and Hazrat Umar was the Caliph at that time. The messenger from Sarandeep met him and inquired about the Prophet's life. Hazrat Umar gave him the details. While the messenger was on his way back he died at Makran (near Baluchistan). He had with him a Hindu servant who came back to Sarandeep safe and sound. He described everything about the Prophet, Hazrat Abu Bakr and Hazrat Umar and also how they lived like dervishes. He said that humility marked their character, they wore patched clothes and slept in mosque.

The happy and fruitful interaction between India and West Asian Arabs came to a close with the decimation of the Abbaside Caliphate by the invading hordes of Chengiz Khan and Timur. The resultant flight of leading religious and scientific personalities proved a boon for India as they touched off Sufi and Bhakti movements, introduced a number of crafts like shawl-weaving and produced a beautiful synthesis in the form of Indo-Saracen architecture, Mughal style painting that forms an integral part of India's cultural mosaic and, no less significant, the development of a language, Urdu. It has got such a hold on the minds of people throughout the country that, despite all the vicissitude of fortune, it continues to flourish, almost like an unacknowledged *lingua franca*. The source of all this ingest was Iran and not the Afghans, Turks or Mughals whose role was confined to being the medium of transmission or carriers of the pollen. It can as such be called indirect contact with West Asia.

The introduction of Islam in north India was the contribution of Afghans, Turks and Mughals who had themselves imbibed it as destroyers of the Caliphate at Baghdad of which Iran was a part. This interface was not as pleasant as that of the earlier Arab period. For a long period, says Nehru, the Afghan raids 'overshadowed Islam in India and made it difficult for people to consider it dispassionately as they might have done otherwise.' He, in fact, rues the fact that Arabs came a bit late in the day:

> If the Arabs had come to India with Islam in the early days, the rising Arab culture would have mixed with the old Indian culture and the two would have acted and reacted on each other with great consequences. It would have been the mixing of two cultured races; and the Arabs were well known for their toleration and rationalism in religion (*Glimpses of World History*, p.186).

This interval is marked by an abatement of the ardour in the relationship that was seen till the decline and fall of the Abbaside Caliphate. It however reappeared with the common perception of the impact of European imperialism that had appeared on the world scene as an unprecedented engine of exploitation, oppression and tyranny, a barbaric force masquerading as a civilising agency. The Islamic *ulama*, from Shah Valiullah to Maulana Qasim Nanautvi, realised the common danger it posed to the Islamic world and to India and felt that the independence of India held the key to resisting this new threat. They made first conscious though tentative attempts at uniting the different religious communities of India to overthrow the aliens who had usurped state power through deceit, wile and cunning. It is significant that the Turkish Caliphate, itself in conflict with European imperialists, advised Indians who sought cooperation with them to unite all the inhabitants of the country to achieve the goal of complete independence.

This early perception came to fruition with the Khilafat movement that developed bonds of unity on the basis of anti-imperialism. Gandhi, Nehru and Maulana Azad, the leading triumvirate of the mainstream of India's freedom struggle, built close relationships with the freedom fighters of West Asia. Gandhi denounced the plan to plant a Zionist entity in the heart of the Arab world as a bulwark against imperialist designs. Nehru evolved the concept of non-alignment in cooperation with leaders of the newly independent Arab countries. Maulan Azad, with his erudition and penmanship, acquainted India with the rich cultural treasures of West Asia and brought home to Indian Muslims, in particular, the need to elicit the cooperation of non-Muslim compatriots to safeguard their religion and culture against the vicious and treacherous onslaught of the West.

Gandhi had supported Khilafat as he felt convinced that the unity of the Indian people, a percondition for the success of the freedom struggle, could be brought about by each community evincing empathy for the religious sensibilities of the other. He argued with Hindus that they must appreciate the Muslim concern for Khilafat to ensure that they reciprocated by showing similar appreciation for their religious sensibilities. To the Muslims he said:

> Whilst every good Muslim must strive to retain the temporal power of Turkey, it is obligatory on him to see that unequivocal Muslim control is retained over the 'Island of Arabia' which includes Mesopotamia, Syria and Palestine as well, and the spiritual sovereignty over them of the Caliph whoever he may be for the time being. No other term can satisfy Muslim opinion. They will not tolerate any non-Muslim influence, direct or indirect, over the holy places of Islam.

There could not be any more strident support of the West Asian struggle against foreign domination.

Nehru extended support to the Khilafat on a purely secular, political basis and pointed out, through the daily *Independent* (a newspaper launched by his father to promote the cause of freedom) that the British had destroyed Khilafat 'because Britain and other European powers wished to divide the Turkish Empire amongst themselves and the Khilafat movement was part of the political struggle for the freedom of Asia'. Nehru strongly denounced the canard that Khilafat was a pan-Islamic movement and that it was being supported to appease the Muslims. In a letter, quoted by his biographer S. Gopal, he wrote:

> Some people living in a world of their own creation imagine that there is a pan-Islamic block which may threaten India. This is pure fancy. Every one of the Islamic countries is developing on intensely national lines and there is absolutely no room in them for an external policy based on religion. The interests of these countries are and will continue to be our interests.

In view of such sentiments dominating Indian politics it is no surprise that India was highly respected in the countries of West Asia who shared the new nationalist, anti-colonial impulses with India. The West Asian response is epitomized in the poetical tributes paid to the Father of Indian Nationalism. Ahmad Shauqi, the famous Egyptian poet, exhorted Egyptians to accord a welcome to Gandhi in a long poem of which a verse reads:

> Stop to welcome him, from close quarters sitting in boats and also from a distance in whatever way possible. He is a guide and path finder like Confucius. In his word and deed he is like the great prophets. He has preached perseverance and truth. He has inspired in Hindus and Muslims the spirit of mutual love and with his spiritual powers, brought the two swords in one sheath. He is a great power house which generates the power to tame and train predators.

Another poet, Ahmed Taimur, likened him to 'the fragrance of the flowers of old civilization' and called him 'conscience of humanity which made no distinction of Indian, Egyptian, and Roman, etc.'

Unitary Histories, Epistemological Divides
A Summing Up

GULSHAN DIETL

'One who knows one, in effect knows none.' What Max Mueller had said about religion is equally true about history, culture and society. It is in this context that the IIC Asia Project needs to be understood and appreciated. Today, the *mantra* is universalism: universal values and habits, consumer goods and services, looks and outlooks. The headlong rush towards linear progress excludes the whole humanistic world of religion, culture, beliefs, artistic expression, anthropological richness: the things that express the deep inner feelings and aspirations of the people. The things that need to be cherished today and preserved for the future. 'Transversalism' rather than universalism is the way to that future. Modern technology need not pose a challenge in its pursuit; in fact, it could be harnessed to provide support towards retaining diversity and attaining unity.

The two-day seminar on 'India-West Asia: History, Culture and Society' was held in that spirit. It was devoted as much to self-introspection as to exploring commonalities, sharing experiences and admitting differences. We agreed to disagree and we decided to continue the dialogue. There were no definitive conclusions reached; nor were they attempted. What this summing up proposes to do, therefore, is simple: recapitulate arguments; capture moods and moments; and recreate the romance. It is an effort to record in a linear text what is essentially a mosaic.

A word about the participants, to start with. There were Indian scholars of eminence. There were also the West Asian scholars: academics, historians, philosophers, a princess, and so on. What was special about the guest-participants was that they were there in their personal capacities and on the basis of their personal capabilities. They did not represent their countries. What they contributed, therefore, was beyond the realm of international diplomatic niceties. And they were all Asians. The organisers of the seminar had taken a policy decision in advance that even if one had to suffer the Orientalist discourse, it had to come from the oriental Orientalists! And since we were all Asians, none could have said, 'The natives all look alike.' We were not just different, but diversely different. Even as individuals, each one was aware of his/her own distinctions, eccentricities, and angularities—a sum total of his/her individual identity plus the legacy of history, culture and society. And each was more than receptive to those of the others.

Let us then begin at the beginning. A popular legend among Arabs has it that Adam had descended in Sri Lanka (at the time a part of India) with the leaves of a paradise tree on his body. When dried, the leaves were scattered by wind throughout India, which is why there are so many perfumes in this country.

Historically speaking, the beginnings of maritime networks across the western Indian Ocean date as early as the third millennium B.C. These range from contacts between boat-building and sea-faring groups along the littoral, to merchant groups involved in the exchange and trade of a range of commodities, and travel by religious functionnaries. In most cases, these networks transcended national boundaries and functioned as somewhat autonomous traditions. Aromatics and dyes, metals and medicines, spices and foodstuff, wood and textiles, gems and ornaments, and plant and animal products constituted a variety of items exchanged. Dilmun (the Bahrain archipelago), Magan (the Oman peninsula) and Malukkha (the Harappan settlements) were the most important ports involved in the trading network. Indian teakwood was used for constructing the boats and the Indian coconut (*al-jawz al-Hindi*, lit. the Indian nut) provided the coir-rope for stitching them.

Is it possible to term these encounters an example of globalisation or world system in antiquity? Maybe, maybe not. The uncritical fixation with the modern world system thesis of Immanuel Wallerstein has undermined the possibility of studying the world system on a much longer time scale as well as in a much broader civilisational anchorage. One could hold on to his world economy argument, but reject the five-hundred-year modern world system as the only world system. Understanding long-term India-West Asia relations demands an approach that is beyond Wallerstein. The relations did transcend national boundaries and functioned as somewhat autonomous traditions. And they led to the movement of maritime communities and cultures in the ancient period and the emergence of distinctive identities as well as cultural transformations within a wider Indian Ocean sphere.

The South Arabians, the Yemenis of today, established their caravan trade across the Arabian Peninsula around 1000 B.C., which was dependent on their discovery of a camel's ability to subsist without food or water for up to four days. Enhanced by their command over the Strait of Bab al-Mandeb, they required trading ships from India, Egypt and East Africa to bring their wares to the Arabian ports for exchange and trade. These seasonal encounters between India and Egypt took nearly a thousand years to transform into direct, regular relations. The discovery of the monsoon winds and their use for navigation empowered the Egyptian merchants to bypass the Arabian ports and sail off directly across the Indian Ocean to the rich Indian markets. The Romans supported the trade and invested capital in it. The Egyptian navigators enjoyed unrivalled dominance in the Red Sea and the Indian Ocean as a consequence, and also provided a link between India and the Mediterranean.

By the latter half of the first millennium B.C., there was efflorescence of an urban milieu in India resulting in the emergence of the *nagaraka* or urbanite of Vatsyayana's *Kamasutra*. The *nagaraka* was exhorted to reside in a city or town, to pay attention to his appearance and to participate in social gatherings and popular festivities. There was a melting pot of sorts in the larger Indo-West Asian region, with peripatetic merchants fueling and feeding needs, wants and urges of consumption. There are references to *yavanas* indicating Greeks in the northwest, though the term remained ubiquitous, referring to a range of non-local groups. And then there were Turuskas or Turks, Tajikas, and Arabs. Swamy Dayanand Saraswati writes in *Satyarth Prakash*, 'In Mahabharat, when Kauravas planned to burn Pandavas in a lac-house, Vidurji informed Yudhishthir in Arabic and Yudhishthirji replied in the same Arabic language.'

The copper-plate from the year 849 recording the grant of several rights in the reign of King Sthanu Ravi to the Tarisapalli church built by Maruvan Sapir Iso bears witness-signatures in Arabic, Pahlavi and Hebrew. The Sasanian king Bahram V married an Indian princess and received as a dowry the port of Daibal in the Indus delta, together with the adjacent parts of Sind and Makran. That was in the fifth century A.D. The emergence of the cult of the Boddhisattva Avalokitesvara as the saviour of mariners and travellers in distress propelled the Buddhists to seafaring activities.

Arabia witnessod the rise of Islam in the seventh century. Immediately thereafter, it set out on an unprecedented career of empire-building, stretching from the Indus river to the Atlantic coast of North Africa, and on to South Europe. Philologists have traced three Sanskrit words in the Quran—*mishk* (musk), *zanjbil* (ginger), and *kafur* (camphor). Prophet Muhammad is believed to have used Indian medicine and recommended it to his followers. An Indian raja is reported to have sent Indian pickle to the Prophet. The Prophet's remark that 'he received sweet fragrance from India' has been quoted by many later writers. Allama Iqbal, the poet-philosopher of modern Islam, sang:

Meer-aye Arab ko ayee thandee hawa jahansay
Mera Watan wahi hai mera watan wahi hai
(The land from where came/Cool breeze to the Chief
of the Arabs/That is my country, that is my country.)

With the conquest of the Fertile Crescent—Persia and North Africa—within a few decades of the Prophet's death, Muslim Arabs came in contact with the peoples of the older religions and civilisations. While Islam is a revealed religion, its followers demonstrated a remarkable catholicity of outlook in their understanding of Hinduism. It was a natural and not a revealed religion, they reasoned. Some nations derived their laws not from the divine revelations through prophets but through the reason and wisdom of their kings and sages, they accepted. The hosts reciprocated the feeling. The Arabs brought

Islam to India and then on to Malaysia, Indonesia and China. A near-total absence of hostile feelings towards its message indicates that it was welcomed as a new way of contemplating man, society and God that appealed to the catholic spirit of its hosts. In India, the impact was felt not only in terms of winning more adherents to Islam but also as a catalyst for Vedantic thought.

In the early Abbasid period, i.e. the eighth century, the Arabs had established *Bait al-Hikmah* (The House of Wisdom) in Baghdad and begun to translate books from Greek, Syriac Persian, and Sanskrit. The town became a hub of learning. Within a few decades, its scholars began to develop sciences and philosophies. Some of the noteworthy Sanskrit works like *Brahmsphuta Siddanta, Aryabhatiya* and *Khandya Khadyaka* in mathematics and astronomy; *Susrata Samhita* and *Carak Samhita* in medicine; collections of stories like *Triya Chāṛitṛ* and *Panchtantra* were translated from Sanskrit into Arabic. Games like *chausar* and *shatranj* were enthusiastically learnt and played. Nehru paid fulsome compliments to the scientific spirit of the Arabs: 'Among the ancients we do not find the scientific method in Egypt or China or India. We find just a bit of it in old Greece. In Rome again it was absent. But the Arabs had this scientific spirit of inquiry, and so they may be considered the fathers of modern science.'

The Arabs taught us the concepts of monotheism and adoration of one's teacher. In turn, they learnt medicine, astronomy, mathematics from us. And they passed them on to the Europeans. It is not for nothing that the Arabs call the numbers Hindi, as they learnt them from us; the West calls them the Arabic Numerals since it learnt them from the Arabs; and we, the largest English-speaking country, count them in English!

The decimation of the Abbasid Caliphate by the invading hordes of Chengiz Khan and Timur led to the flight of leading religious and scientific personalities. Many moved to India. The results of the phenomenon were far-reaching: the flowering of Sufi and Bhakti movements, a number of crafts like shawl-weaving, Mughal style painting, Indo-Saracen architecture, and the birth of Urdu.

Al-Biruni, who has left an exhaustive legacy of scholarship on India, studied Hindu religious literature and observed the society during his long stay in the eleventh century. His commentaries on the Vedas, the Puranas, *Mahabharata, Ramayana*, Patanjali's Yoga Aphorisms, etc., reflect his profound understanding and abiding interest. Even where his comprehension of the texts is inadequate and his reading of the situations inaccurate, his admiration never falters. The Hindu caste system and the practice of idol worship were some of the things he observed and explained. No author before him or after him until modern times studied India in such depth and with such sympathy. He also strove to bring about an atmosphere of reconciliation and amity between King Mahmud Ghaznavi and his Hindu subjects. Like all coins since the Ummayads, the coins of Ghaznawi were inscribed with the *kalima 'Lailaha Illalah Muhammad Rasulullah'* (There is no God but Allah and Muhammad is His Prophet) in Arabic. What was unique about the Ghaznawi coins was that, on the reverse side, they had a Sanskrit inscription *Avayaktum Ekum, Muhammada Avatara* (The Unmanifest is One and Muhammad is His Incarnation). It was not a literal translation; rather a Hinduisation of Islamic creed, according to Suniti Kumar Chatterji, one of the renowned Sanskrit scholars. Some scholars attribute this extraordinary feat to Biruni.

By the thirteenth century, the area between the east Mediterranean and the Indian Ocean constituted the fulcrum that balanced the East and the West. A non-hierarchical world system had evolved in which the Arab-Persian imperial centres, the Mongol empire, the Delhi Sultanate, the trading centres of coastal India along with the towns of western Europe formed the nodal points. Their mutual trade and civilisational links formed a core activity in that historical world system. If we agree on pushing the modern five hundred-year old world system of Immanuel Wallerstein back in time, then the history of India-West Asia relations can be retrieved with immense consequences in terms of reinterpretation and empowerment. To break the shackles of unitary national-societal histories on the one hand and the West/non-West epistemological divide on the other, it is imperative to talk about systemic aspects of history so that linkages rather than the perceived hierarchies of temporal and spatial dimensions could be studied.

By the sixteenth century, all the three empires in the world—the Moghul in India, the Safavids in Iran and the Ottomans in Turkey—were located in Asia. The Europeans could have easily accused the historiography of this period of being Asia-centric!

The arrival of the Industrial Revolution in Europe and of Europeans in our parts of the world disturbed the age-old patterns of interactions between the neighbours. In their pursuit to secure the Indian jewel in the crown, the British proceeded to turn the Gulf into a British Lake. The Indians resisted, and so did the Arabs. At times, they coordinated their moves; at times they extended helping hands to each other. In the late eighteenth century, Tipu Sultan, the ruler of Mysore, reached out to the Ottoman Sultan, the Shah of Persia, the King of Afghanistan, the Sultan of Oman and other Gulf rulers in order to off-set British pressure on his kingdom. The Ottoman Sultan accorded permission to Tipu to assume the title of an independent monarch, to strike coins and to have the Khutba read in his name. Tipu attached great importance to foreign trade and commerce as he viewed them to be the bases of state power and prosperity. Towards that end, he established factories in Muscat, Hormuz, Basra, Bushire, Bahrain and Jiddah. It was also a time of resistance against economic hegemony and imperial subjugation in the Gulf. The British were engaged in widespread 'pacification' of the tribal chiefs, who they accused of trading in slaves and arms as also of piracy. The al-Qasimis of Sharjah, the King of Oman, Nadir Shah of Persia and many other local leaders were seeking to throw off the yoke of European presence and unifying their people to that end.

The two-way migrations between the people continued uninterrupted during the colonial period. The Yemenis came to India, especially to Hyderabad; and the Indians went to the Yemeni port towns of Shihr, Mokalla, Mokha, Hodeida and even Socotra, apart from Aden. 'The resonance of Bombay hypnotizes Aden', observed Harold Jacobs, the British Officer posted there. The notices and instructions in public places were written in Arabic, Hindi and Gujarati. The British, in the meanwhile, forged linkages of their own between India and the Gulf. For most of the period of British rule, the Gulf emirates were under the political and administrative authority of the British Administration in Bombay, and the Indian rupee remained a legal tender there till their independence. In all the treaties between the British Indian Authorities and the Gulf Principalities, there were articles asserting protection and privileges for the Indian merchants. Gradually, the Indians came to occupy government positions and jobs in the oil companies and enjoyed better wages and conditions than the local employees. In Bahrain, there were disturbances and strikes against this in the 1930s and 1940s.

On a broader level, though, the Indian freedom struggle inspired the nationalists across the Arab world. Fraternal delegations from Egypt, Syria and Palestine were invited to the Indian National Congress sessions in pre-independence days. The Arab delegations also participated in the Asian Relations Conference hosted by India in 1947. The Indian policy *vis-à-vis* the creation of Israel and the subsequent Arab-Israeli wars was based on principles of justice and international law. When Israel, Britain and France attacked Egypt in the wake of the nationalisation of the Suez Canal in 1956, Nehru was quick to lend support to Nasser. And quicker to grasp the larger context of the event. In a message to Nasser, he wrote, 'If colonialism succeeds in coming back to Egypt, it will reverse the entire course of history and return to every other country from which it had been forced to go.' The Nehru-Nasser friendship, the Afro-Asian solidarity and the Non-Aligned movement brought India and the Arab world closer together and strengthened their positions during the crucial period of nation-building.

What does the present look like in the light of such an inter-woven past? What are the forces shaping our national life, inter-regional cooperation and international standing? If we survey the current trends, there is much to celebrate and much to complain. How we navigate this early phase of post-Cold War globalisation would be critical to our future. A single world with a single agenda formulated according to the value system of one culture—to the exclusion of others—will be a world in which injustice and marginalisation will inevitably lead to conflict and war. The 'one world of ten thousand cultures'—a world in which commonalities are the foundation and particularities are the cornerstones—will be characterised by cooperation. Are we well-equipped, are we on the right track, are we looking ahead and moving on?

From high culture to mass culture, the Indian influence is pervasive in the entire region. Aspects of Indian culture and heritage have been cordially subsumed in the local ethos. The Bollywood films are all-time favourites: in Sudan with its strict Sharia law and their application in every facet of life, the Indian films constitute as high as 82 per cent of all the films screened there. And the fallout is visible—and audible: the influence of Indian music, language, and cuisine; and a fascination for India in general. In the field of education, the India-educated elite is emerging alongside the degree-holders from the US and Europe. Faisal al-Rfou'h, a participant in this seminar, is one such. He was twice a minister in Jordan, and is now an academic at the university there.

There has been a distinct surge of revitalisation of old economic ties between India and the Arab world since the oil boom in the seventies. Today, 75 per cent of our crude oil imports come from West Asia. The surging demand for gas will be supplied almost exclusively from there as well. There are estimates of nearly 3.5 million Indian expatriates in there—contributing to lessening of pressure on the job markets here, sending remittances to the tune of $4 billion annually and subscribing overwhelmingly to the bonds and deposits schemes and monetary collections in times of need here. Our Information Technology (IT) industry is poised to make a big arrival in the form of software development, onsite services and joint ventures. As the oil states move from rentier to production-based economies, the relations will acquire a new context. Geo-economics will remain the prime mover of relations among the countries in the twenty-first century; and it will be within the growing expanse of economic interactions that politico-strategic understanding will be reached.

Demography, minorities and women in the Arab context and secularism in the Indian context were articulated as areas of deep concern during the deliberations.

The population of West Asia-North Africa is about 345 million today. The rapidly falling mortality rates and only a slow decline in fertility levels have resulted in a three-fold increase since the 1950s. As a consequence, the population profile is young. The dependency ratio (i.e. the ratio of population under 15 years and over 64 years to the population aged 15-64) is one-to-one. Also, the region is one of the most urbanized in the Third World with 53 per cent of its people located in the cities. Various kinds of youth activism and urban violence, which may in turn lead to increased state authoritarianism, is a credible future scenario in the circumstances.

Some of the brutal conflicts in West Asia are rooted in the inability of the states to recognise social diversity and their unwillingness to accommodate the demands of the minorities. Affirmative actions in favour of officially recognised minorities ensure significant representation in the parliaments and provide certain constitutional protections and safeguards, but are inadequate to deal with the question of power sharing. In a few exceptions, ethnic or religious minority groups actually control the state apparatus; for example, Syria, Iraq, Jordan and the Gulf Sheikhdoms.

During the pre-oil period, when many male members of Kuwait spent several months of the year away from home travelling on their merchant ships to distant lands, it was the Kuwaiti women who held the fort. The Kuwaiti women showed an extraordinary resilience and fortitude during the Iraqi occupation of Kuwait. Despite the equality of participation guaranteed by its Constitution to all Kuwaiti citizens, the women are denied the right to vote. The historical initiative of an Emiri decree granting full political rights to women failed to receive parliamentary approval in 1999. The move was lost by a slim margin of two votes. The struggle continues, even as lessons from the first round are being learnt.

In India, our rich composite culture has been threatened at two moments in the history of the country. The first moment arose when the strategies of the colonial power fragmented the idea that Indian society had built by means of various cultural resources to create a shared multi-textured culture. The second moment arises in the 1980s, when a series of historical events, most notably the consolidation of majoritarianism or Hindutva, challenged the notion that Indians across all religious and cultural persuasions have much in common, and that this unites them in projects of social co-existence. It is time that we reiterate the right of every individual to live a life of dignity as guaranteed by the Constitution, and his/her right to be respected not despite but because he/she belongs to a different culture. The right which accrues to a human being by virtue of being human.

There was disagreement on the use of the term West Asia. Reservations were expressed about its usage on three grounds: one, that it leaves out Egypt and the whole of North Africa; two, that it neglects the Mediterranean dimension of the people's self-perception. Alexander the Great, Hellenism in general, the Roman Empire, Muslim Spain (Andalusia), the Christian Crusades, the shared experience of Ottoman rule with Eastern Europe, European modernity—history has bound the region to the Mediterranean all along its evolution. And three, that the people there have used and been used to the term Middle East for their part of the world. There were counter-arguments to these, but ultimately, we agreed to disagree.

There were two specific suggestions offered at the seminar. One, that centres of crisis avoidance need to be established in the larger frame of 'arc of crisis', taking in the Horn of Africa through the Congo, Central and West Asia and the Indian subcontinent. It is time to move on from the culture of mere survival to a culture of non-violence, participation and peace. Two, that India should seek to strengthen its ties with the member-states of the Organization of Islamic Conferences (OIC). The OIC unites not only the Muslim countries, but also other countries with Muslim communities. The Indian presence will be beneficial to the Organization as also to the Indian subcontinent.

The seminar did not seek a consensus on any issue. There was nonetheless a complete agreement that it was an intellectually enriching experience for each one of us—differently and for different reasons. Differences after all, sustain dialogue, they need not cause conflict.

Contributors

ABDUL ALI is Professor in the Department of Islamic Studies, Aligarh Muslim University, Aligarh.

ABDULAZIZ OTHMAN ALTWAIJRI is Director General, Islamic Educational, Scientific and Cultural Organization (ISESCO)

ABDUL BARI is Professor and Chairman, Department of Arabic, Aligarh Muslim University, Aligarh.

ABDULLA ELMADANI writes weekly articles on Asian affairs from Bahrain for journals in Qatar, Bahrain, UAE, Saudi Arabia, and London. He is an academic by training.

AKHTARUL WASEY is Professor in the Department of Islamic Studies, Faculty of Humanities and Languages, Jamia Millia Islamia University, New Delhi.

A. K. PASHA, Professor, is Director, Gulf Studies Programme, Centre for West Asian and African Studies, Jawaharlal Nehru University. Among his publications are *Libya in the Arab World: Qadhafi's Quest for Arab Unity* (1988), *India and West Asia: Continuity and Change* (1999), and *Aspects of Political Participation in the Gulf States* (1999).

A. K. RAMAKRISHNAN, Professor, is Director, School of International Relations, Mahatma Gandhi University, Kottayam, Kerala.

FAISAL ODEH AL-RFOU'H is currently Visiting Professor at Bayt al-Hikmah Institute, Al-Bayt University, Mafraq, Jordan, and Associate Professor, Department of Political Science, University of Jordan. He was formerly Minister of Culture (1999-2000).

GIRIJESH PANT, former Professor at the Centre for West Asian and African Studies, Jawaharlal Nehru University, is currently the Vice-Chancellor of Guru Ghasidas University, Bilaspur, Chattisgarh.

GULSHAN DIETL is former Chairperson and currently Professor, Centre for West Asian and African Studies Programme, Jawaharlal Nehru University, New Delhi. She was the Coordinator of the 'India and West Asia: History, Culture and Society' seminar.

HASSAN MEKKI is Professor, Africa International University, Khartoum, Sudan.

HIMANSHU PRABHA RAY is Professor, Centre for Historical Studies, Jawaharlal Nehru University. Her publications include *Archaeology of Seafaring in Ancient South Asia*, *The Winds of Change: Buddhism and the Maritime Links of Early South Asia* (1998).

JAFFAR MIRGHANI AHMED, Dr, Director General of Institute of Sudan Civilization, is an academic and linguist by training.

KARAN SINGH, Dr, Member of Parliament, is Founder Trustee and former President of the India International Centre, and the Chairman of the IIC's Asia Project.

M. A. SALEEM KHAN retired as Professor from the Centre of West Asian Studies, Aligarh Muslim University.

MOSTAFA EL-ABBADI, Dr, is Professor Emeritus of Ancient History at the University of Alexandria. He has authored *Egypt from Alexander the Great to the Arab Conquest*, and *Life and Fate of the Ancient Library of Alexandria*, and co-edited *India and Egypt: Influences and Interactions*.

NEERA CHANDHOKE is Professor, Department of Political Science, Delhi University. She is the author of *Civil Society and the State: Explorations in Political Theory* (1995).

PRAKASH C. JAIN is Professor in the School of International Studies, Jawaharlal Nehru University. His publications include *Racial Discrimination Against Overseas Indians: A Class Analysis* (1990) and *Population and Society in West Asia: Essays in Comparative Demography* (2001).

P. R. KUMARASWAMY is Associate Professor, Centre for West Asian and African Studies, Jawaharlal Nehru University.

RAFIQ ZAKARIA, Dr, is the Chancellor of the Urdu University in Aligarh. Dr. Zakaria has held several distinguished positions in government. A former Cabinet Minister, he has thrice represented India at the United Nations.

RASHA AL-SABAH, Professor, is Undersecretary, Ministry of Higher Education, State of Kuwait.

SADIK J. AL-AZM is Emeritus Professor of History of Modern European Philosophy, Damascus University, Damascus, Syria

SALEH ALI BASURRAH is Rector, University of Aden, Republic of Yemen. Professor of History, his current research is on the history, art and culture of Yemen, and Yemen-India relations.

SHEREEN RATNAGAR, was Professor of Archaeology and Ancient History at the Jawaharlal Nehru University.

WAIEL S. H. AWWAD, Dr, is Chief of the South Asia Bureau of the Syrian Arab News Agency, New Delhi.